SECOND
EDITION

CHINESE
ETIQUETTE
& ETHICS
IN BUSINESS

**SECOND
EDITION**

CHINESE
ETIQUETTE
& ETHICS
IN BUSINESS

Boye Lafayette De Mente

Boston   Burr Ridge, IL   Dubuque, IA   Madison, WI   New York
San Francisco   St. Louis   Bangkok   Bogotá   Caracas   Kuala Lumpur
Lisbon   London   Madrid   Mexico City   Milan   Montreal   New Delhi
Santiago   Seoul   Singapore   Sydney   Taipei   Toronto

First Printed in 2004

Other books by Boyé Lafayette De Mente
Chinese Etiquette & Ethics in Business
Chinese in Plain English
Japanese Etiquette & Ethics in Business
Japanese in Plain English
Korean in Plain English
NTC's Dictionary of Japan's Cultural Code Words
NTC's Dictionary of Mexico's Cultural Code Words
The Japanese Have a Word for It
Chinese Have a Word for It
Everything Japanese

10   09   08   07   06   05   04   03   02   01
20   09   08   07   06   05   04
FC   BJE

Library of Congress Cataloging-in-Publication Data
De Mente, Boyé.
    Chinese etiquette & ethics in business / Boyé Lafayette De Mente. — 2nd ed.
      p. cm.
    ISBN 0-8442-8524-2
    1. Business etiquette—China.   2. Business ethics.   3. Industrial management—China.   4. National characteristics, Chinese.   I. Title.   II. Title: Chinese etiquette and ethics in business.
HF5384.D4   1994
306'.0951—dc20

    94-6700
    CIP

When ordering this title, use ISBN 007-144817-9

Printed in Singapore

"Do not be in too much of a hurry to get things done. Do not see only petty gains. If a man hurries too much, things will not be done well or thoroughly. If he sees only minor advantages, nothing great is accomplished."

—CONFUCIUS

Contents

Westerners as Aliens • The Chinese Advantage •
The Roundabout Way • The Importance of *Keqi* •
Human Feelings and Face • Facing the World •
Overseas Chinese

Symbols • Face Versus Efficiency • Two + Two
Does Not = Four • Limiting Your Obligations •
Apologies and Revenge • Masked Emotions •
Showing Respect • Criticizing Indirectly • Dress and
Punctuality • Restaurant Bill Taboos • Projects That
Have the Best Chance • Keeping Your Guard Up •
Power Plays • Structuring the Workplace •
Expanding the Chinese Mind • Using the Strategies
of War • Dealing with Your Head Office

Acknowledgments

I am greatly indebted to the following people for sharing with me their experience and knowledge of living and working in China:

Irene M. Park
Michael Levin
G. P. Cove
Carmond Hui
Peter Khan
May Law
Ernst Mayer
Ian J. Stones
Frank Hawke

Major Dynasties of Imperial China

The Five (Mythical/Neolithic Age) Dynasties   ?–2000 B.C.
Evidence of agricultural communities in Yellow River Valley.

Hsia Dynasty (Bronze Age)   2000–1600 B.C.
Gradual growth of population, appearance of cities, development of various technologies.

Shang Dynasty   1550–1030 B.C.
City states emerge, writing developed, wheeled vehicles invented, irrigation applied to agriculture, slavery institutionalized, society divided into "vertical" classes made up of peasants, merchants, the military, scholars, and the aristocracy.

Chou Dynasty   1030–256 B.C.
Feudal states emerge, with hereditary military rulers; salt and iron industries developed as government monopolies; glass invented; metal coins and chopsticks in common use; wealthy merchant class emerges. Age of Confucius, Taoism. Gradual breakdown in social classes.

Qin (Chin) Dynasty   221–207 B.C.
Feudal states merged into unified China; construction begun on Great Wall; books burned to break hold of past traditions; uniform legal code created; written language, weights and measures, length of cart axles standardized; scholarship made basis for government service; vertical class society (peasants, merchants, military, scholars, aristocracy) reestablished.

Han Dynasty   206 B.C.–A.D. 220
Bureaucratic government becomes feudalistic; civil service instituted to run government; Buddhism introduced from India; Confucianism becomes state religion; paper invented; empire expands; Yellow Turban Revolt; private enterprise made taboo, stifling innovation.

Three Kingdoms, Southern and Northern Dynasties   A.D. 221–581
Social, political discontent; revolts against feudal government; Buddhism spreads; tea becomes popular beverage; numerous contacts with Korea and Japan.

Sui Dynasty   A.D. 581–618
Empire reunified; north and south joined by Grand Canal; growth of Buddhism suppressed; influence on Korea, Japan grows.

Tang Dynasty   A.D. 618–907
Empire continues to expand; state examinations for elite scholar-officials; trading vessels penetrate Indian Ocean; printing developed; footbinding begins; art, music, and scholarship flourish among the rich and ruling classes. Affluence breeds decadence and weakness in the imperial line; the dynasty falls.

Five Dynasties   A.D. 907–960
Period of turmoil and short-lived dynasties.

Sung Dynasty   A.D. 960–1127

Northern tribes become serious threat, forcing capital to move south; compass used routinely for navigation; paper money in use; size and sophistication of cities grow.

Southern Sung Dynasty   A.D. 1127–1279

Incursions by nomadic northern tribes continue; Sung rulers move south, new dynasty set up in north.

Qin (Chin) Dynasty (Northern China)   A.D. 1115–1234

New northern dynasty cannot match military power of the nomadic Mongols, and is defeated.

Yuan Dynasty   A.D. 1280–1368

Mongol horsemen capture all of China, set up Yuan Dynasty; expand empire into Central Europe, attracting Western travelers, including Marco Polo. Mongols twice invade Japan, failing both times to subdue the island kingdom; novels published, opera developed.

Ming Dynasty   A.D. 1368–1644

Mongol rulers absorbed by Chinese; replaced. Chinese trading ships reach Africa; foreign missionaries become active in Beijing; Portuguese traders set up outpost on Macao; peasant revolt.

Qing (Ching) Dynasty   A.D. 1644–1911

Weakened Ming Dynasty falls to the Manchus, another northern people. Empire reaches its peak; population explodes, bringing economic and political stress. Western powers begin to encroach into China, taking concessions, forcing unequal treaties. British forces defeat Chinese to protect opium trade. Revolts by peasants and political dissidents. Uneducated, superstitious, isolated empress dowager and successors fail to lead. Dynasty falls.

Modern Times   1911–1949

Empire breaks up into battling factions. Warlords compete with new republic. Chinese Communist leaders begin vying for power; civil war begins between Communists and Nationalists. Japan invades and captures most of eastern China. Nationalist leader Kai-shek Chiang continues to war against Zedong Mao's Communist forces, ignoring the Japanese. Chinese loyalists capture Chiang, force him to join battle against the Japanese. When Japan defeated, Chiang resumes battle against the Communists, ignoring needs and desires of China's farmers, who make up bulk of population. Failing to win popular support, and plagued by corruption, bad planning, and military ineptness, Chiang's Nationalist forces are defeated, despite American help. The leaders, their families, and hard-core followers flee to Taiwan, oust the island government, and declare themselves the legitimate government of China. The People's Republic of China founded by Zedong Mao October 1, 1949.

Introduction

The New China

The gravitational center of the global economy has shifted to East Asia, and there is a growing possibility that China will reemerge as the centerpiece of this part of the world—despite the political and economic setbacks that followed freedom demonstrations in the spring of 1989.

It is not only China's size, natural resources, and huge population that could give it an overwhelming edge in the future; there are also the racial and cultural factors linking China with Japan, Korea, and the other countries of East Asia. China was the wellspring for much of the traditional culture and civilization of all of these countries, including their Confucian-oriented social and moral systems. This gives them a special intellectual and emotional bond with China that, coupled with their proximity, makes them natural trading partners.

This Confucian cultural sphere is already competing head-on with the Christian sphere of Europe and the Americas. Technology, management expertise, and capital are flowing into China from the Confucian East (as well as from the West), helping to fuel the political, social, and economic revolution now transforming the country. There are many who believe that this joining of East Asian countries into a new economic community that dwarfs the West is the wave of the future. The only question seems to be the continued willingness of China's leadership to let market forces shape the national economy.

Of course, any consideration of China as a market for export products, a source for imports, or as a location for a factory site must include an acute awareness and appreciation of several realities, among which are that China is the world's oldest and most pervasive bureaucracy, that the country is still in the process of shedding a feudalistic skin that is layers deep and tanned by a strong dose of communist ideology, and that the business structure of the country is in the throes of "reforms" that are an attempt to create an entirely new economic order.

The aim of this new order is "to effect a coexistence of diversified economic sectors"—meaning that the economic system China is now trying to build is a combination of state-owned, privately owned, household-operated, and Sino-foreign joint-venture enterprises, all directed by the market under the guidance of the state.

Often more important than the bureaucratic and political aspects of doing business in China is the basic character of the Chinese. Their attitudes and behavior are rooted in a culture that is different from and often diametrically opposed to Western thought. China's age, its relative isolation during much of its long history, and its philosophical and artistic accomplishments—many of which predate comparable developments in the West by more than two thousand years—have given the Chinese a sense of ethnocentrism that is unsurpassed among the peoples of the world. For more than a thousand years, China was the largest and in many ways the most advanced civilization on earth.

Because of a variety of internal and external reasons, however, China lost its place on the center of the world stage. Unable to adapt to changing times brought on by the Industrial Revolution in Europe, it ended up as one of the world's most backward countries. As part of its subsequent confrontation with an outside industrialized world, the country was then savaged both physically and intellectually by a series of foreign invasions and civil wars that began in the mid-1800s and did not end until 1976.

Memories of a Holocaust

The 1920s, 1930s, and 1940s, still within the memory of the senior generation, were a long-drawn-out holocaust for most Chinese. Millions of people—men, women, and children—were coerced slave laborers. Millions of farmers, already at the barest existence level, were cheated out of their plots of land by moneylenders in collusion with local government-appointed officials. A famine in 1929 killed more than five million people in Inner Mongolia alone. In the mid-1930s, bodies of babies, children, and the destitute littered roadways and streets like fallen leaves. Millions more were killed by Japanese troops and by Chinese Nationalist and Communist forces.

Today's China is working desperately hard to overcome the handicaps of its own cultural and political history and the damage wrought upon it by Japan, Western colonial powers, and its own internal struggles. Rapid progress is being made, but there is a long way to go. Still today, as during the seemingly endless dynastic ages of the past, the bulk of China's great population lives in rustic simplicity, far removed from the Fifth Avenues and Ginzas of the world. The high-rise office complexes and apartments of the principal cities, the proliferation of factories along the eastern seaboard, and the growing presence of China on the international scene are evidence of the energy and ambition that is remaking China, but this metamorphosis is still in an early and vulnerable stage.

At the same time, there is a growing consensus that China's 4,000-year cultural heritage is its greatest handicap and that virtually all the things that most Chinese take pride in—the Great Wall, the Yellow River, the Dragon— are in fact symbols of the nation's historical weaknesses, not its strengths. This growing doubt about its own heritage was brought into focus in 1988 by a six-part TV series called *He Shang,* literally the painful and inevitable decline of "the Yellow River civilization." The controversial program, written by five people in their twenties and thirties, including two teachers, views the symbols of China's past as signs of blind ethnocentrism, conservatism, and cowardice, and concludes that China must in fact create a new culture if it is going to escape from the bonds of its history.

China's ongoing link with its past is graphically demonstrated in the village of Zhangcun in Henan Province, where the entire population of the village lives in underground caves. China has, of course, long been famous for its cave dwellings, but generally these have been caves carved into the sides of hills and mountains. The caves of Zhangcun are cut into the flat loess plateau of the region.

Construction of cave houses in Zhangcun begins with the excavation of a courtyard some six meters into the ground. Large rooms are then cut into the four perpendicular walls of the courtyard, each measuring four to five meters in width and extending back some ten meters. The arched ceilings of the rooms are whitewashed, slaked with lime, then papered to keep the packed loess from crumbling.

Each of the large rooms (there are up to eight rooms surrounding a courtyard) has a hole cut in the ceiling to serve a multitude of purposes—skylight, air duct, and grain chute (after grain is spread out on the ground above and dried in the sun, it is funneled down the light-and-air duct for storage in the underground chamber). Each family has a private courtyard and a well. Tunnel-like passageways lead from the courtyards up to ground level.

Far from being as primitive as they may sound, however, the cave homes of Zhangcun have many advantages over more conventional housing. They are cool in the summer and warm in the winter, and both windproof and soundproof. More importantly, they are much cheaper to build than ordinary housing and are virtually maintenance free. As far as "modern" comforts are concerned, furnishings in the cave dwellings include such things as television sets and gas stoves.

Chinese political leaders on every level, as well as a significant percentage of managers in the commercial area, are understandably touchy about China's image and about its relations with foreigners and foreign countries in particular. In some areas and ways this touchiness crosses the barrier into paranoia, making it unusually difficult for foreigners, including those whose goodwill and intentions are above reproach, to work smoothly and effectively with their Chinese counterparts.

Foreigners doing business with today's Chinese often must overcome a maze of cultural, political, and bureaucratic barriers that range from irritating and time-consuming to insurmountable. They must also overcome a series of self-made handicaps that they bring along with them—handicaps that range from little or no knowledge of the Chinese way of doing things to ingrained foreign expectations and habits that are incompatible in China.

Close Encounters

Making the initial contact with Chinese companies and agencies follows familiar patterns—participating in trade shows, personal visits, written proposals, advertising, introductions. Many companies, of course, use a combination of these approaches. Whatever method is used, written proposals and follow-up visits are invariably keys to the development of any business relationship.

Some old China hands say the final secret of making out in China today is to learn the art of "chewing sunflower seeds"—which refers to enduring with Buddha-like patience the delays, the irrationalities, the occasional ill will, and more common avarice, and taking what you can get when you can get it. But despite the problems involved in doing business in China, the potential for reward—which for many on both sides goes well beyond monetary gains—is so great that the challenge pales by comparison.

The primary purpose of this book is to identify cultural and political elements that affect the process of business, and in doing so to provide guidelines that will assist foreign businesspeople in day-to-day dealings with the Chinese and thereby hopefully contribute to their reaping some of the rewards.

Boye Lafayette De Mente
Beijing

1

The Land and the People

"By nature men are pretty much alike.
It is their learning and practices that distinguish them."
—CONFUCIUS

China in Profile

In addition to having one of the oldest continuous civilizations, China is also huge in size, encompassing a total of 3.7 million square miles in area (as compared to 3.6 million in the United States). From the Pamir Mountains in the west, it is 2,500 miles to the east coast. From its southern border with Vietnam to the northern border with Russia at the Amur River, it is 2,000 miles. The large city of Urumqui in the autonomous region of Xinkiang, some 1,400 miles from the nearest coast, is the most remote city on the globe.

Geographically, China slopes upward from the eastern seaboard to the high plateaus and mountains of Tibet and Quinghia in the far west, where the average elevation is 4,500 meters and mountain peaks of 6,000 and 7,000 meters are common. The rain and snow in these western highlands feed China's great rivers.

China has common borders with more countries than any other nation—more than a dozen—including Afghanistan, Bhutan, Burma, India, Laos, Mongolia, Nepal, North Korea, Pakistan, Russia, and Vietnam. These foreign borders stretch for a total of 14,900 miles. China is bordered on the east by the Yellow Sea and China Sea, on the north by the high plains of Mongolia, on the west by the Gobi Desert, on the southwest by the great Tibetan upthrust, and on the south by jungle-clad mountains.

1

China occupies approximately the same latitudes as the United States of America, with a similar spread of weather from north to south and from the lowlands to the highlands. It is far more mountainous than the United States, however, with most of the population concentrated along the floodplains of its great rivers.

China is the third largest nation in the world, after Russia and Canada. The *Han* Chinese, or the original core Chinese, occupy about half of the country's overall landmass. The rest is inhabited by Mongols, Tibetans, and over fifty other racial and ethnic groups.

The country is divided into twenty-one provinces and five autonomous regions, with some five thousand offshore islands that range from rocky outcroppings to the large island of Hainan off the southern coast. The autonomous regions are Inner Mongolia, Ningxia, Xinjiang, Guangxi, and Tibet. Three of China's great cities also have provincial status: Beijing, Shanghai, and Tianjin. Altogether, China has 644 cities.

Notwithstanding its huge physical size, the overriding fact is that China is land-poor. Some 80 percent of the landmass is made up of uninhabitable mountains and desert. The country's one billion-plus people thus live in an area that measures approximately 740,000 square miles, or an area about the size of Mexico. With only about 7 percent of the earth's cultivated land, China has to feed 22 percent of its population.

In addition to its natural border barriers, China is further divided into distinct geographic regions by interior mountain ranges and the mighty Yangtze River, which runs west to east, splitting the country into north and south sections. It is South China that is noted for its intensely cultivated rice paddies and terraced fields, its mist-covered hills and mountains, its abundant rain, swift rivers, and picturesque gorges.

Within South China there are three great level areas of land that form another distinct feature of China—the Canton delta in the far south, the Yangtze delta along the central seacoast, and the Red Basin, 1,400 miles up the Yangtze River in Sichuan Province. These three areas are crisscrossed by some 200,000 miles of canals, and are among the most intensely farmed regions on the globe. The canals in the Red Basin, noted for its terraced hills, were designed and built by an engineer named Ping Li some 2,000 years ago.

North China (everything north of the Tsinling mountain range) is the land of the "Yellow Earth" and the famous (or infamous) Yellow River, and might be called China's dustbowl. The region is cold and snowy in the winter and hot and dry in the summer. Rainfall is infrequent and the area is regularly blanketed by great dust storms blowing in from the deserts of central Asia. The windblown silt that covers a huge portion of this region is hundreds of feet thick and fertile, but in the far west the rivers coming down from the high mountains have cut deep beds into the soft soil, making irrigation difficult or impossible.

Taming China's Sorrow

The Yellow River in particular is noted for the volume of silt it carries out of Central Asia and has traditionally been one of the great blessings as well as curses of China. The river begins in the plateaus of western Quinghai and snakes through nine provinces on its way to Bohai Bay on the Yellow Sea, a distance of 3,388 miles. Each year it picks up millions of tons of silt in the loess (sandy) plateau of western China and deposits it along its central and lower reaches.

Every year the riverbed in these lower reaches is raised another three or four inches and is from thirteen to twenty-three feet above the level of the adjoining land. The water is held back by embankment dikes built up over the centuries. Still in the past 2,000 years it has changed its course twenty-six times and flooded adjoining areas 1,500 times, destroying whole villages and towns and killing millions.

The Yellow River deposits an annual average of 1.2 billion tons of silt at its mouth, adding 50.7 square kilometers of new land to Shang-dong every year and pushing the coastline an additional 1.4 kilometers further into the sea. The river began its delta building in 1855 when it changed its direct-line course in Henan Province and began to snake through Shangdong Province, finally emptying into the Bohai Sea.

China's government spent over a billion dollars in the 1980s in an effort to control the Yellow River's rampages. A computerized warning device, built with help from the United States and the United Nations, gives a twenty-hour advance warning of a potential flood, allowing time to open gates and divert some of the water to retention areas. There is also an ongoing program of planting vegetation in the loess region to help prevent soil erosion by the river.

Besides the perennial danger presented by its many rivers, sandstorms in China's far west, driven by hurricane-force winds, frequently bury miles of railroad tracks and cause other damage despite heroic efforts to deflect the sand by walls, fences, rows of trees, cacti, and grass.

Divisions of China

In addition to the great north-south divisions of China, the country is further divided into seven regions—three in the south, three in the north, and one in the west.

In the south there is Southern China, Southeast China, and Southwest China. Southern China is made up of Hubei, Hunan, and parts of Zhejiang, Jiangxi, Shaanxi, and Anhui provinces. Shanghai, often listed as the most populous city in the world, is in this region. Southern China is also the most densely populated region in the country.

Southeast China, which is very hilly, includes the coastal provinces of Zhejian, Fujian, and Guangdong. The well-known city of Guangzhou (Canton) is the largest city in Guangdong province, of which the New Territories, Hong Kong, and Macao are a part. The two most widely spoken languages in this region are Cantonese and Amoy.

Southwest China consists of the provinces of Yunnan, Guizhou, Sichuan, and the autonomous region of Guangxi. Much of the huge area has very rugged terrain. Sichuan is especially noted for its scenic mountains, rivers, and beautiful valleys, plus its spicy food.

The Chinese consider Qinghai, the autonomous region that borders Sichuan on the northwest, as their wild west. It is remote, made up of mountains, desert, and grasslands, and is thinly populated. The capital, Xining, at an altitude of 2,250 meters, is filled with non-Chinese minorities—Mongols, Kazaks, Hui, and Tibetans—that give it an exotic non-Chinese appearance.

Turpan, in central Xinjiang (which is even farther west and the largest autonomous region in China), with its grape arbors, and donkeys in the streets, has been described by Western visitors as like something out of the Bible. The city is both the hottest and lowest city in China—150 meters below sea level, with summertime temperatures that regularly go well above the 100°F mark.

Northern China is bounded on the north by the Great Wall, on the east by the Huai River, on the south by the Tsinling Mountains, and on the west by Inner Mongolia. This region is frequently compared to North America's Great Plains insofar as terrain and climate are concerned.

The northwest region of China begins with the Taihung Mountains in Shanxi province and extends to the far west of Inner Mongolia. It is the homeland of many of the Aryan peoples of China, including the Kazakhs, Kirghiz, Hui, and Uyghurs.

The northeast region is the area that was formerly known as Manchuria, which borders North Korea and a great swatch of Russian Siberia. China's seventh region lumps Inner Mongolia and Tibet together.

The Han People

China's population, excluding Hong Kong, Macao, and Taiwan, is well over one billion and still swelling at the rate of some fourteen million people each year. The largest racial and ethnic group in China is generally referred to as the *Han* Chinese, Han being the name given to the indigenous group that made its home in the valley of the Yellow River and is credited with being the founders of the Chinese civilization. In addition to this huge core group, China has fifty-five recognized minorities, mostly living in the outlying southern provinces and the western autonomous regions.

China's largest minority group are the Zhuang (some fourteen million), who are concentrated in the Guangxi Zhuang Autonomous Region on the southern border. The Zhuang look very much like the Han Chinese, but speak a language that is related to Thai.

The Uygurs, who number well over six million and are another of China's largest minorities, are more related to the Turks than to the Han Chinese. Their language closely resembles Turkish, their written script is Arabic, and their religion is Islam. Primarily Caucasian in appearance, their ancestral homeland is the plateaus and mountains of Xinjiang in China's far west. The Hui people, numbering approximately one and a half million, live in the Ningxia Hui Autonomous Region of Northwest China, making up about one-third of the population in this area. They are Muslims.

The Yunnan Menagerie

Not surprisingly, a significant percentage of China's minority peoples are found in the far southern mountainous province of Yunnan. A total of twenty-four ethnic groups live in this region—or almost half of all the ethnic minorities in the country. Thirteen of these groups are found in just the Xishuangbanna region of the province, which borders Laos, Vietnam, and Burma.

Xishuangbanna is a subtropical area made up of fertile plains, hills, and mountains that boasts one-fourth of all the wild animal life in the country and one-sixth of its plant species. Elephants, leopards, tigers, monkeys, and an incredible array of birds inhabit the region along with its amazing variety of people.

The ethnic minorities of Xishuangbanna outnumber the Han Chinese in the region. The largest ethnic group are the Dai, an ancient race related to the Thai, who are devout Buddhists. Other groups include the Hani, Bulang, Lahu, Akha, and Jinuo. Each group has its own language, distinctive tribal customs, and elaborate native wear. And there are extraordinary physical differences in the people despite their proximity to each other.

One explanation of why there are so many different ethnic groups of people in one area is contained in a Jinuo legend. This legend says that a great flood covered the earth, and that only two people, a brother and a sister, survived. The couple subsequently gave birth to five children whose offspring became the founders of the five largest groups—the Jinuo, the Han, the Dai, the Hani, and the Bulang.

Other minorities include such groups as the Lisu, Lahu, Yao, Yi, and the Mongol/Caucasian tribes of Xinjiang: Tartars, Uzbeks, Tajiks, Xibes, Dours, Khalkhas, Kazaks (Cossacks), and Talmuks.

With the spread of Mandarin as the national language, rapidly improving communication and transportation systems, and subsequent mobility of the population, the smaller of China's minority groups will no doubt be gradually absorbed into the mass culture. The large groups such as the Uygurs,

Huis, and Inner Mongolians, however, will certainly retain their identities for the foreseeable future.

For the most part, China's minorities, situated on the outer edge of the country in generally remote areas, maintain their traditional lifestyles of farming and herding, following customs that are thousands of years old.

Provinces of Today's China

Provinces	Area (sq. km.)	Population (in millions)	Capital
Anhui	140,000	50	Hefei
Fujian	121,700	26	Fuzhou
Gansu	450,000	20	Lanzhou
Guangdong	212,000	61	Guangzhou
Guizhou	174,000	28	Guiyang
Hainan	34,000	6	Haikou
Heibei	187,700	54	Shijiazhuang
Heilungjiang	469,000	33.1	Harbin
Henan	167,000	75	Zhenzhou
Hubei	187,000	48	Wuhan
Hunan	210,000	55.1	Changsha
Jiangsu	102,600	60.2	Nanjing
Jiangxi	166,600	32	Nanchang
Jilin	180,000	23	Changchun
Liaoning	145,740	36.3	Shenyang
Quinghai	720,000	4	Xining
Shaanxi	195,800	29.1	Xi'an
Shandong	153,300	74	Jinan
Shanxi	156,000	25.5	Taiyuan
Sichuan	570,000	100	Chengdu
Zhejiang	101,800	38.9	Hangzhou

Cities with Provincial Status

City	Area (sq. km.)	Population (in millions)
Beijing	16,800	9.4
Shanghai	6,186	12
Tianjin	11,000	7

Autonomous Regions

Region	Area (sq. km.)	Population (in millions)	Capital
Guangxi Zhuang	230,000	40.2	Nanning
Inner Mongolia	1,100,000	20.3	Hohhot
Ningxia Hui	660,000	4.2	Yinchuan
Tibet	1,200,000	2	Lhasa
Xinjiang Uygur	1,600,000	13.8	Turpan

Notes on the Languages of China

Chinese is a family of languages like the Romance languages of Europe, notes Timothy Light, professor in East Asian languages and literature at Ohio State University. Light explains that China's famous "dialects" (Cantonese, Shanghaiese, Fukienese, etc.) are not mutually understandable, and are therefore just as much "real" languages as Spanish and Italian. Altogether there are ten major languages in China, including Mandarin, Cantonese, Shanghaiese, Fukienese, Hokkien, Hakka, and Chin Chow, plus several dozen minority languages, including a number in the far west that are related to Turkish.

The vitally important difference between the Chinese family of languages and the Roman family is that there is just one writing system for all of the Chinese languages. Despite the fact that the languages are made up of mostly different words with different pronunciations, they all use exactly the same ideographic writing system in which all of the individual ideograms making up the writing system have exactly the same meaning. They are just pronounced differently in the different languages. *This means the Chinese can read each others' languages fluently, without being able to speak them.*

It is this remarkable factor that has held the Chinese peoples together over the millenniums, despite long periods of political separation and physical isolation from each other. This writing system was standardized in the third century B.C. and, with the exception of some simplification in the number of strokes in commonly used ideograms, has remained virtually the same ever since.

Grammatically, Chinese resembles English—subject, verb, object—but there are no other similarities. Chinese words are made up of one, two, three, or more "syllables," each of which requires an ideogram or character to write. The majority of modern Chinese words have two syllables and require two ideograms (characters) to write.

There are numerous cultural differences in the way Chinese and English are used. For one, we have devised a special language for legal purposes that is often so obtuse it is nonsense to the layperson. The Chinese do not have a body of legalistic terms. Their contracts are written in ordinary language, usually in very general terms that make no attempt to cover every contingency. This difference in the use of language and in contracts is one of the biggest challenges facing Chinese and foreigners trying to do business with each other.

All languages are continuously changing, but Chinese is changing a lot faster than most because of the rapid influx of new products and new ideas for which there are no traditional terms. These changes are so rapid and in so many areas that even the most accomplished translators and interpreters are unable to keep current on everything.

There are also significant differences between spoken and written Chinese and between informal and "official" Chinese. Informal spoken Chinese is very loose, very casual. In formal or "official" situations, spoken Chinese becomes very stylized, very refined, and requires great skill and experience to use properly. Written Chinese has even more levels of use and, in the case of government propaganda or official communications, is charged with special meanings and nuances that are difficult or impossible for non-Chinese to fully grasp.

It is also common for the Chinese to speak in flowery, exaggerated terms that can be misleading to someone not familiar with this form of cultural expression. Further, it is also a deeply ingrained Chinese characteristic to speak in vague, often ambiguous terms as part of the process of not directly committing themselves to anything, while also protecting both their "face" and the "face" of others.

Irene Park, an American cross-cultural communications expert with years of experience in China, says: "Chinese is not designed to clearly, concisely communicate information. It is a means of expressing feelings, emotions, and 'polite escapes.' "

Park explains that 'polite escapes,' which she says make up approximately eighty percent of Chinese language usage, are ploys to avoid accepting responsibility or making commitments. "If you ask someone, 'Is this white or black?' a typical response is, 'Well, it isn't very gray.' If you extend this kind of reaction to virtually all other areas of business, you have a pretty good idea of the problems involved in communicating with Chinese."

Because of these language differences, it is important for the foreign businessperson in China to be wary of engaging in a lot of loose chatter and, particularly during business discussions, to use simple, straightforward terms that lend themselves to direct translation and reduce the possibility of misunderstandings. The habit of incorporating jokes and far-out references during speeches and presentations should especially be avoided during the early stages of any relationship.

Only extended exposure to the Chinese way of using language allows one to understand what is really being said. For example, when someone says that something is "inconvenient," the true meaning is most likely that nothing is going to happen or that it is impossible so you may as well forget it. The Chinese habitually use "maybe" and "perhaps" to preface statements that they mean categorically. At the same time, during negotiations there are occasions when these conditional terms are used in their "proper" sense, leaving room for further discussions.

Mandarin (*Putunghua* or "Common Language") is the official language of China and is the language of education in the country's twenty-one provinces and five autonomous regions, but Cantonese, Hakka, and several other Chinese languages are still widely spoken. It is currently estimated that some 75 percent of the younger population understands and speaks some Mandarin. The Beijing dialect of Mandarin is said to be the oldest continuously spoken language on earth, and more people speak Mandarin than any other language.

Chinese is "straightforward" and less complex than most other languages. Some consider it easier to learn than many other languages because it does not have verb tenses, conjugations, declensions, inflections, genders, or moods. Most of the rules of Chinese grammar have to do with word order rather than word changes. However, expatriate businesspeople who have gained considerable fluency in the language say it is far from easy to master.

The biggest problem for most people who undertake the study of Chinese is the existence of tones that change the meanings of words. Mandarin, having only four tones (Cantonese has nine!), is easier than the other related languages which have more tones. The four tones of Mandarin are high level, rising, falling-then-rising, and falling. These are indicated in the romanized spelling of the language by the following marks:

high level — rising / falling-rising v falling \

Another problem faced by foreigners studying Mandarin results from the fact that it apparently has more words that sound exactly alike than any other language. An attempt to remedy this situation was made around A.D. 500 when a tonal system was adopted, but the problem remains. There are hundreds of words that have dozens of meanings. One of the most often quoted examples is the word *i*, which has sixty-nine meanings, some of which are *city, ant, soap,* and *barbarian*.

This situation has contributed to a national habit of punning. Many Chinese constantly spice their conversation with esoteric puns that make the language especially difficult for foreign students to understand—but are an extraordinary vehicle for humor when one knows it well.

Early Western missionaries in China devised a number of systems for writing Chinese phonetically in Roman letters. None of these systems was a true representation of the correct pronunciation of the languages involved, which caused a great deal of confusion. In 1951 the government of the People's Republic of China began working on a new phonetic alphabet for Mandarin, which had been designated as the offical language of the country. This new system, called *pin yin* ("phonetic transcription"), was introduced in 1979. In this system all vowels are pronounced as they are in Latin, but there are several consonants that have totally unrelated pronunciations and, phonetically speaking, make no sense at all as far as English is concerned. See the pronunciation guide below.

Pronunciation Guide

(The official phonetic alphabet for Mandarin)

Pin yin	As in:	Pin yin	As in:
a	far	p	par
b	be	q	cheek
c	similar to **ts** in its	r	rzh
ch	church	s	so
d	do	sh	shore
e	her	t	top
ei	way	u	too
f	foot	v	used only in
g	go		foreign words and
h	her		some dialects
i	eat	w	want
j	jeep	x	she
k	kind	y	yet
l	land	z	zoo (zu)
m	me		sound
n	no	zh	pronounced **j** (jump)
o	law		

Learning how to say a dozen or so things in Chinese can go a long way in China. *Ni hao* (nee how), for example, has several meanings: "Hello," "Good morning," "Good afternoon," "Good evening," "How are you?"

Other especially useful words for the foreign visitor:

Thank you	Xie Xie (*shay shay*)
Very good	Hen hao (*hern how*)
Tasty	Hen hao chi (*hern how chee*)
Cheers (toast)	Ganbei (*ghan-bay*)
Friendship	Youyi (*yoe-yee*)
How are you?	Ni hao ma? (*nee how mah?*)

Fine, thank you	Hen hao, xie xie (*hern how, shay shay*)
Please come in	Qing jin (*cheeng jeen*)
Please sit down	Qing zuo (*cheeng zoh*)
Welcome	Huangying (*hwang-yeng*)
My name is Boye	Wo jiao Boye (*wah jee-ow Boye*)
What is your name?	Gui xing? (*ghwee sheeng?*)
Don't mention it	Meiyou guanxie (*may-e-yoh ghwan-shay*)
Sorry!	Duibuqi (*dewy-buu-chee*)
I don't understand	Wo bu dong (*wah buu dong*)
Toilet	Cesuo (*t'sue-soh*)
Open	Kaimen (*kie-men*)
Closed	Guanmen (*ghwan-men*)
Tea	Cha (*chah*)
Green tea	Lui cha (luu-ee-chah)
Black tea	Hong cha (*hong chah*)
Coffee	Kafei (*kah-faye*)
Boiled water	Kaishui (*kie-shuu-ee*)
Mineral water	Qi shui (*chee shu-ee*)
Beer	Pijiu (*pee-juu*)
Hot (temperature)	Re (*ruh*)
Hot (to touch)	Tang (*taang*)
Hot (spicy)	La (*lah*)
Cold	Leng (*lung*)
Chinese food	Zhongguo fan (*chong-gwah fahn*)
Western food	Xi can (*she tsaan*)
Sick	You bing (*yoh beng*)
England	Yingguo (*yeng-gwah*)
English language	Ying wen (*yeng win*)
British Embassy	Yingguo Da Shir Guan (*yeng-gwah dah shur gwahn*)
USA	Meiguo (*may-e-gwah*)
American Embassy	Meiguo Da Shir Guan (*may-e-gwah dah shur gwahn*)
China	Zhongguo (*chong-gwah*)
Chinese language	Zhong wen (*chong win*)
Chinese people	Zhongguo ren (*chong-gwah wren*)
France	Faguo (*fah-gwah*)
French language	Fa wen (*fah win*)
French Embassy	Faguo Da Shir Guan (*fah-gwah dah shur gwahn*)
Germany	Deguo (*day-gwah*)
German language	De wen (*day win*)
German Embassy	Deguo Da Shir Guan (*day-gwah dah shur gwahn*)
Japan	Ribenguo (*ree-ben-gwah*)
Japanese people	Riben ren (*ree-ben-wren*)
Japanese Embassy	Ribenguo Da Shir Guan (*ree-ben-gwah dah shur gwahn*)

Numbers are vital in basic communication, and fortunately the Chinese counting system is simple and similar to the Roman system. It is made up of combinations of ten elements beginning with zero, plus an additional key word for one hundred, one thousand, ten thousand, and so on. Eleven, for example, is ten plus one; twenty is two tens; fifty is five tens.

0	ling (*leng*)		17	shi-qi (*shur-chee*)
1	yi (*yee*)		18	shi-ba (*shur-bah*)
2	er (*rr*)		19	shi-jiu (*shur-jee-yu*)
3	san (*sahn*)		20	er-shi (*rr-shur*)
4	si (*suh*)		21	er-shi-yi (*rr-shur-yee*)
5	wu (*woo*)		25	er-shi-wu (*rr-shur-woo*)
6	liu (*lee-yu*)		30	san-shi (*sahn-shur*)
7	qi (*chee*)		31	san-shi-yi (*san-shur-yee*)
8	ba (*ba*)		38	san-shi-ba (*sahn-shur-bah*)
9	jiu (*jee-yu*)		40	si-shi (*suh-shur*)
10	shi (*shur*)		50	wu-shi *woo-shur*)
11	shi-yi (*shur-yee*)		100	yi-bai (*yee-buy*)
12	shi-er (*shur-rr*)		200	er-bai (*rr-buy*)
13	shi-san (*shur-sahn*)		500	wu-bai (*woo-buy*)
14	shi-si (*shur-suh*)		1,000	yi-qian (*yee-chee-inn*)
15	shi-wu (*shur-woo*)		10,000	wan (*wahn*)
16	shi-liu (*shur-lee-yu*)			

Chinese addresses and place-names make a lot more sense when you know the meaning of the more common terms. Here is a selected list:

Bandao (*bahn-dah-oh*)	peninsula
Bei (*bay-e*)	north
Chang Cheng (*chahng chung*)	The Great Wall
Cheng (*Chung*)	city
Cun (*tswun*)	village
Da (*dah*)	big
Dao (*dah-oh*)	island
Diqu (*dee-chuu*)	prefecture
Dong (*dong*)	east
Duan (*doo-on*)	section (as in Zhongshan Lu San Duan = Third Section Yatsen Sun Street)
Feng (*fung*)	peak, mount
Gang (*gahng*)	harbor, port
Gaoyuan (*gah-oh-yuu-inn*)	plateau
Gongyuan (*gong-yuu-inn*)	park (Renmin Gongyuan = People's Park)
Gonglu (*gong-luu*)	highway
Hai (*hie*)	sea

Haixia (*hie-she-ah*)	strait
He (*hay*)	river
Hou (*how*)	rear, back
Hu (*huu*)	lake
Jiao (*jee-ow*)	suburb (Dong Jiao = East Suburb)
Jie (*jee-eh*)	street
Jing (*jeng*)	well
Lu (*luu*)	road, street (Yi Lu = First Street, Er Lu = Second Street)
Nan (*nahn*)	south
Nei (*nay*)	inner
Pendi (*pin-dee*)	basin
Pingyuan (*peng-yuu-inn*)	plain
Po (*poe*)	lake
Pubu (*puu-buu*)	waterfall
Qian (*chee-inn*)	front
Qiao (*chee-ow*)	bridge
Qiuling (*chee-uu-leng*)	hills
Quan (*chuu-inn*)	spring
Qundao (*chuun-dah-oh*)	islands
Shamo (*shah-moe*)	desert
Sham (*shahn*)	mountain / mountain range, ridge
Shandi (*shahn-dee*)	hilly land, mountainous area
Shanfeng (*shahn-fung*)	peak, mount
Shang (*shahng*)	upper
Shankou (*shahn-kouh*)	pass
Sheng (*shung*)	province
Shi (*shee*)	city
Shuiku (*shuu-ee-kuu*)	reservoir
Tielu (*tee-eh-luu*)	railway
Tiyuchang (*tee-yuu-chahng*)	stadium
Wai (*wye*)	outer, outside
Wan (*wahn*)	bay
Wenhua Giji (*win-hwah gee-jee*)	cultural and historical site
Xi (*she*)	west
Xia / Xiagu (*she-ah / she-ah-guh*)	gorge
Xian (*she-inn*)	county
Xiao (*she-ow*)	small
Xingzhenqu (*sheen-jung-chuh*)	administrative district
Yang (*yahng*)	ocean
You (*yoh*)	right
Yunhe (*yuun-huh*)	canal
Zhaoze (*jah-ow-zuh*)	swamp

Zhen (*jen*)	town
Zhong (*chong*)	central
Zizhiqu (*tsu-jur-chuh*)	autonomous region
Zizhixian (*tsu-jur-she-inn*)	autonomous county
Zizhizhou (*tsu-jur-joe*)	autonomous prefecture
Zuo (*zuu-ah*)	left

Notes on Chinese Names

Chinese family and given names are often confusing to the foreign visitor. Altogether there are some 438 Chinese surnames, with thirty of these being double, clan names. The three most common family names are Wang, Zhang (Chang), and Li (Lee). Some 10 percent of the total population is named Zhang, or well over one hundred million, which gives a very good indication of the problems of keeping people and their names straight. Sixty percent of all Chinese have only nineteen surnames; 90 percent have only one hundred surnames.

To help diminish both the appearance and reality of this problem, I have chosen in this book to follow the Western practice of placing the first or given names first—which may seem rather odd where well-known names like Zedong Mao or Kai-shek Chiang are concerned, but it quickly "makes sense" and feels natural.

Traditionally all Chinese received a "milk name" at birth, a "book name" upon entering school, and a "style" or "great name" upon marriage. The "milk name" was normally used by members of the family and very close friends. The "book name" was used by teachers and school friends. Both parents and relatives would also use the individual's new "style" name after marriage. In feudal days, scholars also commonly assumed a "studio name," which they used in signing their works.

No doubt because of the profusion of identical names, many Chinese ended up with nicknames—often associated with their physical appearance or characteristics. When the exodus from China began in the 1800s, Chinese who lived overseas often adopted Western names in addition to their Chinese given names. In fact, one of the ways the Chinese seem to be using to distance themselves from their unhappy history is by adopting foreign names (usually American) outright. There have been occasions where one person in an office came up with a foreign nickname, and everyone else in the office followed suit.

When Chinese names are written in Roman letters in Hong Kong and Taiwan, a hyphen generally separates the first name and the "middle" name (Zi-yang). On mainland China, the custom is to run the two names together as if they were one (Ziyang). The explanation is that this is done to prevent foreigners from thinking that the second middle name is the last name.

It is customary to address Chinese by their last name, using the title Miss, Mrs., or Mr. until you become good friends and/or they let you know the nickname or Western name they prefer to be called. In rank-and-status-conscious China, job- or profession-related titles are especially important as badges of respect and recognition. People liked to be called by their titles. One reason for this might be the fact that so many people have the same family names. When there are 100 million Zhangs, who could get excited over being called Mr. or Mrs. Zhang?

It is common, for example, to call any tradesperson or skilled person *Shi Fu* or "master craftsperson," whether the individual is a carpenter, electrician, plumber, chauffeur, or cook. Old people who have no work-related title are commonly called *Lao*, which is more or less the equivalent of "honorable old one." Younger people with no identifiable name or job title may be addressed as *Xiao,* or "honorable young one." *Lao* and *Xiao* may also be used as Mr. or Miss in front of a family name.

The Chinese themselves generally address each other by the family name and an appropriate title, or by both the family name and full given name together, with the family name first—e.g., Li Jiqi (lee jee-chee). The obvious reason for this custom is that it helps distinguish all the Zhangs, Lees, and Zhous from each other.

Some common surnames are Cai, Cheng, Deng, Ding, Du, Feng, Gao, Gong, Gou, Han, He, Hu, Jiang, Lei, Liang, Li, Liu, Ma, Mah, Mao, Peng, Qian, Sun, Tang, Wang, Wei, Wen, Wu, Xu, Yao, Ye, Zhan, Zhang, Zhou, Zhu.

2

The Historical Perspective

*"A gentleman understands what is moral.
A base man understands what is advantageous or profitable."*
—CONFUCIUS

The Yin and Yang of Things

The basis for traditional Chinese philosophy, religion, science, astrology, and divination is the principle that the universe is composed of and held together by two forces, the yin and the yang, or the positive and the negative, also referred to as the principle of duality. In Chinese thought, every aspect and facet of nature is imbued with these two forces, which must be in balance, in harmony, for things to be right with the world—for crops to grow, for people to remain healthy and be content, for governments to function, for companies to prosper.

In this concept, there is a plus for every minus and it is the interaction of these yin and yang forces that creates life and gives the universe the form and the cycles that we see.

The view of the world now accepted by most modern-day Western scientists—from protons and electrons all the way up—is based on the same principle expressed in different terms. It can therefore be said that, to a considerable extent, the Chinese divined the now accepted nature of the universe more than two thousand years ago.

Becoming familiar with the yin-yang principle may seem like a very esoteric pursuit to some Western businesspeople, but recognition of the principle and knowing something about its role in Chinese thought and behavior today can be very helpful in understanding and dealing with the Chinese. It is a factor in what the Chinese eat and in the order in which they eat

16

things—which is about as basic as you can get. It also influences many of the day-to-day decisions the Chinese make in business.

Simply stated, the yin-yang principle gives the Chinese a long-range view of things and allows them to accept the bad with the good as the natural order.

The Philosophers' State

China is famous for its philosophers, and rightly so. Over the centuries there have been thousands of them, and they fashioned a body of thought and knowledge that is unsurpassed. The reasons for this extraordinary phenomenon include the long age of civilization in China, a writing system that was developed very early and has remained virtually unchanged down to the present time, and the important role education played in Chinese culture. The work of many of the greatest scholars and thinkers of each generation was thus passed on to succeeding generations.

Among the best known and most influential of these philosophers were King Wen (2953–2838 B.C.), the Duke of Chou (1231–1135 B.C.), Ze Dao or Lao Tsu (604 B.C.–?), Confucius (551–479 B.C.), Tzu Chung (399–320 B.C.), Mencius (371–289 B.C.), and Hsi Chu (A.D. 1130–1200).

King Wen, founder of the Chou Dynasty and credited with being the father of Chinese religion and industry, is known for his inventions of various tools and technology as well as the creation of the forerunner of calculus. His son, the Duke of Chou, added to King Wen's work. Their commentaries make up the bulk of what came to be known as the now famous *I Ching* or *The Book of Changes*. The duke is also said to have invented the first compass.

Ze Dao is known as the founder of Daoism, which is ranked next to Confucianism and Buddhism in its influence on Chinese thought and customs. His primary work, the *Dao-te-Ching (Way and the Power)*, is said to be the second most frequently quoted work in history (the first being the Bible).

Dao's philosophy was that ultimate reality can be perceived and understood only through mystical insight and cannot be expressed in words. Daoism refers to the way of the universe and all things in the universe—the spirit, the driving power, and the order of all things.

The passage of time and later philosophers split Daoism into three levels or forms. The first was Popular Daoism, which emphasized sorcery, magic, and the power of the gods. It appealed to the illiterate masses who were the overwhelming majority in China. The second was Esoteric Daoism, which held that the power that ordered and drove the universe was psychic in nature. Individuals could then imbue themselves with some of this power through meditation and yogic exercises. This category of Daoism, long since gone from China, appealed only to a small educated minority.

The third was Philosophical Daoism, which held that by education, reflection, and intuition, one could achieve harmony in one's personal life as well as with the rest of the cosmos. Philosophical Daoists taught that selflessness and humility were the basis for human conduct, that the ultimate goal of humans was harmony with other people and with the universe—to flow with nature instead of against it and to adapt to it rather than try to change it.

Daoists of this school believed that change was disruptive, that nonaction was better than action, that simplicity was preferable to complexity, that informality took precedence over formality and that the ultimate goal was to conform to the "way" and ride it serenely to eternal bliss. In a Daoist society there would be no classes, all things would be individually or democratically decided, and an all-powerful government would not be needed. It was, therefore, not surprising that Daoism was never embraced by the ruling elite of China.

Followers of Popular Daoism practiced conventional medicine, science, and alchemy, particularly the search for an elixir of immortality. Later Daoists of this school also preached and practiced an extraordinarily active sex life in order to keep one's life balanced. Sexual relations three or four times a day was considered necessary to ensure good health and long life, and manuals were published giving explicit instructions on a variety of sexual techniques, generally couched in poetic terms.

Probably one of the primary reasons for the growth and influence of Daoism over so many centuries was the teaching that older men should choose young women for their sexual partners, and older women should tryst with younger men. Daoists noted that older men and women would benefit from the energy of their younger partners, while the young men and women would learn from the experience of their older lovers.

The Great Sage

The best known of all of China's ancient sages is, of course, Confucius, who began as a bureaucrat and then became a wandering teacher, diplomat, and advisor to princes. His many books include the *Book of Songs*, the *Canon of History*, and the *Spring and Autumn Annuals*.

As a young man, Confucius is said to have gone to the capital to study ceremonial rites under the famous Ze Dao, the "old master." Later, after he himself became a teacher, Confucius taught courses in six "arts" that were carefully selected to produce the ideal administrator: ceremonies, music, archery, carriage-driving, writing, and mathematics. The proper foundation for society, according to Confucius, was propriety based on respect for human dignity, which in turn is based on two principles: fairness and reversibility.

Confucius, who was born in 551 B.C., when Ze Dao would have been about fifty-five years old, did not follow in the master's footsteps, however.

Taking his cue from long-gone dynasties during which peace reigned, Confucius based his teachings on absolute respect for tradition and on a carefully ranked hierarchy founded on primary relationships between members of families and between people and their rulers.

All of these relationships were defined by a strict code of conduct known as *Li*, or "etiquette," which was founded in filial piety, strict observation of the prescribed rituals, and obedience to a ruler who governed with the consent of the subjects in recognition of his goodness and ability. The final foundation of Confucius's system was training and ongoing experience in such cultural arts as music, calligraphy, painting, and poetry as part of the moral education that is essential to raise people above the level of savagery.

This latter teaching resulted in the quality of one's handwriting being equated not only with cultural refinement but with one's morals as well. The skilled calligrapher was therefore a "good person," whose morals were visible for all to see. Conversely, of course, those who were unskilled in writing were looked down on as base people whose proper role was to be ruled over by people with morals. And, of course, it was this Confucian commandment that helped spark the prodigious outpouring of literature, painting, and other works of art in China during the succeeding generations.

Eventually, the teachings of Confucius were compiled in a large volume called simply *The Analects*, which was to become the bible of the Chinese way until modern times.

Soothing Savage Beasts

Educated Westerners are usually familiar with the old belief that "music soothes the savage beast," an obvious reference to the fact that a long time ago someone in the West recognized the subtle power that music has to influence behavior. In the West, however, this new-found wisdom was neither clearly defined nor utilized in a knowing, comprehensive way to aid in civilizing people or in controlling antisocial behavior.

Well before 1200 B.C. the Chinese government was already using music as a means of helping to regulate life in the country. Confucius not only recognized the power of music; an integral part of his teachings was that music could and should be used to improve the morality and behavior of people. He noted: "Nothing can ease the higher-ups and govern the people better than propriety, and nothing can reform manners and customs more effectively than music."

A later philosopher said that promoting decorum through music leads to the unity of mind and action, and another added, "The best music heals; the best rites administer." After Confucius, music became an important factor in the moral education of the Chinese, and contributed greatly to the preservation and enhancement of the civilization.

Another key principle taught by Confucius: In societies that are governed by politics and where people are disciplined by penal laws, no sense of morality or shame is instilled in their citizens, and people in such countries will break the laws when it suits their purposes. On the other hand, in countries that are led by virtue and regulated by etiquette, the people will develop a sense of morality and will conduct themselves properly without force or the threat of punishment.

Confucius commented on just about everything in human behavior, and his concept of sincerity is still the ideal of cultured Chinese. The sincere person, Confucius said, "does not take advantage of a dark room." In other words, this person is moral and upright at all times, not just when on public display or involved with others, and strives always for a totally clear conscience. Another descriptive phrase that Confucius used to define sincerity was "freedom from self-deceit"—being honest to oneself.

Mencius, who came after Confucius, believed that human beings were naturally endowed with four good instincts: compassion, abhorrence of indecency, a sense of right and wrong, and a sense of propriety—but that this inborn tendency could be fulfilled only by education and constant self-examination. He humanized much of Confucius's philosophy. He believed that each individual was responsible for his or her own morality, with responsibility to one's family being the paramount duty. He taught that the rights of people took precedence over the rights of rulers and that people had the right to overthrow unjust governments.

Philosopher Zi Xun taught that proper behavior was vital in economic prosperity as well as in politics, religion, and other disciplines. He taught that to achieve economic success the masses had to be clearly divided into classes and ranks. "Without a sense of hierarchy, the masses become mobs. Social functions can be fulfilled and prosperity can be assured only when the difference between high and low is acknowledged in a hierarchy of power," he said.

Tzu Chung, a Daoist philosopher, disagreed with Confucius and taught his followers that since the mysteries of heaven and earth were unknowable, it was better to sit back, do as little as possible, and attempt to stay in harmony with nature rather than change things. His thinking contributed to the development of Zen Buddhism some one thousand years later.

Hsi Chu, who came some eight hundred years after Mencius, is known as the Great Synthesizer. He extracted what he thought was best from all of the great philosophers of antiquity, further humanizing Confucianism and building on the work of Mencius. His four books of commentary came to be known as *The Four Classics* and in A.D. 1313 were adopted by the government as texts for the civil service examinations on which the country's whole administrative system was based. *The Four Classics* were to remain the basic instructional material of China's civil service examinations until the exams were abolished in 1905.

Much of the philosophy of China's greatest masters is as modern and pertinent today as it was two or three thousand years ago. Tsu Mo in the fifth century B.C. said, "Spread love, do not make war." Confucius, in the sixth century, said, "That which you do not desire, do not do unto others." In the third century B.C., Tse Hsun wrote; "You glorify nature and meditate on it. Why not domesticate and regulate it?"

The Great Sage Today

Confucian ethics remain the bedrock of Chinese thought and behavior throughout Asia today, perhaps more so in Singapore and Taiwan than in mainland China, but if you look closely at the average Chinese businessman or bureaucrat anywhere, the influence of the great sage is unmistakable. It is the underlying belief among Chinese that the "human-heartedness" and righteousness, along with the rituals of etiquette and ceremony taught by Confucius are the proper base for all business relationships. A contemporary Confucian scholar, Dr. Sinn Whor Shu of Singapore, adds that Confucian philosophy is particularly appropriate for modern-day business, despite a popular belief that Confucius did not address himself to money or economic matters. "Confucius strongly advocated making money to the best of one's ability," Dr. Shu said.

Other Singapore authorities on the teachings of Confucius say that businesspeople should study and follow The Analects as a foundation for their business conduct, since commercial laws and contracts are not completely binding and must be based on deeper principles, such as the virtues propounded by Confucius.

In Confucian terms, the ideal man was described as a "gentleman," meaning one who was upright and moral in all things, and observed the proper rituals of etiquette in his behavior. To be described as a gentleman in Chinese terms, therefore, means much more than it does in the West, where just being polite is often enough to earn the title.

Propriety, as espoused by Confucius, is based on three principles: respect for human dignity, fairness (what is unfair to one is unfair to all), and "reversibility" (willingness to be the recipient of one's own manners and actions). Another ingredient always added to these principles is "duty"— one's duty to parents, to employers, to customers, to the state.

Patterns of Chinese Thought

At the beginning of the Chin Dynasty (221 B.C.–207 B.C.), the first Chin emperor, Shihuang Chin ordered that virtually all books be burned. The only books exempted from his order were those in his own library, those of seventy court officials, the history of the state of Chin, and a few books on medicine and agriculture. He also had many of the scholars of that period buried alive. His purpose was to eliminate possible criticism of his reign, thereby removing any threat to his authority.

The destruction of some of the greatest and most important writing in history did not perpetuate Chin's reign, however. His dynasty fell to the Han only fourteen years later, becoming one of the shortest in China's history.

Pang Liou, the founder of the Han Dynasty, following the advice of his prime minister, Chungshu Tung, ordered that all schools of thought except that of Confucianism be banned. This "unification of Chinese thought" by the Han emperor, says Ding-Ho Wang, a Taiwan scholar-actor-businessman, was to become the key in the development of Chinese character as it is known today. This is demonstrated in the failure to exhibit individuality and accept personal responsibility and the tendency to blindly obey those who are in authority.

Wang said that, when individuality is suppressed from childhood, when rebellious behavior of any kind is blotted out, when there is no freedom of speech, no freedom of self-expression, no freedom to disobey, all of one's natural desires are choked out of existence. Thus, when people achieve a position of authority, they typically expect to exercise absolute control over everyone under them, that nothing will be done without getting their approval, and that everything will be done their way.

Under these circumstances, Wang added, the average Chinese employee, deprived of esteem and any semblance of authority, is unwilling to accept responsibility, takes every possible opportunity to cut corners, and simply gives the appearance of working; thus, making it much more complicated and difficult to accomplish anything.

One of the favorite ways in which the Chinese pass the buck, Wang says, is to write an official document asking for instructions from their superiors. This system goes way back to the Ch'ing Dynasty, when there would often be no response to such requests for many months—a situation that was referred to as "documentary travels."

Historically in China, the difference between those in power and those without official authority was vast and absolute. Government officials on all levels had the power of life or death over the people at large. The only way people could get out from under this pervasive control was to become officials, and this was limited to people who passed the great civil service examinations after years of intense study.

The father in every family was an absolute despot. His word, his every whim, was law. The dutiful son not only followed his father's specific instructions in everything, but did absolutely nothing without his father's approval rather than take a chance on doing anything the father might dislike. In the Chinese context, an unfilial son lost his place in society and became an outcast.

Within the confines of this system, virtually all ambition, all courage, all curiosity, all esteem was smothered. Sons were conditioned in a perverse inferiority complex, unwilling to try anything new, to accept any responsibility—until the death of their father, when they fell heir to the status and power of the supreme authority. At that time, Wang said, their inferiority complex was suddenly converted to a superiority complex, and they repeated the same process with their own sons and daughters. This was the foundation of Chinese society for generation after generation—frozen in time.

Wang added that part of the heritage of the Chinese is that they have a deep compulsion to somehow get into positions of authority. They have been conditioned to believe that having authority over others is the most important thing in the world. But, he adds, achieving authority does not mean that the individual will act in a responsible manner; people in authority are invariably more interested in their special privileges than in fulfilling the obligations that come with their authority.

China's traditional educational system reinforced the concept of unquestioning obedience to authority and to the status quo in the social, economic, and political systems. Students were required, on the pain of punishment, to accept the attitudes and standards of their teachers. To dispute any state-approved precept was a serious crime. Blind obedience was the only acceptable type of behavior.

This stultifying educational system, although greatly diminished, is still alive in Taiwan and still turning out students who are little better than robots, students who are still expected to blindly obey their parents, their teachers, government officials, and their employers, Wang adds.

The Ultimate Bureaucracy

The national civil service examination system that was to create a privileged class of powerful bureaucrats in China was established during the Sui Dynasty (581–618). This class was to administer the day-to-day affairs of the country with an iron fist for the next 1,300 years, molding the character of the intelligentsia as well as the peasantry and becoming the primary influence in the development of the country thereafter.

Only sons of the better-to-do with the luxury of time and money could afford to devote much of their lives to the intensive study necessary for the exams, thus creating a situation in which the ruling class perpetuated itself. The examinations were held on a local district level, then on the provincial level, and finally on a national level at the capital. Those who passed the exams became known as *Chuuargyuan*, or "Mandarins," and were assigned administrative posts in either the capital or elsewhere in the country.

Upon passing the first examination on a county level, the fledgling scholars received the title of *Tung-sheng*, qualifying them to sit for the First Degree examinations on the prefectural level and advancement to either *Lower Grade Syoutsai* or *Ordinary Syoutsai*. Those who achieved only the lower grade of this level had to take additional examinations periodically. Failure to pass resulted in punishment.

Scholars who achieved the rank of *Syoutsai* were then eligible to sit for Second Degree examinations on the provincial level for the rank of *Jyuren*. Passing still another examination meant the scholar was eligible to go to the capital and compete for the coveted title of *Datyau*. Last were national examinations at the Third Degree level and the title of *Jinshr*, which was the equivalent of a doctorate.

According to extant descriptions, the exams could last up to nine days. One part of the exams was the copying of two themes for essays and one for a poem. The themes were attached to the ends of long poles. Part of the grade was determined by how rapidly the candidate wrote the essays and the poem.

Power of the Scholars

At any one time in China's history, the number of Mandarin scholar-officials, who for the most part made up the gentry landowning class, were never more than about 2 percent of the population. But their power and influence over the rest of the country was absolute.

The scholar-officials were more than just bureaucratic administrators. They also functioned as jury and judge, as architects, engineers, and project managers. Officially they were in charge of and responsible for everything that took place or was planned for their districts. In reality, most also were masters at avoiding responsibility, placing the blame for any problem on their subordinates.

One of the prime rules of the mandarinate system in dynastic China was that any change in any activity, social, economic, or political, had to be approved by the Mandarins and the higher echelons of government. And generally speaking, change of any kind was regarded as upsetting and therefore undesirable. The Mandarins and the Imperial Court wanted nothing that might interfere with their power or privileges. They therefore demanded and enforced passive obedience, humility, respect, and strict adherence to all established rules and ways.

Thus the lives of the mass of Chinese remained virtually the same for century after century. Curiosity, ambition, innovation, creation—all were antiestablishment and therefore taboo among the common people.

Mandarins as Villains

Critics of the Mandarin system point out that it created a bureaucracy that was rigid to the extreme, that it did not inspire or teach management ability or leadership, and that the Mandarins lacked any kind of practical experience, and instead of being outgoing and interested in really learning about the needs and interests of the people, most were opinionated, arrogant, and dedicated to protecting their special privileges and the status quo. Being the only educated segment of Chinese society, the Mandarins tended to have little or no respect for the opinions of the people under their control.

Since power, privilege, money, and the pursuit of earthly pleasures were strictly limited to the ruling class, and the only way into this class was through the examinations, study became exalted to the exclusion of almost everything else. But since the overwhelming majority of the population was totally illiterate, superstitions, spiritualism, and taboos flourished. Not being able to read, receiving no instructions in anything beyond household and farm work and proper behavior toward superiors, the bulk of the Chinese population were simpleminded people who were easily influenced and controlled.

Members of the royal court spent a great deal of their time and energy competing against each other for favor with the emperor and higher members of the court. The emperor was godlike, omnipotent, but the empress was in constant competition with three classes of concubines and a large cadre of eunuchs. Ministers competed against each other and against the emperor's relatives, all of whom were embroiled in intrigues and battles to protect and extend their power and privileges.

In this atmosphere, your connections were often the most important things in life, and to this day among the Chinese everywhere, connections are the oil of business and the basis for most professional and social relationships.

Since position and authority were not based on talent or learning but on connections, asking for and dispensing favors became the modus operandi for what passed as management and business, not only in the imperial government but on a provincial district level as well. Because maintaining good connections meant maintaining good relations with large numbers of people, particularly those in superior positions, the Chinese were forced to become very circumspect in their speech; to go to extraordinary extremes not to give offense to anyone, even inadvertently; and to protect their "face" and the "face" of their contacts in everything they said and did.

Another factor in the molding of the traditional character of the Chinese was the all-encompassing pressure for obedience without question. The emperor, his ministers, the Mandarin officials, military officers, teachers, and fathers were to be obeyed absolutely, regardless of the circumstances. Questioning, much less disobeying, any authority figure was a serious crime against society and the government. Punishment was certain, swift, and usually severe, as an example to others. Within the confines of this highly structured, emotionally, intellectually, and spiritually limiting system, the ordinary people of China endured for one generation after the other.

Baggage from the Past

During the two thousand years between the beginning of the Han Dynasty in 206 B.C. and the fall of the Qing (Ching) Dynasty in 1911, primitive communication and transportation systems isolated most of China's population from the direct influence of the Imperial Court. The people at large were basically left to the not-so-tender mercies of the Mandarins who ruled in the name of the emperor, according to precepts set down at the beginning of the period.

Present-day critics, including many Chinese, say that the heritage of the Han education and social systems lives on, that the biggest handicap facing the Chinese today is a school system still based on forcing students to accept the thinking of others without expressing their own opinions and to blindly obey those in authority. This, the critics add, curtails the development of any sense of responsibility and leads to the perpetuation of insensitivity to the rights of others.

One of the manifestations of these age-old concepts is that many Chinese employers will not share authority. This results in employees not taking any kind of responsibility, even for the most routine actions within their own company and always waiting for the boss to make the necessary decision. Examples abound. A piece of equipment breaks down. The worker reports the problem to the immediate boss who passes it on up the chain of command, often to the president himself—a process that can take days. Then the procedure is reversed and more days elapse before a replacement is bought and delivered to the worker, who has not been able to do the job properly since the breakdown.

Not having responsibility for the operation within a company, it is common for employees to be unconcerned about the quality of their work or about meeting deadlines. It is also common for them to have little if any loyalty toward the company. Even among employees who do feel a sense of loyalty to their firm, many will not go beyond a very limited scope for fear of exposing themselves to criticism. People in this category will often not make any commitment at all when presented with a problem or proposition.

It is still common for Chinese workers, including some managers, to equate business decisions with political decisions of government officials.

Since they have no political power, the idea of making decisions either doesn't occur to them or they pass the responsibility on to someone higher, slowing down the business process.

"The whole problem boils down to the fact that Chinese are still conditioned to obey instead of take responsibility, but in business today just being obedient is not enough," said a Chinese commentator. "In fact, people who are just obedient are the ones who are the most apt to make mistakes when anything happens that requires some thought," he added.

A further extension of this attitude is that departments within the same government ministry, agency, or company often do not or cannot communicate and cooperate with each other. Competition between departments also contributes to this basic problem. Each department wants to look good in the eyes of the boss. To cooperate with another department in some project that would make it look good may run counter to this feeling, resulting in little or no cooperation.

Origins of Chinese Etiquette

Throughout most of China's long history, the relationships between people in all classes were based on carefully prescribed forms of behavior that covered virtually every aspect of conduct—so much so and to such a degree that learning and following proper etiquette was one of the major facets of life. The higher one was on the social ladder, the more meticulous and demanding were the rules of etiquette.

The Chinese word for etiquette, *li*, which originally meant "to sacrifice," refers to the fact that following legally sanctioned etiquette required extraordinary sacrifices, not to mention detailed knowledge of hundreds of correct forms of behavior. Training in this highly prescribed way of living was so thorough, so pervasive, that people were judged first, last, and sometimes always on how closely they followed these rules of behavior. Etiquette came to be equated not only with learning in general, but with culture and morality—even nationality and nationalism.

The Chinese eventually came to believe that their behavior was the only correct etiquette in the universe, that all who did not follow the same meticulous rules of conduct were uncivilized barbarians. Of course, the rules of etiquette in China today are no longer enforced by harsh feudal sanctions and they have been considerably relaxed, but they remain very important. There are still formalities, particularly in business and formal situations, that are ingrained in the behavior of the Chinese.

At meetings, for example, the leader of the group acts as spokesperson for the whole group. Whatever differences of opinion the members of the group may have are resolved beforehand or afterward. The American custom for everyone to speak out during meetings and for differences to be hashed out on the spot goes against the Chinese grain.

The Chinese attempt to control every aspect of meetings, from the first greetings and introductions, to the order of seating, the content of the discussions, and how they are conducted. This is not entirely a ploy to take and keep the advantage, although that is surely a primary aim. It is also to ensure that the meeting goes smoothly and that there are no surprises.

One of the essences of Chinese relationships that play a key role in meetings, negotiations, and ongoing relationships is that the basic relationship is not between individuals or people per se. It is between bureaucratic organizations, with all that this implies—meaning that the relationships are conducted on a higher, abstract level, with the individuals taking little or no personal responsibility.

This approach means that the individual Chinese businessperson or government official can never be pinned down personally, that he or she always has an out and can delay things, stop things, or do other things in the name of the organization, no matter how irrational or stupid they may appear to be to the outsider.

While foreign businesspeople on a high executive level generally have the authority to make decisions on the spot, to make changes in company policy—or at least in what the company will accept in particular situations—the Chinese either do not have such authority or will claim not to have it when it suits their purpose. Generally they must in fact refer the matter to their organization to get consensus agreement, or they use this as a way of gaining time and/or their own ends.

The Chinese negotiating technique has been likened to both guerrilla warfare and psychological warfare—strike, retreat; strike, retreat; confuse the enemy, get them off guard, weaken their will, make them feel guilty for opposing you, make a "final offer" that is considerably below what they know is acceptable.

Unlike most foreign businesspeople, Chinese officials and managers have often had considerable experience in psychological tactics, in cross-examining and intimidating opponents. It is also typical Chinese behavior to withhold information, to reveal as little as possible about their own situation, putting the foreigner at a further disadvantage.

The use of the strike-retreat technique while opponents thrash about trying to defend themselves and mount a counterattack at the same time is apparently drawn from the same principle as the *dai ji juan* martial art. This is said to have been created by a priest after he watched a bird of prey attack a snake. In its attempt to strike the snake, the bird eventually wore itself down, made a mistake, and was nailed by the writhing reptile.

Of course, some of the rules of behavior sanctioned in the Chinese system were common enough and benign. For example, during the early genera-

tions following the invention of eyeglasses in China it was considered exceptionally rude for a person wearing glasses to speak to someone without first
removing the glasses. The Western parallel, of course, is removing one's hat
before speaking to someone.

While the handshake is now a common form of greeting among most
Chinese, the traditional greeting is to cup one's own hands (left over right),
chest high, and raise them slightly while bowing. In earlier times when
greeting someone of superior social standing, it was customary to raise the
hands as high as the forehead and to execute a low bow.

When offering an object such as a gift or a drink to someone, as well as
when receiving something from someone, it is polite to use both hands.

At hosted meals, it is the responsibility of the host—not waiters or servants—
to see that the guests' drinking glasses are refilled. It is also mandatory in
Chinese etiquette for the host to accompany each guest to the door when a meal
or party ends. Ranking guests are normally accompanied all the way to their
automobiles, and the host waits until they drive away before going back inside.

It is Chinese etiquette to say no when offered a drink, a meal, a gift, or
a favor. It is up to you the host to politely persist, without being crude or
rude.

In Chinese etiquette, there are prescribed manners for everyone at meal-
times, when in the presence of superiors, and when greeting and seeing
guests off. One always accompanies guests to the entrance or to the upper-
floor elevators if they are leaving your office building. The host normally
pushes the elevator button, then waits until his guests are in the elevator and
the door closes before returning to his office.

There is growing concern among some Chinese that the one-child-per-
couple system in China will end up causing its own kind of serious social
problem in the future, including a breakdown in traditional Chinese etiquette. This dread is based on the tendency of parents with just one child,
especially when the child is a boy, to seriously spoil him. The symptom is
clearly discernible among the more affluent families, so much so that the
children of such families are commonly referred to as "Little Emperors."

This new generation of "un-Chinese-like" children is usually dated from
1978, when the country's new Open Door policies began making it possible for
better-off parents to indulge their children, allowing them to become selfish and
demanding. Since most of these children are in the educated upper class, they
will move into positions of leadership early in the twenty-first century.

Questioning the Genius of China

Given the nearly 5,000-year history of the Chinese people, many have commented on their apparent lack of inventive genius. This lack was certainly

not brought about by any failing in intellect or imagination, at least on the part of the intelligentsia. It was, instead, brought about by a social system that not only did not reward technological innovation or invention, but for the most part opposed such changes by custom and law.

Over 90 percent of China's population throughout the ages was totally illiterate and existed at a level of subsistence and in a social system that precluded the kind of tinkering and trial and error that is the hallmark of the inventive bent. Even the intelligentsia lacked both the motivation and the kind of background that encourages inventiveness. Virtually none of them ever had any hands-on work experience (with the exception of paperwork). Their formative years were spent in the intense study of classical literature and philosophical treatises. Most lived lives of nonproductive bureaucrats, priests, or dilettantes.

Still, the list of technological discoveries and inventions created in China is long and impressive, and predated similar developments in the West by more than a thousand years. Some of the things that the world owes to the genius of China are paper, eyeglasses, silk, the printing press, mariner's compass, paper money, porcelain, umbrellas, fans, fingerprinting, watertight compartments in ships, gunpowder, rockets, automatic lock-drive on astronomical telescopes, the mechanical clock (invented by two scholars in A.D. 725), sugar, cooking stoves, the washboard, the magnetic needle. The first printed map was produced in China in A.D. 1115, showing the western regions of the country.

Mathematics was already a well-practiced art by the second century A.D., when the abacus is said to have been invented. It is mentioned in the *Shu Shu Chi I*, or *Memoir on Some Traditions of the Mathematical Art*, published around the end of the second century. The first surviving drawing of the abacus, in its present form, appears in a book published in 1436. The device, still widely used throughout Asia, was described in detail in a 1593 book.

Early Chinese Traders

During various periods in its long history, China was very active in foreign trade. Its first known ongoing link with the Western world was the fabled *Silk Road* that began in Xian, capital of the present-day province of Shaanxi in central China, and snaked westward, exiting China near Kashi. There it continued on through territory that is now part of Russia, northern India. Afghanistan, and Persia, ending at what is now the port city of Tyre in Lebanon. The road began in Xian, which is near the geographical center of China, because when the road was opened Xian was the capital city of the reigning dynasty, and in fact was the capital of China during the course of eleven dynasties over a span of 1,100 years (until the end of the Tang Dynasty in 907).

No one knows exactly when the great road was established but it was in use during the earlier years of the Roman Empire, and it was along the road that Buddhism traveled from India (where it was soon to die) to China around A.D. 65, found a lasting home, and became a main thread in the culture of the country.

During the first two hundred years of the great Tang Dynasty (A.D. 618–907), Chinese and foreign merchants, adventurers, students, and missionaries traveled the Silk Road to and from the fabled Middle Kingdom, their caravans and nightly stopovers an important part of the pulse of the country.

The ancient Silk Road became news again in 1988, when the Silk Road International Auto Rally was established with the approval of the International Motor Sports Federation. The annual rally starts in Beijing and runs approximately eight thousand kilometers to Urumqi, capital of the Xinjiang Uygur Autonomous Region, over some of the roughest roads in the world. While the rally brought renewed attention to the famed trade route, the province of Xinjiang took more substantive steps by linking the Silk Road with a series of development programs, including ninety-three joint-venture projects. The province, China's largest, abolished a number of its more restrictive foreign investment laws and passed a series of new ones, making its business environment more attractive to foreign investors than many of the more developed regions.

Chinese junks were known in the ports of Southeast Asia and as far west as Africa more than a thousand years ago. A description of one of these trading junks indicates a degree of sophistication and comfort that would not be out of place today. The ship had four decks, and there were private cabins for the officers and ranking passengers as well as members of the crew. The cabins for those of rank had closets, private toilets, and other conveniences. Upper-class passengers often brought their wives or concubines along; even crewmen were allowed to have their families aboard with them, and grew fresh vegetables in large wooden tubs.

The naval/commercial voyages of the Ming admirals from A.D. 1405 to 1433, for example, were formidable in their size and strength and brought great wealth and prestige to China. The first of these voyages included sixty-two ships, the largest of which was 444 feet long and 180 feet wide. There were 27,870 men in the expedition, including clerks and buyers. The fleet was called the "Star Raft" in reference to the starlike glow attributed to the emperor's court.

But China decided it did not need anything the outside world had to offer, and suddenly ended its trading activities and closed its doors, forbidding its citizens from traveling abroad or communicating with foreigners. By withdrawing into itself, China cut itself off from a vital source of wealth, leaving a vacuum in Asia that was soon filled by Japanese buccaneers, the Portuguese, the Spaniards, the Dutch, and other Europeans who began pouring into the area in the 1500s.

This was not the first time that China had closed its doors to the outside world. During the latter third of the Tang Dynasty (618–907), the emperor, fearing for the survival of the dynasty, banned all foreign religions and barred all foreigners from China's ports. For some four hundred years afterward, the country was almost completely isolated from the rest of the world.

It was not until the Yuan Dynasty, founded by Kublai Khan in 1280, that China once again opened its borders to foreigners, including the intrepid Marco Polo, whose stories of the greatness of China were assumed by most to be fiction. Then with the downfall of the Mongolian Yuan regime in 1368, the succeeding Ming Dynasty resolved that China would never again be conquered by foreigners. For the second time, it closed off virtually all contact with the West, allowing only the famous expeditions of eunuch Admiral Chen He to Arabia and Africa. This, if anything, proved to the Chinese that they were so far ahead of the West there was nothing they needed from the outside world. Even the famed Silk Road, which in the meantime had brought Buddhism, Islam, and material wealth to China, was abandoned. This second period of isolation was to last for nearly three hundred years.

It was to be the eunuchs of the Imperial Court of Ming China who in the 1640s opened China's doors the third time by maneuvering to let the Manchus breach the Great Wall and destroy the now weakened court. The Manchus, founders of the ill-fated Qing (Ching) Dynasty—which was to be China's last—were unable to contend with the new forces now being brought to bear on China from the industrialized West. For the third time they attempted to cut the country off from the rest of the world, this time with disastrous consequences that resulted in the fall of the dynasty and the eventual triumph of the revolutionary forces of Zedong Mao.

The first European trading ships to arrive in China were Portuguese in 1516. In 1557 Portuguese traders were given permission to set up a trading base in Macao. Shortly thereafter, British, Dutch, and English ships began flocking to China, but it was 1685 before the Imperial Court opened Canton to foreign trade. European missionaries followed closely on the heels of the traders.

Still, rather than take an aggressive approach to dealing with the outside world, the Ming Dynasty turned inward, and devoted all of its energy and resources to restoring the traditional infrastructure and culture of the country—thousands of bridges, temples, tombs, stupas, rock gardens, and city walls were built; canals were deepened and lengthened (large vessels could go all the way to Peking from the mouth of the Yangtze via the Grand Canal). Altogether, some 50,000 water and waterway projects were completed.

But administrative evil (much of it stemming from the large number of eunuchs* who virtually controlled the government), corruption, and other weaknesses brought the Ming Dynasty down. After a great deal of turmoil it was replaced by the foreign manchu tribesmen who set up the Ching Dynasty (1644–1911), which also tried to keep China closed to the outside world and to maintain the style of government and life that had persisted for more than two thousand years.

As the centuries went by and the Western world was remade by the Industrial Revolution, China was wracked by internal discontent and strife, making it an easy matter for the Western powers—and Japan from the 1890s—to continue carving up the empire to suit their own economic and political designs. China's unworldly court and its advisers tried to continue the country's policy of isolation. The government designated Canton as the only international trading port and gave a monopoly on foreign trade to a small group of Chinese merchants. This resulted in Britain's demanding Hong Kong as a crown colony and the base for its operations in China, along with the opening of five other ports. Other nations followed Britain's lead, demanding the opening of eleven additional ports as well as extraterritorial rights for their nationals and many other special privileges. Uprisings in China became more common and more destructive.

From the mid–1840s until the final victory of Zedong Mao and his Communist forces over Kai-shek Chiang and his Nationalists in 1949, China was ravaged by peasant rebellions, marauding warlords who controlled great segments of the country, and finally by an invasion by Japan and a disastrous civil war between the Communists and the Nationalists. During this period, huge areas of the country were laid waste and millions died horrible deaths from wars and, near the end, mass starvation.

The first Western product to make significant inroads in China was opium, despite opposition from the government of China, which passed a

---

China's Imperial Eunuchs: The practice of maintaining eunuchs in China's Imperial Court was already well-established by the Tang dynasty (618–907). The first eunuchs were servants. There were apparently two reasons for depriving them of their manhood—to keep them from becoming sexually involved with the emperor's harem, and as a safeguard for the emperor, since the operation made them less inclined toward physical violence. Over the generations, the power of the court eunuchs grew, and on more than one occasion in succeeding dynasties, eunuchs were the power behind the throne. Soon after eunuchs became a fixture at court, the eunuch masters themselves took over replenishing their ranks. In earlier decades, only the male's gonads were removed, but it later became the practice to remove all the male genitalia. Prior to the operation, boys who had reached puberty were sometimes given a final opportunity to lie with women. Before the genitalia were severed, the pubic area was painted with a liquid made of the hottest peppers. After the operation, the cavity was packed to stop bleeding, and the patient was sometimes buried in sand in an upright position, with his legs apart, until the wound healed or he died.

law prohibiting opium smoking in 1729 and banned its importation in 1800. In 1772 the new British governor of India, Warren Hastings, authorized the export of opium and later took it over as a government monopoly. Before long, opium exports to China represented one-seventh of the total revenue of British India (Leonard P. Adams, *China and the West*).

In 1834 American traders joined the rush to export opium to China. Virtually all other prominent foreign traders of the period also became active in the trade. A few years later Chinese authorities began confiscating and burning shipments of opium brought into the country. The British government declared war (the Opium War of 1840–1842) to force China to accept the shipments and guarantee the British other trading rights. In 1856 England, aided by France, again went to war against China to force new trading concessions from the now virtually powerless Chinese government. With millions of Chinese addicted to the deadly drug and the drain on the country's currency bringing social and economic havoc, China became an easy victim for the predatory colonial powers of the day.

More enlightened groups in China worked feverishly to begin the transformation from a feudal kingdom to a modern industrial nation. In the 1860s these leaders came up with a slogan that said a lot about their reaction to the idea of industrialization in the fashion of the West: "Chinese learning for substance; Western learning for practical utility." But the country was too big, too split by rivalries, too xenophobic for the slogan to be turned into reality.

With the establishment of the Communist "dynasty" in 1949, Mao and his "court" followed tradition by shutting out all of the West except for fellow Communists. This time, the doors remained closed for only a brief period but the question remains—will they be closed again? There are those who fear that China will once again find the outside world too destructive to its culture and traditions and close its doors as it has done several times in the past.

Memories of the Opium Wars

The Chinese have long memories. Part of the image they have today of foreign businesspeople and their efforts to sell consumer merchandise in China is the opium trade that was forced onto China and was a key factor in the country's being divided up into spheres of influence by Japan and several Western powers (excluding the U.S.). The West, particularly Britain, continued to export opium in great quantities to China until 1911, when Parliament finally outlawed its shipment. At this time, somewhere around 90 percent of Chinese men and 60 percent of the women in many southern cities were opium addicts. Still in the 1920s, upwards of two-thirds of the land cultivated in a number of provinces was devoted to growing poppy plants. It was not until after the Communists took over China in 1949 that the opium scourge was finally eradicated.

Mao's Great Purge

In an insanely misguided effort to "purify" China by eliminating every vestige of capitalistic thought and enterprise and to squash political opponents, Zedong Mao in 1966 virtually turned the country over to radicalized students known as "Red Guards." All schools were closed. The millions of students were urged to attack and destroy the "four old elements" in Chinese society—old thinking, old habits, old customs, and old culture. This meant attacking teachers, school administrators, party leaders, and parents; and destroying old buildings, temples, and art objects throughout the country. Anyone who had ever had any connections with Westerners or Western education was especially targeted.

The Red Guards first appeared at Beijing University in May 1966, apparently as an independent student uprising. They were quickly suppressed by government forces in June; however, Mao endorsed their action. In August he unleashed them, resulting in the so-called Cultural Revolution—one of the worst periods in China's long history. It was *Lord of the Flies* on an unimaginable scale.

The Red Guards turned loose on China by Mao were not a new invention. They had their origins in the student uprisings that began in 1919, when high school and college youths took to the streets in an effort to influence national policy. The fascist-oriented "Blue Shirts" organized by Kai-shek Chiang in the early 1930s (when Chiang preached that the fascism of Nazi Germany and Italy was a "wonderful medicine" that could save China) were also a major influence.

The creed of Chiang's Blue Shirts was that the Chinese should totally renounce all freedoms and all thoughts of individuality and give their bodies and souls to the state, with absolute obedience to Chiang, the supreme leader. Chiang was thus the godfather of the concept that radical students could be used to shape the destiny of a nation.

It was not until around 1987 that people in China began to feel safe enough to talk and write openly about the nightmare of the Cultural Revolution. One of the most shocking and poignant of the stories to appear in print at the end of that year was that of Bo Ma, under the title *Bloody Dusk*. When the Cultural Revolution began in 1966, Ma, a high school student, became one of the most fanatical of the Red Guards, turning in his own mother, Mo Yang, a celebrated writer, and personally destroying their home.

Volunteering to carry the revolution to the countryside, Ma went to Inner

Mongolia with a group of other students in 1968. There his violent temper got him into trouble with his superiors and political instructor, and in 1970 he himself was accused of being an enemy of the revolution. Just as so many other victims before him, Ma was mercilessly interrogated, his friends betrayed him to save themselves, and he was convicted of a series of crimes he had never even thought about.

Stripped of his humanity, Ma was used as a beast of burden, starved and mistreated for the next five years. Still in his twenties, he became known as the "Old Ghost" because of his terrible appearance. As the Cultural Revolution began to wind down, Ma started writing about his experiences. Freed after eight years, he entered Beijing University, majoring in journalism. He completed *Bloody Dusk* in 1979, but it was rejected by thirteen publishers before finally being accepted by the Workers Publishing House in 1987 and becoming a best-seller as soon as it appeared.

Older Chinese who have read Ma's book say it captures like no other both the high points and the unimaginable cruelties of the revolution, helping them, somehow, to put the nightmare behind them.

The Communist Crucible

The holocaust that the Communists and Kai-shek Chiang and his Nationalist forces loosed on China in the 1930s—the millions dead, the anguish and suffering of additional untold millions—eventually had one positive side effect for which future generations should be eternally grateful. It was to help reveal the bankruptcy of both communism and socialism in a way that could not be disguised or debated.

Capitalism in China

In a very real sense, capitalism is still a new concept in China. During the imperial dynasties, which did not end until 1911, none of the legal infrastructure for capitalism existed. The imperial courts did not grant the merchant class the rights of deeds, charters, franchises, titles, claims, privileges, immunities, or any of the other legal foundations on which to engage in business. All such rights, powers, and privileges remained in the hands of the government (and later in government-controlled guilds), which exercised them only on the most basic level as a means of maintaining the status quo between the rulers and the ruled. In this environment, the relationship between government officials and producers in the economy was often based on corruption in the form of bribery and "squeeze."

In an essay on why capitalism did not develop in imperial China, Etienne

Balazs (*China Yesterday and Today*, Bantam Books, 1984) says it was simply because of the superabundance of cheap labor and the fact that there was no scope for individual enterprise, no individual freedom, no security, no guarantees against the predatory actions of the state. He adds that probably the supreme inhibiting factor was the overwhelming prestige of the scholar-based government bureaucracy, which absorbed the aspirations and energy of the affluent and educated, and the almost total passivity of the common people in seeking any real change in their lifestyle.

Capitalism did not spring into being overnight when the last dynasty fell in 1911. The laws were changed and an environment that would support a degree of capitalism was established, but there was little knowledge of and perhaps less appreciation for capitalism in the China of that day. The country remained in a state of constant turmoil from the beginning of the first republic on January 1, 1912, until 1976, when for the first time the government began to take practical steps to introduce a careful measure of capitalism into the country.

When the Communist party took over China in 1949, most industry that had survived the war years was on a cottage and home level. The economy was still based on a feudal agricultural system, with Western-style enterprises limited to small enclaves. Seventy percent of the land was owned by less than 10 percent of the population. Mao's disastrous "Great Leap Forward" and the Cultural Revolution (which some people say set China back one hundred years) were still to come. It was not until 1978, two years after the end of the Cultural Revolution, that China finally broke with the past and took the first bold steps toward creating a "New China," utilizing the power of capitalistic enterprise.

3

The Awakening Dragon

*"It can be harmful to come, without thought,
under the sway of utterly new and strange doctrines."*
—CONFUCIUS

Seeing Beyond the Facade

Part of the image that most educated Westerners have of China is derived from books, movies, paintings, and various other works of art and handicrafts passed down from the ages. This is "Cultural China," the great center of civilization that stretches back nearly five thousand years, and is awesome to contemplate.

This image is the source of some of the problems facing foreign businesspeople now dealing with or trying to deal with China because it suggests (to both foreigners *and* Chinese) that the run-of-the-mill Chinese of today are the recipients of China's great cultural heritage—that they are culturally sophisticated and in many ways superior to people with much shorter and much less impressive historical backgrounds.

The truth of the matter is that the overwhelming majority of China's population over the millenniums has been uneducated, illiterate peasants, virtually untouched by the refinements of China's lengthy civilization. The intellectual accomplishments of China have always been the products of a tiny portion of the population, and for the most part enjoyed only by them.

Neither the universal education system nor other conditions that have existed in China since 1949 have transferred a mantle of historical culture onto the mass of Chinese. Most Chinese today have no real link with the culture of China's past, the philosophies of the sages, the accomplishments of the great artists. They are instead products of the times—of their times—with all the ignorance, misinformation, misunderstanding, and confusion that is typical of people even in highly developed countries. They are also

38

further handicapped by the lingering influence of Confuciansim, Daoism, and Buddhism, which are incompatible with an internationalized, competitive world—*plus* the baleful influence of Communism.

In fact, higher education in China virtually stopped in 1966 with the advent of the notorious ten-year Cultural Revolution, and more than twenty years later had not recovered, leaving the generation of Chinese born after 1950 seriously deprived of even general knowledge of specialized subjects and the world at large. Many of the older generation of educators, managers, and other professionals did not survive the revolution. Many who did survive found their lives so changed that they were unable to utilize their knowledge and experience in the new world that emerged. China practically started over from scratch in 1978.

The recent "Westernization" of the skyline and the hemline, along with such surface symbols as Kentucky Fried Chicken (adjoining Beijing's famed Tiananmen Square), is not necessarily a reflection of the basic mentality or behavior of the people. These symbols may make the foreigner in China feel a lot more comfortable, but they do not always make it easier to do business there.

Turning Traditions Upside Down

Despite the weight of their cultural and political heritage, however, the Chinese have literally turned traditions upside down since inauguration of the latest Open Door policy in 1978. The Confucian concept of restraint and moderation in all things has been thrown to the winds. The age-old sanctions against common people accumulating wealth and living ostentatiously have been repudiated. The pursuit of wealth has not only been given official approval, it is now the "duty" of every Chinese to become as rich as possible. "To become rich is glorious" sums up the new mood.

By the late 1980s the income-leveling policy instituted by the government of New China—known colloquially as the "Big Pot"—had become virtually obsolete and was being ignored on a massive scale, despite vehement criticism from intellectuals and employees of state-run enterprises, whose salaries were very low in comparison with those in privately run organizations and independent entrepreneurs, and who had no way to supplement their incomes.

Not too long ago it was illegal for any Chinese to take a second job for the sake of more income. Now a significant percentage of all specialists and technicians in the country have side jobs. A growing number of college students have become "infected" with what the press calls "business fever," and are working at part-time and even full-time jobs. More and more are going into business on campus, operating food and drygoods stalls, or acting as salespeople for nearby factories.

The order of the famed "three paths" of labor—the so-called red, black, and yellow paths, referring respectively to political, academic, and commercial fields of endeavor—is rapidly being reversed, with more and more of the political cadre and educators switching to business.

On the government side, both communism and socialism now take a backseat in China's commitment to a technologically advanced economy in the shortest possible time. The Chinese neatly sidestep the problem of differentiating the political coloration of present policy by saying, "If it works, we call it socialism!"

Officially the Chinese call their mixture of economic systems "market socialism," which is described as a system in which the government sets the goals and guidelines, then leaves it up to business to achieve those goals within the framework of regulations established by the government. In this respect, China's "market socialism" is similar to Japan's "administrative guidance" system. Major differences, of course, are that the Japanese have more than a hundred years of experience with their system, have honed it to an art, and deal with a much smaller, more homogenous, more manageable social base.

One of the great challenges of the Chinese system of "market socialism" is devising an effective relationship between government ownership of economic enterprises and management based on market factors, since the two concepts are basically contradictory. A partial solution was the introduction of a contract relationship between the state and state-owned enterprises in the mid–1980s. Under this approach, the government sets an annual production and profit quota for each state-owned enterprise, and provides it with some of the necessary raw and semi-finished materials and energy at fixed prices. The manager of the enterprise agrees to remit profits to the state in the form of taxes. If the annual quota is not met, the manager agrees to reduce the shortfall at a predetermined rate each year.

Soon thereafter, in a further refinement of this system, the cities of Beijing and Chongqing and the provinces of Jiangsu and Liaoning were authorized to retain all excess profits and to function more or less as private enterprises. In 1988 China's ruling body agreed that thirteen additional provinces and municipalities could adopt this financial contract system on a trial basis as a means of enhancing production and reducing costs. Critics of this system say it will have to change after price reforms are carried out. (At present, China has a "double-track" pricing system—state-controlled prices and market-regulated prices.)

Another step taken in August of 1988 was the abolition of twenty-eight administrative laws and regulations, some of them dating back to 1949, which were deemed incompatible with the current government policy of developing an export-oriented economy.

China's various ministries behave very much like huge commercial conglomerates. Each is made up of bureaus that operate dozens to hundreds of companies. Except for the government control, they resemble the zaibatsu groups of Japan and the chaebol of Korea.

Typical of China's headlong rush toward various forms of private enterprise is the "scientific invention area" in the Chaoyang district of Beijing. The largest nongovernment scientific information consulting organization in the country, the center helps private companies develop new products based on current technology. Known as "Invention City," the consulting organization emphasizes its services to businesses in rural areas.

Entrepreneurship Is In

Pure entrepreneurship, a concept that was historically regarded as antisocial and undesirable by the ruling classes of China, has taken root in the very fertile soil of the masses. There are now well over twenty million registered private and individual businesses in China, ranging from tiny hole-in-the-wall barbershops to elaborate restaurants, and more are sprouting daily. (In the Chinese context, a private enterprise is one financed by private funds with eight or more employees; an individual business is one financed privately with seven or fewer employees.) The stories of opportunity and entrepreneurship are endless and are reminiscent of new settlements in the American West of the early 1800s when whole towns and businesses would mushroom overnight.

One example of China's new entrepreneurs is Zhangguang Zhao, an ex-farmer who spent ten years concocting a hair-restoring tonic, opened his first factory in 1986, and by early 1988 was well on his way to becoming a millionaire. Zhao's clinic, at the Jinsong Hospital in eastern Beijing, treats an international clientele. One Japanese medical firm sponsors regular tours to the clinic, bringing customers in by the busload. Zhao's tonic, called *101 Hair Liniment*, is a liquid said to be made from a recipe of some thirty medicinal herbs. He claims a 92 percent success rate in growing new hair on previously bald pates. The success rate for people who have lost hair in patches is said to be 100 percent.

Then there is the twenty-one-year-old former factory worker who quit to open a tiny shoe store. "I am already making ten times more than I did in a state factory!" he bragged. He uses a new motorcycle for transportation and employs his eighteen-year-old girlfriend (a bus conductor) to tend the shop when he goes on trips to replenish his stock.

Abhorrence of anything smacking of commercialism has long been a hallmark of China's intellectuals, but in today's heady atmosphere of rising expectations, this ancient tradition is dissipating like early morning fog exposed to the sun. In the forefront of this radical break with the past was a group of professors at Quinghua University, the largest in Beijing. In 1988 they set up an enterprise called the Electronic Technology and Products

Group (ETPG), made up of more than four hundred professors, to develop new high-tech products and bring them to market.

The group included the software and audiovisual education centers of the university and the electronics and electrical machinery research centers. "In the past, teachers had to be content with doing research only as part of the process of trying to become professors. Now the trapped human researchers have been released," said a spokesman for the university.

Financial rewards promised by such entrepreneurship were not the only motivation for Quinghua's going into business. It was also a desperate move to prevent its professors from being enticed away by the so-called "4–3 Formula" used by many enterprises in which high-tech knowledge was in demand. Under this formula, a professor who signed a three-year contract with a company immediately received a large cash bonus and a three-room apartment, and was put on a monthly retainer.

The Golden Seat Café, one of the most popular cafés in Chengdu, Sichuan Province, was founded by a twenty-four-year-old single woman who gave up a position as lecturer on Marxism-Leninism at the Southwestern Finance and Economics University in Chengdu for the uncertain life of an entrepreneur. Besides food and drinks, the café features fashion shows, art exhibits, song-and-dance troupes, and lectures on literature and good food. "Running the Golden Seat Café is an experiment for me," the young entrepreneur told *China Daily*. "It gives me the experience I will need to run big enterprises in the future." Within a year after this, the enterprising young woman had taken over the management of a garment factory and a beverage factory.

By 1988 the new entrepreneurial spirit in China had reached even the ancient order of Daoist priests. A Daoist health drink, based on a formula that had been kept secret for over a thousand years, is now available to the general public for the first time. The drink, developed by Daoist priests on famed Mt. Laoshan, was strictly reserved for the senior priests of the order; and the formula was known only to the chief priest, who passed it on to his successor each generation.

In keeping with the new order of things in China, eighty-five-year-old Changxiu Kuang in 1988, then head priest of Mt. Laoshan and vice president of the Shandong Daoist Association, donated the formula for the health drink to the Quingdao "Yellow Sea" Brewery, which now sells the drink as "Laoshan Daoist Beverage."

Not to be outdone, beer brewers in the far-northern city of Harbin inaugurated the country's first international beer festival in July 1988, with the expressed intention of turning it into a "Chinese Oktoberfest," patterned after the world-famous Munich event. The Harbin beer party attracted brewers and brewing equipment suppliers from the United States, Canada, Denmark, and South Korea.

Even pawnshops, outlawed by the Communist government in 1949 as being in the same category as brothels and gambling dens, are once again flourishing and are rapidly increasing in number. The first one, the Huamao Pawnbroking Firm in Chengdu, Sichuan Province, opened to the tune of firecrackers, gongs, and drums on December 31, 1987, and was an immediate success with overstocked and cash-short businesses as well as individuals.

In addition to pawnshops, credit cooperatives are also flourishing, along with licensed agents who are doing everything from importing and exporting to product distribution, recruiting domestic servants, and helping people exchange homes. Lotteries were also rehabilitated (although this time, some 50 percent of the funds generated goes to social welfare projects, and winners get only 35 percent of the pot).

Also as of 1988, Chinese who have legal income in foreign currency were authorized to begin using credit cards, the epitome of capitalistic tools, on their trips abroad. China's first foreign currency credit card, the Great Wall MasterCard, was introduced by Mastercard International and the Bank of China (where users must have a foreign currency account) the same year. At the same time, American Express was permitted to begin marketing its green and gold cards in China for domestic use, in collaboration with the state-owned Bank of China, the Bank of Communications, and CITIC Industrial Bank.

Soon after Zedong Mao took over the government in 1949, the design and construction of all private homes was brought under control of the state. Architects and planners designed standard, generic "box" houses without any reference at all to the needs or desires of the people who were going to live in them (only the color of the front could be changed). Under pressure from frustrated architects and entrepreneurial builders in outlying provinces, this too is changing, reducing some of the dreadful sameness of cities all over China.

In another move to improve on the housing situation in China, the Beijing Managerial Bureau of Housing in 1988 set up a housing exchange where people wanting to move could register their names.

There are also new examples each year of foreign entrepreneurs creating a niche for themselves in China. One of the distinguishing marks of virtually all of the first of these foreign entrepreneurs was that they spoke Mandarin*

---

*The Chinese are ambivalent about foreigners speaking their language. Like the Japanese, they have traditionally regarded their language as a barrier against intrusion into their personal affairs by foreigners, and on the one hand did not want foreigners to learn Chinese. A common saying was *Tian du pa. Di bu pa. Zhi pa yanguo quizi shuo Zhongguo hua.* (Do not fear the sky. Do not fear the earth. Fear only foreigners who speak Chinese.) Amy Konvolinka, an American in Beijing studying Mandarin, said springing this saying on taxi drivers was usually enough to cause guffaws. While she had never heard a Chinese use it, she had been made aware directly and indirectly that many Chinese feel uncomfortable around Chinese-speaking foreigners and regard it as an unwelcome intrusion on their privacy.

and knew a great deal about China. Among this new generation of old China hands (most of whom were young) was Malan Jackson, the founder of Celestial Yachts Ltd., which manufactures pleasure boats in Xiamen; Roberta Lipson, founder of the U.S.–China Industrial Exchange in Beijing, which began selling medical equipment to hospitals all over the country and later added scientific instruments and industrial equipment; Martha Fitzpatrick, founder of a trading company in Xiamen that handles furniture, electronics, and satellite equipment.

Harvard-educated American-Chinese Doris Wan Cheng made a name for herself in China as the producer-host of "Global View," which began airing on Beijing TV in 1987, and for a twelve-part series introducing Western-style management that began on Shanghai TV in 1988. Cheng, who is known in Chinese as Wen Zhang, said her primary goal was to let China's managers know what the business and political leaders of the world are thinking as a way of helping to inspire the Chinese.

All of these new China hands emphasized that patience, personal attention to customers, and being willing and able to do business with the Chinese on their terms was essential for success. And one of the more conspicuous aspects of these foreign successes in China is that a large percentage of the principals were women.

Helen Katsoulas, an Australian of Greek ancestry, is another example of the exceptionally bright, capable, and ambitious young women who were attracted to emerging China in the 1980s. The daughter of an émigré family that achieved enviable success (the father as a diplomat and the mother as a well-known fashion designer), Katsoulas was raised with a strong emphasis on being self-reliant and persistent in achieving goals. She traveled the world with her family, learning several languages and the art of communicating and getting along with people of different cultures. When her father was transferred to the Australian Embassy in Beijing, she came along, went to work for the commercial department of the embassy, and quickly proved herself a whiz in helping to market Australian goods in China.

Later, Katsoulas was offered a job by IBM China Corporation in the marketing department of its Beijing office, where she was equally successful. "Things are done differently here and accomplishing anything is a challenge, but if your goals are valid and reasonable you can achieve whatever you set out to do. It is just a matter of a positive attitude, patience, persistence, and goodwill toward China," she said.

She also advised: "Learn the language!"

Katsoulas attributed some of her success to having been taught humility and understanding as a child and being determined to make a genuine contribution to China. "Many people who come here are totally self-centered; out only to benefit themselves. Most of them are unable to 'take' China and just wither away," she said. "You have to get involved outside of your company obligations; you have to do things; make things happen. To succeed here as a foreigner, it is very important that you have a sense of accomplishment; that you feel you are being amply rewarded over and above your salary for your personal sacrifices and efforts.''

Katsoulas added: ''The Chinese are very smart. They know what they are doing. Before they were fighting to survive; now they are fighting for success. The challenge they face is to keep it all together; to not let it get away from them. They are trying to create a totally new society, and must go slow and be careful.''

Another female expatriate, Miyuki Ishii, a twenty-eight-year-old Japanese woman from Yokohama who came to China as a language student, then went to work for a joint-venture company in sales, said she found the Chinese way of doing business totally different from the Japanese. ''But,'' she added, ''I have found that there are many ways of doing things.''

Ishii said she felt that many of the differences—and problems—in the way the Chinese behave and do business are primarily a result of disruptions caused by the Communist and Cultural Revolutions, and what is now seen as ''Chinese behavior'' is not normal and will change significantly as their economic situation improves.

''The young, especially, are frustrated by the present system and feel that their lives are being wasted. They realize that things are changing rapidly but not rapidly enough for them. They can't wait,'' she added.

A national entrepreneur association was founded in 1988 to encourage entrepreneurship by recognizing the most outstanding individuals each year. Candidates are recommended by local enterprise management bodies and professional groups in the cities, provinces, and autonomous regions. They are then rigorously screened for pioneering spirit, originality in management, and success in business, ''regardless of their political backgrounds.'' The final approval committee is made up of officials from China Enterprise Management Association and the China Factory Director and Managers Union.

Energized by the entrepreneurial spirit, the first recorded attempt on a provincial level to eliminate red tape that had been slowing the industrialization process was on April 2, 1988. The city of Luoyang applied for the status of ''open city'' to allow it to solicit domestic as well as foreign investors to build factories there—a process that would normally have taken several months to years. This time, however, the governor of Henan Province called the fifteen department chiefs concerned with such applications to a special meeting and got the project approved in one day.

This set a precedent that other provincial and city governments immediately began emulating. Many bureaus were combined and others were eliminated altogether. Shortly after this movement began, the director of a cement factory was able to get approval for a new plant in thirty minutes—as opposed to the months it normally would have taken. The old saying, "With one monkey in the way, not even ten thousand men can pass," could soon be a thing of the past.

Another sign of the new times was the first Western-style beauty contest attempted in Beijing in 1988. Cosponsored by the Beijing Television Studio and *Contemporary Television*, a magazine published by the China Television Artists Association, the contest was staged with the title "Girls of Youth and Elegance," and emphasized "talent and intelligence—not just physical beauty." The contest was open to women between the ages of seventeen and twenty-seven, both single and married, and attracted several hundred entrants. Remarked one contestant, "There are such contests in foreign countries, so why can't we have them?"

Unfortunately, at the last moment the state clamped down on this extraordinary demonstration of Western-style behavior. The show was held but did not get on the air. Now beauty contests are commonplace.

Another aspect of changing China: popular songs from Hong Kong, Taiwan, and the West, as well as songs written by Mainland Chinese composers, have been the rage since 1981. In the coastal cities, at least, pop songs are at the top of the charts and attract larger audiences than classical concerts. In 1988 the State Council began relinquishing control of the performing arts to social organizations, collectives, and individuals.

Ever-increasing numbers of tourists are another common sight in the New China. The largest group of travelers was the Chinese themselves. The country's network of trains* was jampacked with sightseers, students, salespeople, peddlers, honeymooners, and city residents visiting their birthplaces. The spring of 1989 freedom demonstrations and subsequent massacre in Tiananmen Square, followed by martial law, drastically curtailed this new Chinese experience, but by early 1990, the tourism industry was already showing signs of coming back to life.

China's New "Gold Coast"

China's coastal lands from the Gulf of Tonkin in the south to Soviet Siberia in the north are rapidly being turned into manufacturing and exporting regions that can compete with Japan, Korea, Taiwan, and Southeast Asian

---

*Because of the large number of trains in China, they are numbered instead of named. The lowest numbers indicate international express trains. The next series of higher numbers are national express trains. The higher the number of a train, the more stops it makes en route. Those with numbers of 500 and above are the "milk trains" of China, stopping at every station. Most trains have dining cars, and apparently all trains in the country provide hot water for tea, with passengers providing their own tea leaves.

countries. Guangdong Province, which borders Hong Kong and is China's largest exporter, was already being compared with the "four economic tigers" of Asia (Korea, Taiwan, Hong Kong, Singapore) by 1987.

In 1988, a watershed year, the government of Guangdong enacted new laws authorizing privately owned businesses to enter into joint and cooperative ventures managed by foreigners. These laws also allow local companies to process imported materials, parts, and patterns and engage in compensation trade; and permit individuals to organize stock companies. The province also began giving preferential treatment to foreign-funded enterprises seeking Chinese managers. A new law stipulated that Chinese organizations must release any manager who receives a job offer from a foreign-financed firm.

This "Gold Coast" program began in 1979 when the government designated the first of several southeastern seaboard areas as *Chu Kou Techu* or Special Economic Zones (SEZ), where both foreign and Chinese companies were authorized to establish factories and engage in manufacturing for export. The first such zones were Shenzhen, adjoining Hong Kong (1979); followed by Shantou, 180 miles northeast of Hong Kong, opposite Taiwan (1980); Zhuhai, in the mouth of Pearl River adjoining Macao (1980); and Huli, in the city of Xiamen, Fujian Province (1980).

In 1985, the SEZs were rocked by a scandal involving the misuse of funds on a major scale, but the overall benefits of the special zones were obvious enough that they survived the criticism that followed and have since served as models for the rest of the country.

The second phase of the program was the designation of several cities and counties as "open," giving them the authority to engage in both domestic and international business on their own account.

Another district first made into an "open area" in the early 1980s and then in 1988 given more economic freedoms than the first four Special Economic Zones was the tropical island of Hainan, forty-eight kilometers off Leizhou Peninsula in southeast China in the South China Sea. At the same time, the State Council, China's executive ruling body, changed the status of Hainan Island from a perfecture of Guangdong Province to full provincial status.

Once a place for criminal and political exiles, Hainan is the country's largest island (34,000 square kilometers) not counting Taiwan (which is 36,000 square kilometers) and the largest of the Special Economic Zones. Directly east of Vietnam in the South China Sea and facing Leizhou Peninsula across the Qiongzhou Strait, the island has been best known in recent decades for its military installations, as a base for oil exploration in the Gulf of Tonkin, and as the site of the South China Academy of Tropical Crops. The academy is a high-tech research center that uses genetic engineering to improve such crops as bananas, coffee, and rubber trees. (It has also introduced a number of new products, including aloe mineral water and aloe cola.) The population of Hainan Island consists of about five million Han Chinese, 750,000 Lis, and 45,000 Miaos tribesmen (who mostly inhabit the central mountains). There are also fairly large contingents of ethnic Chinese refugees from Indonesia, Malaysia, and Vietnam.

When converting Hainan to the nation's thirty-first province, the State Council also adopted a new policy for the island, giving it more autonomy than any other area in the country. In fact, the list of laws and guarantees in effect for the island makes it sound like a potential second Hong Kong.

About the only areas of responsibility in the nation's newest province that were reserved by the national government were conducting foreign affairs, defense, public security, customs, and the postal services. The province has the right to regulate itself in all other fields, including the so-called three freedoms—to import and export goods, to import and export capital, and to import and export foreign staff. There are numerous guarantees pertaining to foreign investments, and foreigners may invest in joint ventures—contractual joint ventures as well as wholly owned enterprises. Tax exemptions, low income taxes, the free repatriation of profits by foreign investors, and reduced duties on imported goods are part of the regulations issued by the State Council.

The Chinese themselves are free to go to or leave the island province at will, and almost immediately after the new province was established, people young and old began flocking to Hainan from all over the country. Within the first several months of its existence, the Hainan Talent Exchange Centre received more than 125,000 job applications from other provinces and the autonomous regions—even Taiwan. Also within the first few months, over one hundred contracts had been signed for the establishment of foreign-funded enterprises on the island. One zone on the island is reserved exclusively for investors from Taiwan, and plans were announced for a free port in the Yangpu Development Zone, with free foreign trade policies.

There are reasons to believe that the development of Hainan may be even more rapid than what has occurred in some of the other Special Economic Zones and that it could indeed become a second Hong Kong. (Some enthusiastic promoters of the island call it "the Hawaii of the Orient.")

In a further move to attract additional foreign investment into Shenzhen, the first of the SEZs, a bonded industrial zone was established in the Shatoujiao area of the SEZ in 1988. The zone incorporated five "new reforms" in the nation's economic development program: (1) Applicants for investment in the Shatoujiao Bonded Industrial Zone (SBIZ) need to submit documentation to only one department, which is required to act on each application within one week; (2) goods brought into the zone from Hong Kong or going to Hong Kong are duty free—factories have only to make a monthly declaration of such shipments; (3) foreign investors have the right to choose their Chinese contractor if they buy land in the zone (tenure for which is fifty years with free transfer rights); (4) foreign investors are not required to obtain employees through the Labor Bureau (but may ask the bureau to act as their agent if desired); and (5) polluting industries are not allowed in the zone.

The SBIZ has its own regulations, which are administered under the supervision of Chinese Customs and a joint committee made up of officials from the city of Shenzhen and the zone.

Determined not to miss any bets, the city of Beijing joined with the Ministry of Foreign Economic Relations and Trade (MOFERT; now known as MOFTEC) in 1988 to establish the Beijing International Barter Trade Company as a means of developing more trade relations with the Soviet Union, Eastern Europe, Southeast Asia, and Latin America without having to use foreign exchange. Beijing was first authorized to engage in barter trade in 1985.

Forward-thinking Fujian Province "opened" the three islands of Meizhou, Pongtan, and Dongshan, all facing northern Taiwan, in 1988, authorizing them to engage in international trade. It was announced at that time that special emphasis would be given to developing business relations with Taiwan—obviously part of a long-range Chinese plan to reintegrate the island into the homeland as an autonomous region. Shanghai continued its own open-door policies by setting up the Shanghai Caohejing Hi-Tech Park, its third special economic zone, which is surrounded by twelve universities and colleges, twelve research institutes, and dozens of factories that specialize in electronics, aeronautics, telecommunications, and precision instruments. Sino-US Foxboro Company Ltd. and a Sino-Canadian printing circuit venture were the first two joint-venture firms in the park.

China is continuing to add to the several hundred counties and cities in the coastal provinces that have already been designated economic development zones where export-oriented industries are emphasized—and by the end of the 1980s the differences between some of these "open" areas and the previously favored Special Economic Zones had virtually disappeared. But favoritism shown by the government toward the coastal provinces upset the less developed inland provinces. Provincial governments as well as individual cities clamored for the same rights and one by one began winning them.

The population among China's eastern seaboard is well above that of Japan, constituting not only a significant workforce but a large consumer market as well. It is also serving as the engine that is propelling the country into the twenty-first century as an industrialized nation.

Other Breakthroughs

China has made significant progress in bringing its copyright protection into conformity with international standards. The basic copyright law was revised in 1988 for the eighteenth time in nine years. In April 1988 the State Copyright Bureau of China established the Copyright Agency of China in Beijing to provide services to copyright applicants and users throughout China as well as Hong Kong, Macao, and Taiwan. The services of the agency include handling copyright disputes. Also in 1988, the city of Shanghai opened the Shanghai Municipal Copyright Office to help local writers obtain copyrights and resolve disputes. It also gives copyright advice to foreign individuals and companies on books printed in China.

The country's trademark protection law went into effect in 1985, and the first court case under the law was settled in May 1988. The holder of the patent won the case.

By 1987 Chinese consultants by the thousands were offering their services to foreign clientele. But generally they do not offer expert management or marketing advice. Their primary service is acting as go-betweens and agents, providing liaison between foreign companies and the various government ministries and agencies—a vital service to say the least.

The Beijing Administration for Industry and Commerce (BAIC) began accepting the registration of foreign companies and liaison offices in Beijing in 1980. The annual average number of registrations since that time has been 122, with Japanese companies leading the way, followed by companies from Hong Kong, the United States, Germany, and France, in that order.

Government policies permitting land sales and subleasing to foreigners in coastal provinces are speeding up the process of turning eastern China into a "Gold Coast." If these policies do not change, they will help concentrate the activities of most foreign businesses along the eastern seaboard of China, with the very real possibility that it will become the biggest "tiger" of all.

The variety of Chinese entities authorized to engage in foreign trade now includes various ministries, the provinces, cities, and private companies. Among the ways foreign companies can do business with China is in the form of basic trade, countertrade (barter), licensing, joint ventures, equity joint ventures, contractual joint ventures, processing, and assembling.

Sale of stock in state-run companies was inaugurated in 1984 (with the Beijing Tiangiao Department Store). Since then the shareholding system has spread to thousands of other firms and is continuing to pick up speed. There are presently three kinds of stock in China—state stock, enterprise stock, and individually or privately owned stock.

The first development bank to break the government monopoly also opened its doors in late 1988. Located in Guangdong Province, the Guangdong Development Bank is a shareholder bank funded by the Bank of China Group in Hong Kong, the Industrial and Commercial Bank of China, the Agricultural Bank of China, Guangdong Provincial International Trust and Investment Corporation, and Guangdong Provincial Development Company.

China's first semiprivate insurance company also dates from 1988. It was set up in Guangdong Province to break the monopoly of the People's

Insurance Company of China and bring competition into China's insurance services, according to General Manager Mingzhe Ma. The new firm, Pingan Insurance Company, began with links to three hundred agencies in other countries that deal with all kinds of insurance except life and automobile insurance.

As of mid–1988, new regulations gave foreign-funded enterprises more freedom in hiring and firing employees. The new rights include being able to openly recruit workers, technicians, and managers outside the areas where the companies are located. A scene that frequently occurs at the Beijing Railway Station epitomizes the New China: construction contractors holding up signs in an effort to recruit workers from among farmers arriving from the countryside (and offering them more money than highly educated government employees get).

In July 1988, the State Council abolished the rule that all wholly owned foreign investments had to be approved by the central government, making it possible for approval to be made on a provincial, regional, or city level—which meant a much faster and less expensive procedure—as long as certain requirements were met.

Approval from the Ministry of Foreign Trade and Economic Cooperation (MOFTEC) is still required in any of the following circumstances: (1) a portion of the product is to be sold in China and the import of such products is restricted by the state; (2) if the product to be exported requires a license from MOFTEC or the products fall under a state quota system; and (3) if the industry or the product is restricted by the government.

When such ventures are approved at the local level, local authorities are required to submit a copy of the approved application to MOFTEC within thirty days. If MOFTEC raises no objections within an additional thirty days, the approval is final. Different cities and provinces are authorized to approve joint-venture investments valued up to a certain amount without any reference to MOFTEC.

While new policies continue to be announced regularly, China's basic stance toward business is contained in the Revised Enterprise Law adopted in May 1988. The 158-article law is available in English.

The same year, when the Legislation Bureau of the State Council reexamined some 550 laws pertaining to the internationalization of the economy and foreign investment, it found that 110 of the laws were contradictory and that 15 of them were totally obsolete. Committees were set to improving the contradictory laws and those found invalid were discarded. Several new laws making it easier and faster for foreign businesspeople to invest in China were also passed. These included the Import and Export Commodities Inspection Law and the Foreign-Invested Enterprises Income Tax Law.

In mid–1988, the Ministry of Light Industry announced new freedoms for joint ventures with foreign firms, and emphasized the already existing favorable terms offered to foreign investors: total exemption from business taxes for the first three years, payment of only 50 percent of the applicable taxes for the next four years, and a preferential rate of 15 percent on income tax.

The China National Light Industry Products Import and Export Corporation in 1988 abandoned its role as a government trade administration organization and became a multifunctional international enterprise group, setting the stage for other state organs to follow suit.

Individual provinces are also continuing to improve the legal structure, safeguards, and incentives for foreign investments in their areas. Another significant sign was the inauguration of a Workshop on International Enterprises in Beijing, with visiting professors from the United States and Switzerland. The purpose of the workshops is to make Chinese businesspeople and economists more familiar with foreign management theories and practices. Topics that were discussed at the first workshop were separating management from state ownership and giving workers more of an interest in the long-term success of their enterprises. A spokesperson for the workshop noted that one of the major problems China now faces is that demands for higher wages and bonuses are not related to the profitability of enterprises.

In a step to bring about rapid and significant improvement in quality control, the government set up the China State Bureau of Technical Supervision in July of 1988. Operating under the direction of the State Council, the bureau has jurisdiction over the production of technical products, scientific research, and distribution. The bureau is authorized to organize, manage, and adjust national standards, as well as to inspect all import and export products, along with medicines, food, ships, and boilers.

The Final Stage

A projection of the new level of reforms needed to speed up liberalization of the economic system was also announced in 1988. The crux of these new ''deep'' reforms was as follows:

1. The state would no longer directly control every enterprise. Instead, it would seek to regulate and guide all enterprises in a manner to create a fair, competitive market.
2. The state would conduct its economic planning and guidance by regulating prices, tax rates, interest rates, exchange rates, and wages.
3. The chief functions of the state's planning departments would be changed from providing financing and materials and setting targets to researching and formulating economic policies to be applied to the regulation of wages, taxes, interest, prices, and exchange rates.

Direct control, the announcement continued, would be applied only in certain economic activities of vital concern to the immediate welfare of the nation, such as key construction projects and those providing commodities in short supply.

The state noted that to achieve these goals, a number of other reforms would have to be designed and implemented, including the freeing of all enterprises from government control, an open market system with roughly competitive prices, a modern information-handling system, the development of a cadre of economists skilled in macroeconomic management, and a democratic decision-making organ—things that would take time.

Burial at Sea

China's reforms have even affected the dead. With ground burial almost entirely replaced by cremation since 1958, the construction and maintenance of huge "bone ash mausoleums" has become vogue. Thousands of people flock to them to pay respects to their dead. The Guangzhou Funeral and Interment Service alone currently operates eight large "bone ash buildings," stores some 100,000 ash-caskets, and has some 1,500 new "residents" coming in each month. Experts predict that if this custom continues, there will soon be large villages of ash repositories all over the country.

The latest trend, started in Guangzhou (China's equivalent of Los Angeles), is for sea burial, and debate about the merits of burying the dead at sea have reached the national level. Conservatives say traditional rituals for paying respect to the dead require the ashes of the deceased, and that there is no way to stop the building of more and more bone ash high rises. Others say that burying the ashes on the sides of mountains and planting trees over them might be an alternative to sea burial.

In the meantime, in such a large "market," burial at sea is bound to become a major business.

Dealing with Chinese-Style Laws

Reading English-language translations of Chinese laws and policies, particularly new ones having to do with economic and business reforms, can be misleading, and foreign businesspeople are advised to approach them with caution. Many of the things that are in the original versions are left out in the translations, and both the nuance and the intent can be quite different.

Veteran expatriate businesspeople in China say many of the business reform laws of the country often turn out to be more of a facade than anything else. The government may enforce them when it is convenient and beneficial or when there is no choice. On other occasions, individuals interpret the laws to suit themselves or ignore them altogether. New laws or regulations that are promulgated often have riders attached that they are on a trial or test basis for varying periods, sometimes up to ten years. There are apparently several reasons for this approach. One is that there cannot be any guarantees that the laws will work. Probably the most important reason is that new top officials want to put their own stamp on the industry and will not want to be locked into place by laws that cannot be easily changed.

This trial provision is attached to virtually everything new, including many products. If there is a failure, no one can be blamed since it was a "test." The result, of course, is that nothing announced or launched (by the government, in particular) can be regarded as permanent. The effect of this is fundamental distrust in the sincerity, integrity, and motives of the government. It is also one of the prime reasons why it is essential to keep close personal contact with high officials in the government and to stay well informed about their fortunes.

Given this situation, foreign businesspeople in China are often operating in a gray area, where they cannot be sure of their status and have to depend on the goodwill and protection of individuals with political influence.

Another consideration having to do with government officials is the amount and quality of the information they have and release to the public, and how individual officials interpret the information they do release. The amount of information (new rules, laws, and policies) released by the State Council and top ministry officials shrinks each time it is passed to a lower bureaucratic level. Therefore, by the time it gets down to the average businessperson, it is often unclear. The lower the party functionary, the less he tends to know—or care—about the policies of the party leaders.

There is also a strong tendency for the lower cadre not to totally commit themselves to policies announced by the government because they do not have all of the facts, are not sure that the policies are going to be permanent, and do not want to put themselves out on a limb.

Avoiding Culture Shock

Foreign businesspeople who have had little or no cross-cultural experience are likely to encounter varying degrees of culture shock on their first and even successive visits to China, regardless of how friendly the political environment might be. Culture shock comes in a variety of ways and degrees. It can be so subtle that it is not immediately noticeable and is often vehemently denied. Or it can be so obvious and "shocking" that one is completely thrown off balance.

The effects of culture shock are accumulative. Like drops of water on the head (an old form of torture), the drop may be hardly noticeable at the beginning but as time goes by it begins to sound and feel like the blows of a hammer. It can be the same with little but persistent irritations or setbacks, such as not getting a direct response when you ask a question, being pressed by masses of people, or not being able to take various small services for granted.

Of course, not being able to read or speak Chinese almost always results in serious cultural shock for average businesspeople. As far as most situations are concerned, foreign businesspeople who cannot speak or read the language become *illiterate* for all practical purposes and are virtually helpless. Their ability to communicate is, of course, dramatically reduced. They become dependent upon interpreters and the few Chinese who speak their language. The cultural differences between China and their own countries are also greatly magnified.

Experiencing culture shock on this level often results in foreigners' becoming either antagonistic and excessively critical or, if they want to make a deal, overly eager to please, less critical than they should be, and highly susceptible to pressure from the Chinese side. The Chinese are also masters at putting newcomers under obligation by treating them to effusive, costly hospitality and weakening their position by the use of psychological ploys.

Foreigners with little or no cross-cultural experience tend to interpret Chinese attitudes and behavior in their own cultural terms, even when they know better. There is also always that strong emotional reaction that Chinese behavior is irrational and wrong, and will not be right until it is just like theirs. In any dealings with the Chinese, it is difficult but vital that foreign businesspeople keep in mind that, from the Chinese viewpoint, they may be the ones who are off base.

Foreign businesspeople should keep uppermost in their minds that business in the Western sense has never existed in China and is only now in the earliest stages of creation. Business does not always have the same sacredness in China that it does in the United States, Japan, or Germany. Among government officials especially, there is often the very strong feeling that business comes second to politics; and when business interferes with political goals, it is business that bites the dust. (Which is not too different from the political attitude toward business in the U.S.!)

The Chinese are also influenced not only by intense feelings regarding their political system but their cultural ways as well, and these invariably play a role in their business relationships with foreigners. Their feelings often take precedence over what foreigners regard as common sense or what Americans, with whom they often appear to have the least in common, fondly refer to as the "good deal."

Contrary to appearances, however, veteran China observers frequently note that the Chinese actually feel more compatible with Americans than they do with most other foreign nationalities. They say the Chinese believe that Americans are more trustworthy and respectful than others. It is certainly true that most Americans are impressed by the incredibly long history of China and the arts and crafts of its civilization, and tend to demonstrate this feeling in their behavior. The Chinese like that.

Westerners as Aliens

Because of milleniums of separation from the West and the Chinese historical concept of China as the center of the world, along with racial and cultural differences, the traditional Chinese image of all foreigners was that they were "barbarians." At first this meant that they were not as civilized or as advanced as the Chinese, and later it simply meant that they were foreigners.

Although many cultured Chinese today may still regard Westerners as less cultured and uncivilized in some ways, it would probably be more accurate to say that they now view foreigners as just different or alien. But there is an odd exception to this general rule. In the countryside, some older Chinese equate being able to speak Chinese with *being* Chinese. Apparently this is because it is impossible for them to conceive of someone's being able to speak Chinese and without being Chinese—their foreign appearance notwithstanding.

At the same time, the Chinese mind-set is so exclusive that the racially different foreigner can be born and raised in China, speak the language perfectly, think and behave exactly like a Chinese, and yet not be accepted as "belonging" in China, much less accepted as Chinese. The only Chinese is a *Han* Chinese. The most that the Westerner can hope for is to be accepted as a "true friend" of the Chinese. Because Westerners can never "become" Chinese or achieve total acceptance, they can never feel fully at home in China—a gnawing, frustrating feeling long-term residents must live with.

The Chinese Advantage

Generally speaking, the Chinese have a conspicuous advantage in dealing with foreigners. Their skills in both impressing and manipulating foreign visitors have been honed since ancient times. It is a deeply ingrained custom for them to be aggressively hospitable, to give the best impression possible, and to get the most out of their cultural accomplishments, in particular, their ritualized etiquette.

By the same token, when Chinese businesspeople visit the local offices of foreign companies or their head offices abroad, they expect the same degree of hospitality. They are often greatly disappointed when it isn't forthcoming and they are left on their own by their hosts. In the interest of establishing and nurturing good relationships, over and above just being thoughtful hosts, it behooves foreign businesspeople to make their Chinese guests feel welcome and comfortable by fulfilling such expectations.

The Roundabout Way

Virtually everything that is accomplished in China seems to be done in a roundabout way, particularly personal things but often business as well. An individual may go through as many as ten different contacts, often all related although distantly so, in order to accomplish one thing. (See *It Isn't What You Know!*, ch. 4.) The Chinese keep close track of the favors they do and receive and expect the ones they do to be returned. The foreign businessperson is strongly advised to also use this obligation-building approach to establish a network that can be called upon in time of need.

Another aspect of the problem of getting things done efficiently is simply that the typical Chinese, especially officials, are reluctant to do anything for which there is no established, officially approved procedure. Americans generally believe it is right to do whatever is necessary to get things done and willingly accept the consequences if there are objections or unforeseen results. The Chinese attitude is to not do anything (or even to prevent anything from being done) that might be criticized or cause embarrassment or that hasn't been fully approved in advance by everyone who might be concerned. This typical Chinese approach to things is a self-preservation mechanism. With their livelihood (and until very recently their lives as well) on the line, self-defense comes first.

Government agencies traditionally regarded business information as state secrets that were to be protected from the prying eyes and ears of foreign businesspeople at all cost. Part of this, however, was that no single individual had or wanted to take responsibility for dispensing such information—even when they appreciated why someone would need and want it.

There was also in the back of everyone's mind the fear that the government might once again do a flip-flop and make such cooperation with foreigners a serious crime. Significant improvements have been made in this regard in recent years, but it can still be a serious problem.

Over and above bureaucratic inertia combined with the practice of avoiding direct answers, the desire of the Chinese to please foreign visitors habitually results in their giving answers they believe the foreigners want to hear whether or not the answers are true. This typical Chinese behavior may be innocuous in some instances, but it generally prevents foreigners from obtaining a true or realistic image of what is going on. In business, it can have a highly detrimental effect if foreigners accept what they hear as correct. The only recourse foreigners have is to continue asking roundabout questions and refer to other sources.

The Importance of *Keqi*

If one had to pick a single word as the key to understanding the Chinese in their social or business life, Wei Yao, a member of the Ministry of Foreign Affairs of the People's Republic of China, indicates that it should be *keqi* (kay-chee). In a booklet called *Communicating with China* (edited by Robert A. Kapp for the China Council of the Asia Society, and published by Intercultural Press Inc. of Yarmouth, Maine), Yao says that an understanding of *keqi* and the ability to follow it is one of the main secrets of Chinese character and behavior.

Yao explains that *ke* means "guest" and *qi* means "behavior," but when the compounds are used together to form *keqi* it means a lot more than "behavior of a guest." When used to describe behavior it means polite, courteous, modest, humble, understanding, considerate, well-mannered— and *moral*.

But all of these definitions are naturally in the cultural context of China. Being humble means not only personal humility, which goes far beyond Western practices. It also means downplaying the status of one's family, friends, employer, and so on. Whereas we have a tendency to brag about our accomplishments and those of the people around us, the Chinese go the other way. The importance of *keqi* also indicates how sensitive the Chinese are to any sign of arrogance or haughtiness.

All Chinese are expected to demonstrate *keqi* in all of their actions, and especially toward foreign guests. In fact, says Yao, the Chinese tend to overdo *keqi* and one most often hears the term used in the negative form— asking people not to be *bu keqi* or *buyao keqi*—too *keqi*.

Yao adds that the force of *keqi* is diminishing in China as social conditions continue to change, but that it is still discernible in the behavior of all Chinese, including overseas Chinese.

There is also a strong tendency for foreigners to overreact to the formalized politeness the Chinese typically extend to them. It makes most foreigners feel somehow inferior and awkward, and as a result they often end up being intimidated by the Chinese and behaving in what for them is an unnatural manner. Part of this overreaction, which, of course, is a form of culture shock, is to be less objective, less questioning, less critical than normal.

Human Feelings and Face

Ambrose King, a professor in the Sociology Department of the Chinese University of Hong Kong, says that one cannot understand Chinese behavior without an understanding of the concept and role of *ren quing* or "human feelings" and *mian-zi* or "face." He emphasizes that traditional Chinese values are based on human feelings—as opposed to religious principles, as in most of the rest of the world. This respect for the feelings, especially as manifested by "face-work," is expected to hold society together and make it function harmoniously.

Professor King adds that one of the cardinal principles of Chinese life since ancient times is summed up in the concept of *mian-zi* or "face"—something that China's Communist party tried desperately to eradicate—without success.

Mian is a sense of social status, what a person thinks of himself or herself in relation to all other people. It has been described as "social prestige," with the implication that it is something that society bestows upon a person. It is measured in terms of how high one is in society, one's wealth and power.

Professor King likens *mian-zi* to a credit card. The more "face" you have, the more you can "buy" with it. He adds that just like a credit card, *mian-zi* can be overdrawn, and care must be taken to keep one's account balanced.

Most people tend to credit themselves with more "face" than they actually have (in the eyes of others). The Chinese tend to be exceedingly conscious of any slights to their *mian-zi* and to the possibility of harming another person's "face." The continuous efforts to protect their own *mian-zi* as well as the *mian-zi* of others is referred to as "face-working" and takes up a great deal of the time and energy of every individual. The higher one is on the social ladder, the more acute is the concern with "face."

In both personal and business relationships, it is critical to the Chinese that they maintain "face" and avoid offending the "face" of others. As Professor King puts it, failure to preserve the *mian-zi* of others is tantamount to robbing them of their social status and bringing great humiliation on them.

He adds: "This is a very grave matter. In Chinese culture it is inconceivable that anyone would dare to disregard *mian-zi*. Anyone who does not care about his own *mian-zi* is considered shameless."

So sensitive are the Chinese to losing their own "face" or inflicting damage on the "face" of others that they have extreme difficulty in being candid and forthright in their dealings with others. As a result, the use of intermediaries or third parties in both personal and business dealings has become a deeply entrenched custom.

When two people have not met or when they have just met and do not know each other very well, they cannot be sure of the relative "size" of each other's "face," making frank discussions virtually impossible. On such occasions, the natural reaction is to do nothing. If they must engage in some kind of business, their first choice is to go through a host or intermediary.

Mian-zi also makes it difficult or impossible for people with a lot of "face" to engage in any kind of direct social or business intercourse with those who have very little "face." This circumstance grew out of the vertical structure of Chinese society and works to maintain the status quo.

Chinese sensitivity to *mian-zi* is apparently the reason whey they attempt to get new relationships on a ''good friends'' basis as rapidly as possible. ''Friends'' has to be one of the most popular words in China today. Foreign businesspeople in particular are bombarded by declarations of friendship and by being described as ''friends'' by those who want to impose on the relationship no matter how new it might be. However, this ''friendship'' is officially regarded by the Chinese as between organizations, not between individuals.

In so many words, maintaining ''face'' is being moral. Disregarding ''face'' is being immoral. In child-raising as well as education, this sensitivity to face is drummed into the Chinese by warnings and a variety of shaming techniques.

In comments on the moral aspect of *mian-zi*, philosopher Shih Hu said that it includes the kind of respect the group or society has for people with a reputation for being upright and moral. They are the people who will fulfill their obligations regardless of the pain or cost, who always conduct themselves as decent human beings. Once people lose this respect, Hu continued, it is no longer possible for them to function effectively in their community.

Facing the World

Life in China was traditionally closely organized. Since it was tied in with family, village, and circle of connections and the correct observation of a meticulously prescribed behavior, one's reputation was of overriding importance. The slightest blemish could have a negative effect not only on one's own life but also on the lives of family members. Even a moderately serious blemish could be disastrous. Thus for the average person, reputation was the most valuable asset. The ultimate in the loss of face was public punishment.

While Chinese society has changed considerably since the fall of the last feudal dynasty in 1911, concern about face is still a vital part of the makeup of every Chinese. In fact, the dimensions of one's face do not stop with the individual's person. It incorporates the whole of China, primarily in a racial and cultural sense, but also nationalistically.

Average Chinese will go to considerable lengths to protect their own face and to avoid harming the reputations of family, friends, and coworkers. This includes withholding information, coloring information, avoiding commitments and responsibility, covering up, and so on. Some of the things Chinese businesspeople do to avoid any possible smudge on their face are totally irrational from the Western viewpoint. This often involves ''do nothing, say nothing'' behavior that can be baffling because it often makes the situation worse.

Foreign businesspeople should take special care not to arbitrarily impugn the face of anyone by public criticism or ridicule, even when such criticism may be warranted. It will not correct the situation, will make the individual angry, and will most likely result in the person's attempting to get revenge in some way. Careful diplomacy that allows you to make your point while preserving the other person's face is invariably the best rule.

Overseas Chinese

Generally speaking, dealing with Chinese businesspeople and officials in Taiwan, Hong Kong, Singapore, and other Southeast Asian countries is a lot easier than it is in the People's Republic of China, if for no other reason than the political climate. Furthermore, a significant percentage of overseas Chinese have had Western educations and years of experience on an international level.

Still, the majority of overseas Chinese, particularly those who were born before 1950, retain many of the traditional attitudes and customs that have shaped the character and habits of the Chinese for more than three thousand years. Some of these similarities and differences are discussed in a separate chapter on Hong Kong. (*Note*: The Chinese government and news media refer to Chinese residents of Taiwan as "compatriots" instead of "overseas Chinese.")

4

Living in a Beehive Society

"Our minds are on the left, but our pockets are on the right."
—a saying that became popular in China in the 1980s

Land of Indentured Servants

The overriding, often overwhelming, factor in the lives of most Chinese today is the *danwei* (dahn-way) or "work-unit" system, which basically means their place of employment. Each of the "units," whether it is a government ministry or agency, factory, hotel, or joint venture in any category of industry, is administered jointly by its managers and by representatives of the Communist party—as if it were an "independent kingdom," to use the terminology of Yaichi Akaboshi, director of a Chinese-Japanese joint venture.

The *danwei* have extraordinary power over their employee-members, and the heads of the larger, more important "units" are treated more or less like monarchs or mandarins of old. Most member-workers are locked into their respective units to such a degree that one expatriate American manager described them as being like servants indentured for life. There is a saying popular in Beijing that the huge capital city actually has no citizens of its own—that all who live there belong first and last to their *danwei*.

The work-units function more or less as political-commercial "communes," and in some areas have more authority over their members than what has traditionally been given to the military services of a country. A confidential dossier is kept on each member of every *danwei*, with detailed personal information going back for three generations. The only people in a unit who have access to the dossier are party officials, and once a black mark has been placed in a person's file it remains there.

Since the late 1980s, people have been free in principle to leave their *danwei* and seek work elsewhere, but this is still very difficult and sometimes impossible to do. As long as a unit will not officially release an individual, he or she cannot go to work for another company or agency. All the unit has to do is refuse to forward the individual's dossier to the new would-be employer. Individuals cannot get married without written permission from their unit. They cannot have children without *danwei* approval. Any item that is rationed must be obtained through the unit. The units provide housing and medical care for their members.

Since people are provided housing by the state through their work unit, they generally have no choice in the type of housing or its location. As a result, many are housed in areas far from their place of work. If they are able to find someone with housing closer to their workplace who is willing to change apartments with them, however, the government allows the switch. In numerous instances, the two apartments concerned are not equal in size or quality or some other aspect. In these cases, the family wanting the better housing offers to add some "boot" to the trade—either cash or something in kind.

The larger the *danwei* the more economic, social, and political functions it controls and the more of the basic services it provides its member-workers. Larger ones operate the schools attended by the children of their members. The largest ones, such as some of the government ministries and major industries, operate their own universities and hospitals.

Severing a relationship with a *danwei* is therefore both difficult and a major step, since it involves far more than just a monthly salary. In all cases, employees who leave units for jobs elsewhere have to give up their housing, and in some cases the *danwei* demand to be reimbursed for any training or other services in kind they have provided.

The workplace is so intimately involved in the lives of many *danwei* members that in some cases they have virtually merged. The employees eat in the unit cafeteria, sleep in unit-provided quarters, bathe at the company facility, bring their older children to the workplace during school vacation, and otherwise depend on the *danwei* in a cradle-to-grave relationship.

Income and privilege within each unit are primarily based on seniority, but the income spread between the youngest apprentice and the head of the *danwei*, no matter how important the unit, is very small—usually no more than ten times. Under this system, veteran nurses at hospitals often outrank younger doctors and receive higher salaries. Engineers often make less than janitors; middle-ranking government officials in their forties may make less than many twenty-five-year-old taxi drivers or young female employees of foreign-operated firms.

Any person in a *danwei* who demonstrates any sign of individual ambition or independent thought or action is in danger of demotion and a permanent black mark in his or her dossier. Those with special training or talents, who no longer fit the standard Chinese mold and stand out from the crowd, are often subjected to criticism and other forms of discrimination by their fellow work-unit members simply because they act different. The envy and ill will this difference causes among other Chinese, particularly members of close-knit *danwei*, can be so strong it is frightening. It is reminiscent of the Cultural Revolution when intellectuals and private businesspeople alike were persecuted and often destroyed because they were regarded as enemies of the people (meaning those who were less educated and not engaged in business). People know that if they criticize the system or attempt to leave and do not succeed they will surely suffer.

While the government repeatedly announces that the country must have better educated, more skilled professionals to help modernize the country, a significant percentage of the population is not able to accept this intellectually or emotionally when the consequences touch them personally and directly.

The atmosphere in many *danwei* is therefore one of frustration and sometimes fear, especially for young people who are well educated. Members still have limited recourse against the system, and have little hope that it will change significantly any time soon. One hears over and over that none of the latest political and economic reforms have had any real beneficial effect on the lives of most *danwei* members. Improvements that have been made are localized and spotty. Residents of the Special Economic Zones and other more internationalized areas generally have it much better than people outside of these still limited districts—a circumstance that is a source for much of the envy and anger afflicting those who are less fortunate.

While the living and working environment for many urban Chinese is improving rapidly, the *danwei* are still the primary economic and social-control factor in the lives of the people.

In 1987 the Beijing Labor Bureau recognized the inefficiency and inhumanity of the system by implementing several new regulations guaranteeing more rights to workers. The following year, the Beijing Labor Exchange Centre was established to help dissatisfied workers find new jobs. The center was immediately deluged with applications from people wanting to change their *danwei*.

The overall quality of life throughout most of China ranges from basic to primitive, despite touches of modernity such as color television sets. Most homes do not have inside plumbing or toilets. Many people in the capital city of Beijing must ride their bicycles for up to an hour to use public shower facilities. This is not a casual thing under the best of circumstances and is a major thing during the bitterly cold winter months. Generally speaking, however, the biggest social disparity in China is between residents of urban and rural areas.

The present system of household registration and the allotment of grain and housing have resulted in a conspicuous difference in the living standards of rural and urban Chinese. People registered in rural areas cannot move to cities to seek jobs and take up residence. The government provides urban dwellers with subsidized grain and other food items at low prices, and state-owned enterprises in cities provide their employees with housing. People in rural areas do not receive any government assistance for food or housing despite the fact that per capita income in rural areas is around half that of residents of cities.

China also remains a hardship post for expatriate businesspeople, particularly those who are accompanied by their families. Many businesspeople still live in small hotel rooms and all still have few recreational choices. Beijing's huge Holiday Inn Lido, flagship of the chain's hotels in China, had a major impact on the capital's foreign community as soon as it opened in 1986. Adopting the Chinese *danwei* approach, the hotel opened one facility after another until it was virtually a self-contained city. In addition to the usual hotel facilities, the Holiday Inn Lido Centre includes a post office, a bank, a supermarket, a delicatessen, a British pub, a disco, a bowling alley, a 318-unit high-rise residential area, a commercial center housing offices of international companies, a school, and a children's playground. Restaurants on the premises include a pizzeria (the first in Beijing), a German restaurant (also the first in Beijing), a large family style Chinese restaurant, an elegant international-class dining room, a coffee shop, and an ice-cream parlor. Some of the hotel's facilities, including the Business Center, are open twenty-four hours a day.

The Holiday Inn Lido's residential center filled up as soon as it opened but there was some turnover during the 1987 flare-up of opposition to China's reforms. Now, said a hotel manager, there is virtually no turnover at all and a long waiting list. "In fact, the apartments are a barometer of the confidence that foreign companies have in China today," he added.

The Holiday Inn complex, a joint venture between Yick Ho Company of Hong Kong and China Travel Service and operated by Holiday Inns International, quickly became an oasis for the international community in a city that was otherwise a social and recreational desert. The Lido was also the first international hotel in Beijing to allow Chinese to enter the hotel freely and to use its facilities—a policy it introduced in early 1988. "The most we have had to do is chase taxi drivers and would-be money changers out of the lobby," said a hotel spokesperson.

Several other large office-residential complexes especially designed for foreign companies and expatriate businesspeople have since opened in Beijing. They are, however, priced beyond the reach of all except the representatives of major firms and ranking diplomatic personnel.

The level of personal service in China varies greatly from place to place and with the situation. One frequently hears of rude service or no service at all in shops, restaurants, hotels, and other kinds of businesses and in government offices, but that kind of behavior is the exception. In explaining one reason for the difference in service provided by a Japanese hotel and a Chinese one, a Japanese hotel man said that labor costs account for approximately thirty percent of the operating costs of a hotel in Japan and only about 1 percent in China.

Another factor in the quality of life in China today is the tendency for those with power to abuse it. Generally, with official power on any level comes a degree of arrogance to match. The lowest cadre (official) can be expected to throw his or her weight around for personal gain as well as for the satisfaction derived from it. With the mantle of authority also comes a disinclination to admit lack of knowledge of anything. The former is something that people without power have to live with. The latter is often the source of problems that can be very big and very serious when people who are not familiar with this syndrome accept what they are told at face value.

A recent two-panel cartoon in a Beijing newspaper was captioned: Idols Change with the Times. The first panel, labeled *Past*, depicted a peasant bowing before an image of Buddha. The second panel, labeled *Present*, showed a present-day Chinese bowing before a government official seated in the same pose as the Buddha.

Dogs are not allowed in Beijing for sanitary reasons, but the citizens of the city often refer to "the three dogs of Beijing." They mean noisy, arrogant police officers, plainclothes part-time security people who wear armbands and are often noisier and more arrogant than uniformed police, and government officials riding in taxis who shout at the drivers and give them a hard time.

Still the preponderance of officials whom the Chinese describe as "old oily doughnuts"—in reference to people who put on a pleasant, cooperative face but are actually deceitful in their behavior and adroit at avoiding responsibility and pretending that what ought to be actually is true—is noticeably diminishing.

Pride is another problem that affects the quality of life in China. The pride that goes with professional status can be as disruptive and destructive as the arrogance of power. A chief engineer, for example, will refuse to go to an orientation about some new technology because it is beneath him. He is a *chief engineer*! He will, however, send young engineers to the orientation. Afterward, when there are problems involved in implementing the new technology he will overrule the young engineers who are the only ones who know anything about the technology to maintain his face as the chief engineer—a situation that often causes major setbacks and can be extrapolated to other situations almost endlessly.

There is no doubt that the new policy of separating government and business and making bureaucrats responsible for their own behavior and performance will lead to more courtesy and service on the official level as well, while ongoing improvements in the remuneration system should bring relief to the professionals who are so important to the advancement of the country.

Bringing the social infrastructure up to a reasonably comfortable and sanitary level is more of a challenge. In describing life in Beijing, a noted Japanese journalist used the Japanese saying, *Sumeba miyako*, which figuratively means that no matter how inadequate or rough a place may be, if you live there it eventually becomes home. His general impressions of life in three key cities: Beijing is too dull, Shanghai is too crowded, and Guangzhou is too much like Hong Kong.

The Chinese Way

Despite the oppressive nature of the *danwei* system and other economic, political, and social restraints, the Chinese are an innately friendly people, gregarious in their likes and relationships—as long as they are free to develop such relationships. While foreigners visiting and living in China during the early post-Mao years often complained of the difficulty of making and keeping Chinese friends (some of them would just disappear into the labyrinth of the Chinese security system), things have changed considerably since the early 1980s and are changing still.

One of the aims of the Cultural Revolution was to destroy all vestiges of traditional behavior, including any suggestions of unequal relationships between people that called for special courtesy, but the revolution failed to change the basic character of the people. Not only do the Chinese continue to recognize the reality of social differences, on the whole they remain a courteous and caring people.

The extraordinary curiosity the Chinese have about Westerners, and the compulsion of many to practice their English, along with their inherent kindness toward visitors, results in what often appears to be a national responsibility for helping foreigners cope with the country and its system. Individual Chinese are always offering to help foreigners who look as though they need it—and sometimes when they don't. It also appears to be a national custom for them to offer to share their food and other possessions with visiting foreigners when they are thrown together on trains and in other situations.

Large numbers of people take every opportunity that presents itself to practice their English on foreigners, sometimes to the degree that it becomes annoying. At the same time, this special interest in foreigners can be reassuring for those who do not speak Chinese and do in fact often get into situations where they need help.

While especially friendly and hospitable to foreign guests, the Chinese balance their custom of hospitality with an age-old habit of frugality. There are numerous stories that illustrate their deeply entrenched habit of thrift. One such story concerns a multimillionaire who took parsimony to the extreme. One day when he was away from home, a friend, Lung Wang, came by unexpectedly.

The millionaire's son, being a chip off the old block, drew the visitor a picture of a pie rather than actually serve him any refreshments. When the father returned home that evening his son said:

"Uncle Wang came to see you this afternoon."

"Were you courteous to him? Did you serve him anything?" the millionaire asked apprehensively.

"Of course, honorable father," the son replied. "I drew him a pie."

With that, the millionaire began slapping his son and shouting at the top of his voice:

"You little squanderer! Why did you draw a whole pie for him? A single slice would have been sufficient!"

In past years the Chinese have typically let the stops out when entertaining foreign guests at state expense, but there is now a trend for this conspicuous extravagance to be curbed, particularly in Shanghai, where the growth rate of the economy has fallen behind that of some other cities. Still, the banquet remains an important aspect of the Chinese business system and is not likely to disappear. It is also a traditional Chinese custom that most foreign businesspeople can readily appreciate.

Foreign tourists in China are in fact often overwhelmed by spontaneous demonstrations of goodwill, hospitality, and affection that is quite heart-rending and leaves them marveling at the courage and character of the Chinese.

A facet of Chinese behavior that has traditionally met with less enthusiasm among foreigners, however, is the tendency to disregard personal privacy. There is no word in the Chinese language for *privacy*, or for the word *intimacy*, because the concept was traditionally alien, virtually unthinkable. The dense population and communal style of living from earliest times conditioned the people to think and behave as a group instead of as individuals. Just like other orders of life, the Chinese lived and functioned together.

The idea and sense of privacy is growing in modern China, but it is still at a nascent stage and is still far below the expectations of Western visitors. Maids and others often blithely enter offices and private rooms at will, ignoring repeated remonstrations against such behavior. They will read private mail and check out anything else that attracts their attention. The foreign businessperson who has served in the military, with its barracks life and communal sharing of showers and toilets, no doubt has an advantage over those who have never been called upon to share their "private" space and time with others. The obvious solution, of course, is to do your best to pretend that you are alone.

Another area that Westerners tend to think of as private but is generally considered to be public in China is the amount of salary received by *danwei* members. Everybody wants to know that everyone else is making to make sure they are all being treated equally. The amount they receive is normally written on their pay envelopes and any attempt to conceal the amount from other employees is regarded as a serious breach of morality.

For employees of foreign firms and joint ventures, however, where salaries and bonuses are based more on position and merit, there is a compulsive desire to keep one's income private. They keep private not only from fellow employees but from outsiders as well, to avoid conflict—a very significant break in the monolithic face of the country.

Sensitivity to Clothing

What people say, do, and wear can still get them into trouble in China. During the long feudal ages of China, different materials, colors, and styles were strictly prescribed by law for the different social classes. It was possible to instantly determine a person's status by his or her clothing. Common people were required to wear white clothing made of coarse material. Upper classes wore pink, red, and yellow (yellow was the Emperor's color) in ascending order. Failure to wear the colors and materials prescribed for one's station was a serious matter that could lead to a quick, untimely death.

So deeply engrained were the rules and customs concerning dress that the fall of the Han Dynasty in the third century B.C. is attributed in part to the fact that Han soldiers were required to wear ankle-length robes. They greatly restricted their movements and made them easy victims for the horseback-riding trousered tribesmen of the northern and western frontiers. Movies depicting historical periods in China also show the thick, heavy robes worn by upper classes and how they had to manipulate them in order to move about and defend themselves.

The famous Yatsen Sun (Zhongshan Sun), father of the first republic of China, tried to outlaw the long robes of the Qing (Ching) Dynasty in 1911 by introducing a simplified suit that was named after him—Zhongshan Zhuang or the Zhongshan Suit. During the period of Soviet influence in China, a double-buttoned coat called a Lenin Jacket was popular among Chinese women cadre. When the Soviets were kicked out, there was a strong movement against any kind of apparel that suggested Westernism, and the Zhongshan Zhuang, now called the "Mao Suit," in gray, blue, or black, became the official uniform of China.

There was another abrupt shift during the early years of the terrible

Cultural Revolution (1966–1976), when the dress for both men and women of all ages was a green army uniform. In 1974 Qing Jiang, the wife of Chairman Zedong Mao and later a member of the infamous Gang of Four, designed a gown based on a style that was made popular by Empress Zetain Wu during the Tang Dynasty (618–907), and tried to get urban women to wear it as a "political statement." The plan did not succeed and Jiang eventually fell from power.

Apparel worn in today's China has lost most but certainly not all of its political connotations. It is generally taken for granted that anyone who wears Western clothing is "for" the political and economic reforms that are remaking the country into more of a capitalistic society, while anyone wearing the "Mao Suit" is regarded as making a conservative statement that could and often does indicate resistance to the changes—or at least, caution.

As late as 1987, when there was a backlash against capitalistic reforms, those who opposed the reforms were quick to criticize those who had changed their clothing as well as their politics, putting a temporary damper on the movement toward freedom of dress.

Social commentators say that even though those born after the Cultural Revolution already look upon the old attitudes linking apparel and politics as ancient history, this deeply entrenched outlook will probably not disappear from China for several decades.

Women in New China

Women are playing an increasingly important role in China, after long centuries of chauvinistic abuse. Sexual segregation among upper-class families and the general degradation of women into second- or third-class citizens was late in coming to China, however. Historians are uncertain, but it seems to have begun during the Sui Dynasty (A.D. 581–618), picked up momentum during the Tang Dynasty (A.D. 618–906), and become a deeply entrenched feature of society by the early decades of the Sung Dynasty, (A.D. 960–1279). In upper-class families, girls were raised separately from boys. Binding the feet of women in the Mandarin class was also a well-established practice by the beginning of the Sung era.

Love marriages also seemed to have been totally replaced by arranged marriages during these long dynastic ages. Men of means were legally allowed to have as many concubines as they wanted. A number of China's emperors were notorious for the size of their harems. One had twenty-seven beds in his sleeping quarters and is said to have "used" well over one thousand girls between the ages of eight and fourteen during his reign.

The government of the People's Republic of China has gone a long way toward remedying this failure but Chinese women are still far from having achieved equal rights with men. Although over one hundred million women work, China's first law protecting women workers dates only from July 21, 1988, and this was passed because previous regulations pertaining to female employees were mostly ignored. Many of China's miners are women, and they have the same work quota as male miners. Yet Chinese women must still take primary responsibility for running the home and raising the children. This puts the familiar double burden on them.

Chinese women are caught in the vortex of the cross-cultural winds sweeping the country. Educated women in particular no longer accept the age-old idea that they are "the moon reflecting the sunlight"—subordinate to men. Surveys show they are rapidly absorbing the Western concept of individuality, independence, and personal responsibility. The majority say they want to dedicate themselves to their careers, the improvement of their country, world peace, and the development of the human race.

Noted one survey of female university students: "They pay more attention to their own moral welfare without thinking of others, and have no interest in school activities, apart from dance parties. Some students are obsessed with making friends."

The model woman in China today does not see herself as just tender, virtuous, and obedient according to traditional Chinese values. She believes that she should work hard and have her own professional career without sacrificing her femininity. Western role models most often mentioned by young Chinese women today: Britain's Margaret Thatcher and France's Marie Curie.

Most young Chinese women who go to university *say* one of their primary goals is to find a boyfriend whom they will later marry. They add that the relationship they want with men must be based on true love, and that if they later discover they do not really love their partners they will end the relationship without hesitation.

Despite the Western veneer coating college-educated women, however, the majority of them still suffer from a deeply rooted inferiority complex in their attitudes toward men. They express concern about how they will be able to juggle a career and the responsibilities of a housewife and mother.

As part of their own liberation, many female as well as male students now work part-time in a variety of jobs and take special pride in their ability to help support themselves and in the fact that they are gaining experience that will benefit them after they finish school.

One of the biggest worries of female students is how they will integrate what they are learning in school with society at large after they finish their education. Chinese society, they say, is not yet able to accept independent-minded, educated women into its economic and political ranks. Job discrimination on the basis of sex is rampant. Male personnel directors and managers readily admit that they discriminate against female applicants for certain kinds of jobs because they fear the women will get married, become pregnant, and have to leave.

Students who major in such things as language, history, political theory (including communism), and literature generally experience special difficulties in finding jobs. When and if they do finally find work, it usually has nothing to do with what they studied in school. In earlier years, employers had no choice but to accept whomever the state sent to them. Now that this system is being phased out and both employers and potential employees are being given some choice in the matter, problems of a different type are common.

Employers sometimes turn down job applicants because they do not like their hairstyle or clothing, or because they think their college major is irrelevant to modern industry. Another problem is caused by students with connections using "the back door" to get desirable jobs, making it impossible for other students to compete with them. Still, most students say they prefer to have some say-so in the matter of job selection. In Shanghai the practice of giving students some options in job-hunting is called "mutual selection" or "free marriage."

In the case of "mutual selection" or "free marriage," the graduating students as well their potential employers are able to exercise a choice, assuring that both parties are pleased.

Black July

China's annual three-day college entrance examinations, held in July each year for enrollment in September, have resulted in the examination month being known as "Black July." Just as in Japan, parents bring intense pressure on their children to study from early morning to late at night in preparation for the examinations. During this writing, one mother beat her son to death for failing to get a grade of ninety or above in all his subjects, while another high school boy who failed the exams killed his parents to avoid having to face them. One seventeen-year-old girl from Henan Province summed it up for many: "I am no longer naive and happy. I have become indifferent to the outside world. I am just a slave to exams. Only when I die can I be totally free."

In many schools, teachers stop covering regular class subjects some six months prior to the examination period to help their students cram for the exams. Said one teacher: "Both students and teachers have to work like slaves. The entrance exams are destroying the mental and physical health of students and teachers alike."

Seventy-five percent of the students who take the national examinations each year fail and are unable to enter any college. Some of them retake the exams three or four years in a row. One student commented bitterly: "The first thing I did after taking the exams this year was to burn all of my books and school supplies. They pressed me so hard for so many years, I hated them in my heart."

Very much like feudal times, the students study exam topics by rote, attempting to memorize masses of material that does them little good in the outside world and dulls their ability to think and act spontaneously. Parents say the regime is so intensive that many eighteen-year-olds have had very little experience in taking care of their personal needs.

Not surprisingly, growing numbers of China's youth are opting for vocational schools instead of college, while others are dropping out of school altogether. Educators complain that even those who remain in school are losing their enthusiasm for study and that more and more students who succeed in getting into colleges and universities are not studying and are cutting classes, or dropping out. The reason, say the educators, is that students no longer see any future in education. "They know they can earn more working as a peddler or a taxi driver than they can as a professor or an engineer," said a university lecturer.

Despite these problems and concerns, the situation regarding students returning from studies abroad is changing rapidly. More and more ministries, agencies, and enterprises, on both the national and regional levels, now specifically request returned students to fill key job openings. Students who are in the most demand are those who took postgraduate degrees, especially in scientific and other high-tech areas. Chinese students are presently studying in over seven hundred colleges and universities in the United States alone.

Also in 1988, the State Education Commission announced an expanded policy of providing state funds for postgraduate study in several areas where specialized training is needed, including scientific research and business management. The program was first initiated in 1986. In the new program, preference was given to applicants who have worked for four or more years after graduating from college or university. China resumed postgraduate training in 1978 after a gap of ten years.

Income levels in today's China are symptomatic of the problems rising out of the "big pot" approach to achieving a socialist utopia. Taxi drivers often earn more than top ministry officials. Some barbers receive higher salaries than neurosurgeons. The frustration this engenders among highly educated and experienced professionals is visible. Rank and authority, both of which are important in any efficient society, have also been upset by the utopian fantasy of everyone being equal (but some more equal than others). When nurses who have more seniority than doctors refuse to take instructions from them, health care is jeopardized. When workers refuse to listen to engineers, projects are endangered. Recognizing the weaknesses of an army without a hierarchical structure of rank, the Chinese military in 1988 reinstituted the age-old system of ranking its members from recruits up to generals.

Among the most envied of all people in China today are those who work for joint-venture companies and other foreign enterprises. Their salaries are two, three, four, or more times higher than the less fortunate Chinese. The fringe benefits they receive often include amenities that are available only to high cadre and successful businesspeople. This situation naturally creates a great deal of envy and ill will among the majority who have no such opportunities and requires that the fortunate ones exercise considerable care not to flaunt themselves and their relative wealth.

Working in the environment of an international hotel is an especially exciting and sometimes traumatic experience for a young Chinese. It is like being in a foreign country and creates psychological pressures that some of them cannot cope with. "Smelling the life of foreigners every day makes them question all their values and acutely feel the shortcomings of their own country," said a Hong Kong Chinese. "After even a short period, they cannot imagine themselves going back to the way most Chinese live and begin dreaming of somehow getting out of China."

While intellectuals, on the one hand, may still be in the doghouse, by the mid-1980s technicians and scientists had been rehabilitated. Still, like many other countries that have traditionally put a high premium on academic credentials as opposed to innovative thinking and practical experience, China's headlong rush to modernize itself is still hampered by laws and customs that give precedence to people with diplomas rather than ability. Complaints about this sort of discrimination are especially common because so many Chinese with degrees have only theoretical knowledge without ever having had the opportunity to put it to practical use.

As in Japan, many Chinese students work very hard to get into the more prestigious schools and then study very little or none at all after they get in because their graduation is guaranteed. By the same token, students accepted by second- or third-choice universities often study very little—frequently only for exams—because they are disappointed with the school and know it is not going to be that much help to them in getting a desirable job (because those jobs are more or less reserved for graduates of the higher-ranked schools). Many students say they are avoiding challenges presented by the "outside world" by taking postgraduate courses and "hiding in the haven" of their universities.

At the opposite end of this spectrum are the young women of extraordinary courage who are determined to make their own way and see themselves as equal to if not better than most men. One such group that achieved national notice are the founder-operators of China's first chicken-sexing company. Formed in Beijing by eight women whose average age was twenty, the corporation provides training in chicken-sexing for domestic poultry farms as well as foreign companies. The manager of the company won a national chicken-sexing contest when she was twenty-two years old, sexing one hundred baby chicks in three minutes and thirty-three seconds, with 100 percent accuracy.*

While claiming that Chinese women have more rights than the women of most countries, Xiaojiang Li, an associate professor at Zhengzhou University and director of the university's Center for Women's Studies, adds that Chinese women have not yet achieved liberation in the true sense. Still, she continued, women should not be measured by male standards, since there are inherent differences in the natural roles of men and women.

The traditional segregation of women in a separate world in China is indicated by the fact that they were not allowed to take the family names of their husbands, which in their case was surely more of a matter of their lower status than their independence. Under today's marriage law, the wife may take her husband's name or keep her own, and the husband may take his wife's name if he wishes. Children may take the name of either parent.

Given the traditional Chinese reverence for the family and what the Communist regime has done for women, it is remarkable that during the early decades the government routinely split families by assigning husbands and wives to jobs in widely separated areas of the country. Millions of families were thus divided, many of them for up to fifteen years or more.

The longer a family was separated, the more difficult it was for them to get their workplaces to release them or for the government to reassign them in the same location so they could live together. Sometimes people were able to effect such moves by getting other people to agree to change with them. This was obviously an area in which the good of the state came before personal considerations. This situation has improved considerably since the early 1980s, but people still are not totally free to change their jobs or their homes, resulting in numerous hardships on families.

Sexual Taboos

Already conditioned to the puritanical, chauvinistic sexual system that prevailed during their long feudalistic period, China's new Communist regime, which took over the country in 1949, established a sexual policy that was even more extreme. The Communist approach was spurred by a genuine desire to slow the population growth, but in making anything relating to

---

*For those who are not familiar with the art of chicken-sexing, it is based on the presence or absence of a small protrusion just inside the chick's anus. Chicken-sexers learn how to pick a chick up in one hand and squeeze it in such a way that the anus opens, allowing them to see the protrusion or to insert the tip of a finger or thumb to feel it. Master sexers become so good at this that they do it entirely by feel—the best of them doing chicks in each hand simultaneously.

sexuality an official taboo, the government ended up creating more problems that it solved.

By the early 1980s, sexual ignorance and frustration had become the source of rampant mental and emotional problems, suicides, and the spread of disease. Fifty young women in just one psychiatric hospital in Henan Province were reported to have become mentally deranged after having their first sexual experience. Sex crimes became common again, and small-scale prostitution reappeared.

During the 1980s, health authorities began pointing out that when young parents were asked by their children about the distinctions between men and women, a common response was, "Those who smoke are men and those who don't are women."

Unhappy sexual lives became a primary cause of a burgeoning divorce rate, and a deep compulsion among young people to learn more about their own sexuality and human sexuality in general led to a flourishing black market in pornographic materials. Sociologists began to say in public that the more sexual behavior is restricted, the more people will desire it. By 1988, the problem had reached epidemic proportions, resulting in moves to introduce sex-education courses into the school system.

Age-old taboos die hard, however, and sexual relations between couples, whether married or not, is still a very sensitive subject. Further, any intimate fraternization between Chinese and foreigners, or just the hint of such fraternization, is regarded as a serious offense by more conservative party officials and acts as a barrier limiting the development of close relationships. There are stories in joint ventures of young, attractive women who become friendly with foreign men being transferred, with no word of their whereabouts.

Yet traditional as well as Communist-inspired prudery is diminishing in China, especially among younger urban Chinese who are being strongly influenced by movies that now show people falling in love, kissing, and going off on romantic honeymoons.

Marriage by the Numbers

China's official policy is that each ethnic Chinese married couple will have only one child. They are expected to register with the appropriate authorities for the one-child program as a control technique. If they have a second child, by accident or design, they must pay a fine (*fa kuan*). The fine varies from one region to another but generally is 1,000 yuan or more a year for five years—a huge amount of money for the average Chinese. There are occasions, especially in rural areas, where couples deliberately have a second child when the first one is a girl. The fine is collected when the wife becomes pregnant.

Laws governing childbirth among ethnic minorities in China vary significantly, particularly among those whose homelands are vast, sparsely populated areas (and who generally ignore such policies in the second place).

By pledging to have only one child, ethnic Chinese parents get all sorts of benefits and privileges, including pay raises, preferential treatment for new or larger housing, private garden plots, medical care, and education. Government records show that 90 percent of China's wives rely on tubal ligations and intrauterine devices to control births.

With predictions that China's population will reach one billion, two-hundred eighty-seven million by the year 2000, the country's birth-control policy (one child per family, with late marriages and late births) was reconfirmed in 1988, but provisions for a degree of flexibility were announced at that time. Rural families whose first child is female were given the option of having a second child in the hope that it would be male, so long as the second pregnancy was well spaced and was done with official approval. It was also announced that "additional flexibility would be given to ethnic minority peoples." For example, an urban ethnic couple in the autonomous region of Xinjiang Uygur may legally have two children and a rural couple may have three. The tribes on Hainan Island can reportedly have up to five children.

Population-control authorities express continued concern at the propensity for couples to marry before the legal age—twenty-two for men and twenty for women—in some rural areas, often without going through official procedures. They say this violation of the policy is especially common in mountainous areas, where the number of unofficial marriages outnumbers those that are legally registered and among members of the nation's growing transient population.

Because of the system of delaying marriage and childbirth, it is common for Chinese men and women in their early twenties to live together before getting married. This arrangement was earlier referred to as *zhu-li*, which literally means "assistant" but came to mean a "live-in" relationship. Now *tong-ju* is the more popular term for unmarried couples living together.

One of the reasons that the population-control system is being ignored by a growing number of people is that some local governments require unmarried employees to pay an "earnest money deposit" to their units (places of work) to guarantee that they will marry late, postpone having children, and have only one child. Those who marry at an age earlier than that specified by their employers forfeit their deposits. This, authorities admit, results in many young couples failing to register their marriages and having children secretly.

Another factor in some regions is the imbalance between eligible males and females, particularly in areas where huge numbers of males have congregated because of work opportunities. This is bringing about a return of "child brides," with preteen girls betrothed to older boys.

Still another barrier presented by the control system is the fee required for a premarital medical examination. Many see it as both unnecessary and too expensive and get around it by marrying unofficially.

Despite the ban on earlier marriage, those who are not married before they are thirty, particularly women, are often subjected to ridicule and sometimes to various kinds of discrimination as well. Arranged marriages, prohibited by law in 1980, have not disappeared, especially in rural areas.

One of the more startling throwbacks to traditionalism are "marriages for the dead," which have been reported recently in the national press and which attest to the underlying strength of age-old customs. Parents whose sons died before they were able to marry literally buy the bodies of unmarried girls who met untimely deaths, conduct symbolic weddings, then bury the dead "bride" with the dead "husband" to provide company for the male soul in the afterworld.

Children Without Identities

The problem of "illegal" children in China—those whose births are not officially sanctioned and not registered—goes far beyond just contravening the one-couple one-child policy of the government. Not being registered, the children officially do not exist and are commonly referred to as "black children." Without registration and an official residence permit, the children are not eligible for rationed foods and cannot officially attend a school, get a job, join the military, or take college entrance examinations.

One of the key ways the government attempts to control the population is by setting specific quotas for each county, based on the number of officially registered couples of childbearing age, with local officials held responsible for the quotas not being exceeded. Once the quotas have been reached, the officials refuse to register any more newborns, adding to the number of "black children."

"Black children" in China number well over one million and are increasing rapidly. Unless the government changes its position and allows the children to be registered the problem will become more serious as they grow up, marry, and have children of their own.

If China's present birthrate of approximately 2 percent stays the same, the population will surpass two billion by the year 2030. The government has been trying to achieve a 1.5 percent growth rate.

Creating a New Culture

Surveys reveal that the political, social, and economic changes sweeping China are altering the way many Chinese view and raise their children—

a process that is creating a new culture. More and more urban Chinese parents are treating their children as equals, fostering independent thinking and behavior—exactly the opposite of the Confucian-oriented upbringing that has marked the country for more than two thousand years. Some social commentators point out that part of this process is a backlash to the Cultural Revolution, which many such parents believe was made all the worse because of the old traditions in which children had no rights and the power of the father was absolute.

The same surveys also reveal a negative side to changes in raising children. While some parents spoil their children by doing too much for them, allowing them to become lazy and arrogant, others are so anxious that their children reap the rewards of their new freedom that they go to the extreme in pushing them to study and to excel in a wide range of things. Many voices in the country are counseling a more rational approach to both child-upbringing and education—one that allows for differences in personality and aptitude and still gives young people the opportunity to be the best that they can be.

As part of its new Open Door policy, China's Civil Affairs Ministry relaxed government restrictions applying to marriages between Chinese citizens and foreigners—with overseas Chinese treated as a separate category of foreigner. This resulted in an upsurge in such marriages, which are now averaging about 10,000 a year. The Civil Affairs Ministry reports that about 90 percent of all international marriages involve overseas Chinese, who are mostly blue-collar workers.

The ministry also noted that there was usually a significant age gap between Chinese women and their foreign spouses, with the most extreme example being a seventy-year-old American businessman and a twenty-year-old Chinese woman. The ministry added that the majority of Chinese women marrying foreigners were college students and those working in tourist organizations and hotels, where they came into frequent contact with foreigners. Many such women marry foreigners just so they can go abroad, the ministry said. Some of the international unions are said to be sham marriages from the start, with divorce following as soon as the Chinese partner obtains resident status overseas.

Consumerism Versus Communism

What one billion new, hungry Chinese consumers could mean to the world, politically as well as economically, staggers the imagination. And even though the China market that exists today is only a fraction of the full potential, it is already exercising an influence that, like gravity, is felt around the world.

There is no doubt that the Chinese people today are more interested in consumerism than in communism. The ideology of consumerism needs no leader, no revolutionary manifesto, no army or Red Guards. Even four thousand years of conditioning in the virtues of austerity was not enough to blind the Chinese to the attractions of life above the subsistence level. They have embraced the consumer revolution with a passion they have never before been free to express.

To say that most Chinese would gladly forget all about communism hardly does justice to the present-day mood in China. In private conversations they leave no doubt that they would prefer to forget all about politics and get on with exercising freedom of choice and improving their standards of living. The popular saying, "Our minds are on the left, but our pockets are on the right," pretty much sums it up.

A very conspicuous sign of the Chinese emphasis on consumerism as opposed to political considerations: More than ten thousand air-raid shelters with a total area in excess of ten million square meters, built during the 1970s, have been turned into hotels, warehouses, hospitals, department stores, recreational centers, and workshops. Most of these vast underground centers are located in Harbin, Shenyang, Quingdao, Chengdu, and Guangzhou.

But there are immense problems involved in the remaking of China. Over and above government regulations and restrictions coloring and controlling the economic system, market-oriented businesspeople are hindered by deep-seated cultural factors, such as the still-widespread belief that aggressive selling is immoral. There are plus factors as well. Because of their long isolation and absence of choice in consumer goods, the Chinese are even more variety- and brand-conscious than the Japanese, which augurs well for marketers.

The Famous "Back Door"

Especially in the beginning of its Open Door policy, China's still-developing consumer industries were unable to meet the demand for consumer goods—and the government kept a tight rein on imports allowed into that country. This quickly resulted in the development of a nationwide "back door" black market as well as a chain of special "Friendship Stores," where foreigners and China's privileged groups could obtain things not available to ordinary citizens.

Taking advantage of the underground economy is known as *zou-hou-men* or "taking the back door," and stories of the experiences of people dealing with or trying to deal with this unofficial market are legion. The two-faced system is not only a testimony to the practical nature of the Chinese, but also a commentary on their economic philosophy.

The most important function of the "back door," in the opinion of some resident foreign businesspeople, is not to provide consumer goods that people cannot get otherwise, but to make available raw materials and parts to factories that cannot obtain them through official channels.

The Need for Revenge

Just as they were during dynastic days, the Chinese are sensitive about criticism, real or implied, of their country. They may criticize the system themselves but criticism from foreigners is not appreciated. Officials in particular are apt to pick up on the slightest sign of disrespect or dislike, and have been known to manufacture such insults when none were intended.

Foreign businesspeople should be especially careful about insulting or slighting individual Chinese, even in subtle ways that may not be regarded as serious from the Western viewpoint. Given the sensitivity and importance of face to the Chinese and also the long cultural tradition of not speaking directly or strongly regardless of the strength of the feelings involved—plus the fact that any overt physical response was strictly taboo—the Chinese developed an often overriding need for revenge when their reputations were impugned or they suffered any injustice from anybody.

This need for revenge became a deeply ingrained characteristic that was unofficially sanctioned by society. People who avenged themselves, especially against great odds and at great personal risk to themselves, were respected and honored. Those who shirked the obligation were viewed with contempt as having no respect for themselves or their families.

Because of the equally strong social sanctions against physical or verbal violence, the Chinese became adept at taking their revenge in more subtle ways, often waiting for years or even generations before acting. Chinese literature is replete with examples of vengeful exploits—so much so that they make up a significant part of the dramatic history of China.

Of course, present-day Chinese are no longer subject to such stringent social controls over their behavior, and many have become masters at verbal defense and counterattacks. But verbal volleys are still not enough to satisfy their deep-seated compulsion to take revenge in more concrete terms. The foreign visitor is therefore cautioned to exercise special tact in any dealings involving criticism, discipline, strong differences of opinion, or outrage of any kind. Whatever the provocation, it is best to remain calm and courteous (and if you also feel the need for revenge, do it the Chinese way).

Another of the biggest mistakes the foreign businessperson in China can make is trying to debate a Chinese official, on any level about anything, on the basis of Western rationality or the principle of right or wrong, fair or unfair, from the Western viewpoint. Like the Japanese, the Chinese base their attitudes and actions on circumstances and policies, not on principles. Without a clear understanding of this concept, it is not possible to engage in a meaningful dialogue with a Chinese official or businessperson.

Hard and Soft

As part of the policy of the Chinese government to present the People's Republic of China as a classless society in which everyone is socially if not economically equal, the designations of first-class and second-class are not used in reference to public transportation. First-class accommodations on planes and trains, for example, are known as "soft seats"; second-class seats are referred to as "hard seats."

"Soft-seat" areas have more than just upholstered chairs. They offer more space in varying degrees of plushness and the windows usually have curtains. Generally, passengers are not allowed to stand in the aisles in soft-seat areas. There are also usually separate waiting rooms and special entrances for first-class passengers. Second-class "hard seats" are in fact mostly padded as far as the seating goes, but they are basic in every other way and tend to be in areas that are very crowded, noisy, and generally uncomfortable.

Age Has Its Privileges

One of the more conspicuous differences in Chinese and Western societies is in the attitude and behavior toward the aged. China was traditionally a seniority-based, Confucian-oriented culture in which the aged were at the apex of society. As people aged, the respect and deference paid to them increased. Age was a symbol of experience and wisdom that grew with each passing year. Further, the ties between parents and children did not end with the adulthood of the children. Children remained subservient to their parents and were responsible for their welfare and upkeep when the parents became unable to support and care for themselves.

This age-old Chinese tradition still prevails in China today, and has been written into the country's family law. Article 15 says that children have the duty to support and assist their parents, and that parents have the right to demand this support. Further, Article 22 makes it mandatory that grandchildren assume responsibility for the support of their grandparents if the parents are deceased.

China's welfare system also favors the elderly. In cities, men can retire at the age of sixty, after twenty years of service; women at fifty-five if they worked in an office and fifty if they worked in a factory. Old-age pensions normally amount to 75 percent of preretirement wages. Older retired people therefore often end up with higher incomes than sons and daughters who are in the prime of their lives and contributing most to the workforce. Since many older people are able to pay for their own upkeep as well as make a substantial contribution to the household, it can be a financial advantage for the entire family. In addition, the family's housing may be in the name of the elderly parents, which adds to the value of keeping the extended family intact.

But there is a downside to exalting seniority. Since one of the primary pillars of the traditional Chinese way of life was the importance of age and seniority, the young were taught to respect and obey their elders, particularly fathers and other male figures in positions of authority, regardless of whether or not the individual concerned merited such respect and obedience. It was an absolute, not subject to interpretation.

Not surprisingly, this system resulted in older people tending to ignore the intelligence and talents of the young, including those who were conspicuously above average, and to give precedence to age and seniority in their personal as well as public affairs irrespective of ability. This attitude and behavior has been carried over into the business world, often with detrimental results. Talented young people are often held back to avoid conflicts with those who are older, and there may be no way the young can make their voices heard. This often blunts the ambitions and energy of the young, and delays or prevents desirable change.

Another aspect of the problem facing both Chinese and foreigners doing business in China is that individuals, particularly younger ones who are smarter and/or more ambitious and harder-working than their colleagues, may be subject to criticism and sometimes extreme jealousy that can lead to acts of revenge. For most, this leads to a "don't rock the boat" attitude that includes: don't make mistakes; don't do anything that might result in making a mistake; don't give anyone the impression you think you are better than they are.

The Iron Rice Bowl

One of the most important facets of the economic system established by the government of New China was guaranteed lifetime employment—a system that was known as the *Iron Rice Bowl* from the connotation that one who had a guaranteed job would not suffer from "having his rice bowl broken" and therefore go hungry or starve. Until the late 1980s, dismissal from a job was rare and usually occured only when someone had committed a serious crime. Under this system there were regular cases in which employees lost their jobs because of factory closings or other circumstances but were kept on the payroll for indefinite periods.

Not surprisingly, the system was regularly abused by workers who had no particular incentive to work diligently or efficiently. In some factories, this factor was blamed for exceptionally low productivity. In other instances it was blamed on the age-old Chinese philosophy that doing nothing is better than doing something, besides being the preferred way of merging one's self with the cosmos. (Dao and other Chinese philosophers taught that *Wu Wei* or "Do Nothing" was the ideal philosophy for man, since by doing nothing one would not do any harm or get into any trouble, and if pursued diligently could achieve nirvana. This concept continues to pervade the thinking of many officials.)

Little by little, however, competition in the new spirit of economic freedom eroded the guaranteed employment system. In the late 1980s the "iron bowl" suffered its first major crack. The city of Qingdao gave all local enterprises authority to dismiss workers whenever they underwent "streamlining" to increase their efficiency and profitability, and to hire new workers without obtaining permission from the state. Workers sacked under this new authority are kept on the payroll for up to three months while they are retrained and look for another job. The central government backs this new policy of making labor more mobile and more responsive to the needs of the marketplace.

Only in China

Remembering the days when lack of a job could literally mean death, the government of the People's Republic of China has adapted an age-old custom to modern times. Instead of the son following in the trade of his father from one generation to the next, the government established a policy that when office and factory workers retire they have the right to turn their jobs over to sons or daughters.

This system was also designed in part to enhance the diligence and loyalty of older employees. It also served to keep families together. (One wonders if the system might ever spread to the West as our countries age and become more crowded and more competitive.) Not surprisingly, however, many young Chinese prefer to make their own decisions about where they are going to work and often ignore the system.

Farmers are allowed to quit working on collective labor teams after they reach the age of fifty, following which they can devote all of their time to raising fruit, vegetables, chickens, and pigs for their families—another reason why having older people in a family is a definite advantage.

Siesta Time!

One Chinese custom that still prevails in some areas and generally comes as a total surprise to many foreign businesspeople visiting the country for the first time is the practice of midday siestas à la Mexico in earlier years. The custom is known as *xiu-xi* (show-she) in Chinese and has its antecedents in the ancient agricultural origins of the culture. Then people got up with the sun, worked in the fields until midday, and took a long break before going back to work and continuing until sundown. Article 49 of China's constitution guarantees the right of all people to their daily midday rest. The article says, "The working people have the right to *xiu-xi*."

This "right" has been banned in a number of cities and regions, however, and in others it has been diluted. In some places, the midday break during summer months lasts for up to three hours, beginning at noon or before. In winter is it usually two hours. Employees in these areas often eat their lunch before noon, on company time.

In the Special Export Zones and "open cities," where a great deal of the business is export-oriented, the length of the *xiu-xi* varies, and in some cases it has been dispensed with altogether. Still, it is surprising to hear very modern Western-educated Chinese say they simply cannot get through a day without their noonday naps. One told the story of how all of the beds were removed from her office as a step to help eliminate the practice. But then efficiency and morale dropped so low that the beds were brought back in and the noon naps resumed.

The Workplace as Big Brother

New China's internal security system, once regarded by some as the most comprehensive and insidious in the world, was originally based on the mass organization of "watchers" down to the small neighborhood level. The lowest level in the system were the small political "discussion groups," next up were the "street committees," and third were the *danwei* or workplaces. On each of these three levels, someone was assigned to watch and report on everyone else. Residents said there was no escape, that every aspect of the daily lives of individuals was monitored.

The system is still in place today, but security is so lax that it is generally not noticeable. Everyone is supposed to attend a political orientation meeting once a week, but the flimsiest excuse is enough to get one out of it and most of those who go pay very little attention to the political lectures.

Members of the street committee can still search one's home at any time without advance warning and without any legal proceedings. They can question anyone anytime about anything. They even have the right to decide which couples in their districts are allowed to have children—and when. But again, there has been a general relaxation of this kind of big brotherism.

China's elaborate internal security system is administered by the Public Security Ministry (PSM), which runs not only the uniformed police and plainclothes agents, but the security agents in each workplace and each street committee. There are said to be thirteen bureaus in PSM, with one of them solely responsible for monitoring the activities of foreigners in China.

In the recent past, government compulsion to control people's thoughts and actions often extended to general information of the kind that is found in libraries. Generally, libraries were not open across the board to ordinary users. This too has improved.

In 1985 a new law was passed requiring all Chinese to carry identification cards. Implementation of the law went into high gear in 1988, and by 1989 some five hundred million people had been issued the cards. Only police with special IDs are authorized to check private citizens to make sure they are carrying their cards.

It Isn't What You Know!

The old saw, "It isn't what you know, it's who you know," is probably more applicable in China than anywhere else in the world. Given the nature of Chinese society and law over the dynastic ages, the foundation for virtually all behavior was personal relations, which in turn were based on familial relationship, sex, age, social class, and rank.

In a very real sense, society was not made up of millions of individuals. It was made up of specific, identifiable groups, from families up to villages, towns, and districts. The lines dividing these different groups were clear and comprehensive, and any crossing of the lines was controlled by rigid customs and rules. There was no public law to enforce social justice (from the viewpoint of individual or human rights) on behalf of the people. Justice, to a considerable extent, was whatever the person in power decided to do in his own best interest.

The only protection that most people had was based on personal connections they had or could develop with individuals who had the power to help them. It therefore became vitally important to have a network of contacts and to continuously nurture them, through various favors, gifts, bribes, or whatever, not only for security but simply to get things done.

Personal connections, *guanxi* in Chinese, are just as important in China today, if not more so, particularly in the business world, where it is necessary to deal with large numbers of bureaucrats and others who can delay, destroy, or otherwise affect a project to suit their purposes. It is therefore important that the foreign businessperson dealing with or in China deliberately establish a network of personal connections, on as many official and private levels as possible, and thereafter carefully cultivate them. This means regular contact, meetings, meals, gifts, and special favors.

Japanese residents of China often refer to the famed *Katsura Palace* in Kyoto when describing living and working in China, saying that all of China is like the palace. "You cannot get into the palace without special connections. In China you cannot get in to see the right officials without connections," explained one Japanese businessman.

In keeping with their Confucian filial piety background, in which the world revolves around family, relatives, and carefully tended contacts, Chinese businesspeople attach great importance to classmates and people from the same village or town, giving them precedence in hiring, networking, and doing business in general.

This approach stems from a family-oriented society in which individualism and independence, both of which are essential in dealing with outsiders, were totally suppressed for generations. With little or no experience in dealing on an equal basis with anyone, the Chinese traditionally kept their outside involvements as limited as possible.

Other Communication Problems

In addition to inherent linguistic problems and other cultural considerations, there are other obstacles to efficient communication in China. The country's telecommunication system has made great strides since the early 1980s and is improving steadily, but it remains far from comprehensive. Businesspeople are still in the earliest stages of learning how to take care of a lot of routine business by phone. Maintaining an appropriate level of contact and cooperation with the numerous government offices concerned with business continues to require extraordinary skills and experience and to be time-consuming.

It is also time-consuming, difficult, and often impossible to carry on business negotiations with Chinese by letter, not only because of cultural factors but also because of translation and typing considerations.

The first made-in-China systems for utilizing the complicated Chinese language ideograms on computers, announced in 1988, should eventually reduce some of the problems of communicating with the Chinese. The first system announced, developed by Yongmin Wang, a senior engineer at the Keli High Technology Group in Beijing, is based on a five-stroke code Wang had been working on for several years.

Wang's system, in which every character, no matter how many strokes it has, is divided into a logical five-stroke code, makes it as practical to input the ideograms as it is to input English-language words (which require up to a dozen or more strokes per word). Wang immediately began promoting his system in Hong Kong, Singapore, Japan, and the United States.

The second system for processing the simplified Chinese characters, developed by twenty-five-year-old Daozheng Zhang, is based on utilizing the 130 most common character radicals more or less as alphabetical letters. The system, called the Simplified and Complex Chinese Character Radicals

Handling System, is said to allow a skilled operator to type one hundred Chinese characters per minute, using a twenty-six unit keyboard.

The Language Block

Being able to speak Chinese gives the foreigner a wonderful advantage in China, but knowledge of Chinese psychology must go along with knowledge of the language. Chinese-speaking foreigners have to learn how to penetrate the psychological block many Chinese have regarding Chinese-speaking foreigners. Most are so conditioned to the idea that foreigners do not speak Chinese that when one does, they fail to understand. The ear and the brain are simply not connected. There are innumerable stories of such incidents (as there used to be in Japan).

One gimmick some people use to penetrate this mental barrier is to get up close, look the other party directly in the eyes, and say something extremely simple in Chinese, like "Hello," and wait for a flicker of understanding and preferably a response. If there is none, they repeat the word and add "How are you?" or "It's a fine day (or bad day), isn't it?" If this gets no response, they ask very directly, "Do you speak Mandarin?" (or whatever local language is involved). This usually does it. If so, they gradually build up from there.

The Chinese do not normally jump right into a subject. They begin with a "conversational starter" and then work up to it. The most common way they initiate a conversation is to say something that is totally obvious and often doesn't actually call for a verbal response. The idea is simply to open the lines of communication—a common-enough custom in the Western world (like saying "Nice day" when it is obvious for all to see).

Happily, the importance of being able to speak the language of a business partner is finally being recognized by a growing number of foreign businesspeople and foreign service personnel stationed in China. The Chinese Language Centre in Beijing has an annual enrollment of about six hundred foreigners who are studying Mandarin—and in many cases, calligraphy, painting, shadowboxing, and music as well. The center notes that many of its students become fluent in the language.

More and more foreigners, businesspeople as well as full-time students, are also attending the Chinese Language Training Centre of the Beijing University of International Business and Economics. The language training center was opened to foreign students in September 1988, offering courses at the beginning, intermediate, and advanced levels.

Gift-Giving

Most Asian cultures developed traditional societies that were based on hierarchies ruled over by feudal powers. Currying favor with higher-ups was often the only way to protect oneself, get wrongs redressed, or obtain basic rights. Gift-giving therefore developed into a high art. China was no exception, and although greatly diminished today (there is a law forbidding government officials from accepting gifts of any kind or value), the practice remains a vital aspect of creating and nurturing relationships with people.

Foreign businesspeople with substantial experience in China recommend that gifts be "business related," as opposed to items intended for personal use, particularly conspicuous luxury items that are much more likely to suggest impropriety and cause problems.

Looking more closely at gift-giving in China reveals a significant difference in the way Chinese and Westerners express appreciation for favors. Westerners are conditioned to express gratitude verbally with a simple "thank you," casual or emotional, depending on the relative importance of the situation. We automatically say "thank you" for even the most minor actions—when someone opens a door for us, hands us a glass of water, and so on—virtually always in good faith and genuine sincerity.

Chinese, on the other hand, are conditioned to express appreciation in tangible ways, such as gifts and other favors. They regard our frequent use of "thank you" as a glib and insincere way of passing off obligations to return favors. When they do someone a favor, they expect appreciation to be expressed in some very concrete way. If all you *can* do or choose to do is say "thanks," it should be very specific and sincere, and then stop. The Chinese do not like gushy thanks.

Generally, the Chinese are not reticent about letting relatives, friends, or newly made foreign contacts know what they would like to receive as gifts— whether the gifts are in return for favors already received or because they are given from a sense of duty or obligation. They are especially forward and frank with relatives who live overseas and come "home" for visits.

Etiquette of Giving and Receiving

It is the Chinese way to decline gifts, invitations, and other offerings two or three times, even when they want to accept, as a matter of etiquette— expecting, of course, that the other party will persist in the offering. This creates many problems because it is often difficult for foreigners to know how far to go in repeating offerings, and how far to go in declining offers made to them. The very fine line that separates proper etiquette from insensitivity or rudeness is easy to trip over.

In a private home setting, many Chinese guests refrain from accepting tea or any other refreshment until the offer is made at least twice and some-times three times, leaving their hosts puzzled at their behavior.

The Chinese naturally expect foreigners to understand and follow their etiquette to some degree, but they often go too far in presuming that when a foreigner says no he doesn't really mean it. This stretching of the rules of their own etiquette often appears to be a deliberate breach in order to get the foreigner to do what they want him or her to do—which often seems to derive from their belief that they know better than the foreigner what is good for him or her, or perhaps from other motives that are unclear and may never become clear as far as the visitor is concerned.

This "forcing" of visiting businesspeople, at its worst, may not be as insidious as it sometimes feels, but it can certainly be upsetting, particularly when it is pursued to an extreme even by Chinese standards.

Justice in the Eye of the Beholder

There is a good reason why the Chinese do not like taking disputes, whether personal or business, to lawyers or courts of law. During most of China's long past, responsibility was collective. The whole family and often the whole village or even district was responsible for the transgressions of each individual member and could be punished at the whim of the local Mandarin. The local scholar-official himself was held personally responsible for the behavior of everyone in his district. His incentives for maintaining absolute conformity and peace in his area were therefore very powerful indeed.

When unofficial mediation failed and a problem was taken to the court, presided over by the subprefect, the accused person was immediately thrown into jail. The accuser also came under strong suspicion and was subject to strenuous investigation. In addition to being expensive—fees and gifts were heaped upon the court in an effort to gain some favor—prisoners were routinely subjected to cruel and unusual treatment (for one thing, jails were not responsible for feeding prisoners), including the most horrible kinds of torture. Many prisoners confessed to crimes they did not commit just to gain relief from torture. The punishment for a long list of crimes, including ones that today are regarded as relatively minor, was death.

The traditional Chinese custom of applying the death penalty to a long list of crimes continues unabated. These crimes include murder, rape, arson, swindling, robbery, pimping, spying, embezzling, corruption, and organizing secret societies. Executions (generally shooting in the back of the head) presently run between three thousand and four thousand a year.

In addition to instilling a deep fear of officialdom among ordinary Chinese and making mediation and compromise the preferred way to settle all disputes, this system also resulted in the common people becoming extraordinarily passive even when subjected to inhuman abuses, and explains why they continued to accept the cruelest injustices for generation after generation, before finally rising up in revolt and throwing off their oppressors.

The cruelty and injustice of a government gone mad during the Cultural

Revolution is still fresh in the memories of all Chinese born after 1950. Still today their private lives are controlled by strict laws, but most of the real fear is gone and people in general are much more open about defending their rights. Foreign businesspeople in China today do not have to be concerned about their own safety or about the government being any more interested in their affairs than their own governments at home.

The Lowest of the Low

During China's Cultural Revolution from 1966 to 1976, lawyers were categorized as "the worst of the stinking ninth category of intellectuals." They did not begin to recover their prerevolutionary status until the passage of the post-Mao constitution in 1978. At that time, China had to virtually start from scratch in establishing a legal system—new legislation, law schools, part-time courses at night, TV courses, and correspondence courses.

An American, Jerome Alan Cohen, generally regarded as the Western world's leading authority on the Chinese legal system, was to play a key role in this rush to reestablish a modern legal system. Encouraged in 1960 to study Mandarin and the Chinese legal system by Dean Rusk, then head of the Rockefeller Foundation, Cohen was one of the scholars who recommended to president-elect Richard Nixon that he reopen talks with the People's Republic.

Thereafter, Cohen's involvement with China grew. During the 1970s, when he was a Harvard Law School professor and head of the university's Institute of East Asian Legal Studies, he made numerous trips to Beijing. Finally in 1981 the Chinese persuaded him to move to Hong Kong, where he became a partner in the three-hundred-attorney law firm of Paul, Weiss, Rifkind, Wharton, and Garrison, opened an office in Beijing, and began commuting between Hong Kong and Beijing.

Cohen said that during these early years, a primary concern of the Chinese was for laws to guarantee their human rights—rights that the outrageous Cultural Revolution had totally smashed, and that the challenge then was to build on the foundation of economic law already in place.

More than 390 Chinese law professors and scholars labored from 1980 to 1988 to produce 111 volumes of law textbooks, many of which have since been revised after use in classrooms. In 1988 the Minister of Justice approved the use of foreign textbooks about law, particularly those pertaining to international law, and the research and writing of law books continues.

Cohen noted that the traditional Chinese preference for conciliation over litigation and binding arbitration is still strong. If friendly discussions fail, they call in a third party to mediate. Arbitration is a final resort. He adds that the Chinese have a long way to go before their concept of commercial law and civil law reaches that of the West.

Despite the above, the use of attorneys in business negotiations and other international transactions is now fully acceptable. In fact, it seems as if the Chinese have gone overboard in the use of contracts, although the laws covering contracts are still evolving. Foreign businessmen are regularly advised by local consultants to bring attorneys with them for the final stages of negotiations.

The first private law offices in New China opened in 1988. The first one was in Shenzhen; the second one in Shanghai. The Shanghai firm immediately announced that its primary aim was to provide legal services for foreigners and their business interests. Prior to its official opening, the office already had a number of foreign clients, including businesspeople from Japan, then West Germany, Hong Kong, and Thailand. Staff members of the office say they worked twelve hours a day, six days a week during the first years.

China's lawyers are still very much under the thumb of the Ministry of Justice, and it will probably be several decades before they become legally independent. Foreign lawyers may practice in China but cannot appear in Chinese courts.

Notaries Instead of Lawyers

Many of the affairs handled by lawyers in the United States and other Western countries are handled by public notaries in China. Since the profession of notary was reestablished in 1979 under the Notarial Department of the Ministry of Justice, offices have been opened in virtually every county and town. Notaries handle such things as contracts, leases, auctions, wills, rights of inheritance, adoptions, and buying and selling houses. In some provinces up to 80 percent of all business negotiations and contracts involve assistance from notaries.

When to Beware

Official corruption in China became a way of life soon after the civil service examination system was instituted over a thousand years ago. It did not end with the establishment of the People's Republic of China in 1949. With power and privilege vested in the ruling cadre, the modern versions of the Mandarins of old, the conditions for bribery and payoffs have remained intact. Corruption in official places is a major concern.

On a personal level, conniving, cheating, and petty thievery are also rampant in China today, despite a generalized reputation for honesty and integrity that no doubt dates back to feudal days. At that time, a very strict morality was enforced by merciless sanction. Even then, however, thievery of all kinds was commonplace, and walls, iron bars, and locks abounded.

Personal failings in morality in today's China have been exacerbated by the perfidy and ruthlessness of all the governments since shortly after the founding of the first republic in 1912, and by the political control of life down to one's most intimate thoughts as practiced during the first decades of the Communist regime. As the result of these conditions, the Chinese do whatever it takes to survive and to justify any degree of cynicism or immorality in the name of the system. Students and others cheat to improve their grades or enhance their image or gain some other advantage, seemingly without any feelings of wrongdoing or guilt.

Maverick Chinese have also traditionally been master con artists. History is replete with stories of how poor but ingenious people worked cons on each other, on supposedly intelligent high-ranking officials, and especially on unsuspecting strangers. Overseas Chinese street vendors have traditionally been notorious for their cunning and often unscrupulous actions.

First-time visitors to today's China should certainly be wary of the many peddlers that have proliferated throughout the country since 1985, when price controls on some 1,800 items were lifted. Some of the scams these freewheeling vendors pull on customers would win the admiration of the sharpest street dealers in Hong Kong. Within three years there were also over sixty thousand perfectly legitimate free markets in the country.

Laws Made to Be Broken

Having been hedged in for so many centuries by so many rules and taboos, the Chinese have developed a perverse and seemingly contradictory attitude toward regulations and laws. They ignore them and break them any time it suits their purpose, as long as they believe they can get by with it. A great deal of the visible conformity that one sees in China, including the very conspicuous politeness, is mostly role-playing just to stay out of trouble. A significant proportion of public Chinese behavior is based on political expediency, not their true feelings.

Since their public, official behavior is more of a survival technique than anything else, they do not feel guilty about ignoring or subverting the system. It is something they do naturally as a way of getting by.

Another peculiarity of the Chinese as well as other people in the Confucian sphere of Asia is that they are more likely to accept and follow the desires or suggestions of a powerful, respected figure than to obey hard-and-fast laws. This is apparently a throwback to the hallowed age when virtuous emperors ruled by example and opinion rather than edicts and armed might.

Public Etiquette

The first-time visitor to China who uses public transportation or goes shopping in public stores must get used to being pushed and buffeted by the crowds, and to accept this as normal behavior without expecting apologies. (Who would *want* to apologize a hundred times during one shopping excursion?)

There is more to this cultural behavior than just contending with a huge, shifting mass of people, however. The Chinese have been conditioned for centuries to ignore "outsiders," meaning anyone not a member of their family, their work unit, or their circle of friends. This means to behave more or less as if others do not exist. The other half of this concept is that since you have no relationship with outsiders, you also have no obligations to them and are not expected to have any concern for them.

This rationale is not as outrageous as it might first appear and obviously derives from China's long feudalistic history. During this time, the huge masses of people had numerous responsibilities but virtually no rights, and minding only their own business became second nature.

Another Chinese characteristic that the visitor must contend with is the extraordinary amount of noise in the populated areas of China. The Chinese tend to be noisy people when they are in crowds, in part because the tonal nature of the various Chinese languages makes it necessary to emphasize the different tones. Also when other people are talking loudly, you have to speak up in order to be heard. The Cantonese, with nine tones in their language, are especially loud and may sound to unaccustomed ears as though they are having verbal combat.

Perhaps even more conspicuous in the cacophony of noise that characterizes life in urban China is the ubiquitous presence and use of loudspeakers. China still has not entirely lost the image of a giant training camp, where each day begins and ends with loudspeakers alternating between announcements and music.

First-time visitors to China who travel on the country's crowded trains (where public announcements and music are the order of the day) are often surprised to find out that the compartments are coed, and that they are sleeping with strange men or women.

All Those Eyes

Foreigners are still so rare in many parts of China that they are the objects of intense curiosity, attracting sometimes unblinking scrutiny that can be annoying after a while. Such staring also occurs in major cities, at transportation terminals, and on buses and trains, where one often encounters Chinese who have never had a chance to look at foreigners up close. Very small Chinese children also recognize foreigners as being different and strange, but they tend to overcome any feelings of fear or shyness very quickly.

On occasion, however, the sudden sight of a foreigner with blond hair and blue eyes is enough to cause a small child to burst into tears, obviously in extreme fright—which invariably results in a big scene. One wonders what kind of stories such children have been told to bring on this automatic reaction. Blue-eyed American Amy Konvolinka, in China as a student, said that Chinese fascination with her eyes was often so obtrusive that it interfered with her studies as well as her personal life.

Happening upon a stationary foreigner in a public place, some adult Chinese will park themselves within a few feet of the foreigner and stare for the longest time, usually with a totally blank face.

A less-bothersome custom that most visitors encounter, often with embarrassing result, however, is the Chinese penchant for singing. Social parties often end up with the participants singing as a group and individually. Westerners intending to spend any length of time in China should definitely learn three or four songs they can sing with reasonable accuracy and verve. (Trapped in this common situation, four out of five American businesspeople in China invariably end up trying to warble a few stanzas of "Working on the Railroad" or "You Are My Sunshine"—creating the impression these are the only two songs taught to Americans.)

Luck, Superstitions, and Taboos

Folklore, taboos, and *joss* (luck) are integral parts of Chinese life. The Chinese have traditionally believed that spiritual currents, affected by the movements of the sun and moon, influence their daily lives. This "cosmic breath" known as *Feng Shui,* or "Wind and Water," is also affected by the form and size of hills and mountains, the height and shape of buildings, and by the direction of roadways.

Foreign businesspeople who are familiar with Chinese beliefs are well aware of the role and importance of geomancy (divination by means of lines and figures) in the location and orientation of buildings and other structures. To most Chinese, there is an intimate, living relationship between the cosmos at large and the earth, with every spot and direction on the globe having a positive or negative "spirit" that influences anything built or situated on that location. The Chinese "see a golden thread of spiritual life running through every form of existence, and binding together, as in a living body, everything that subsists in heaven above and on the earth below,'' wrote Dr. Ernest Eitel of the London Mission, in a book on the *Rudiments of Natural Science in China,* published in the late 1800s.

The ancient science of divining where buildings (and graves) should be built has also come to be known as *Feng Shui,* apparently in reference to the importance of taking into consideration the flow of water and wind in the area of the proposed site.

Geomancy has been practiced in China since the Chou Dynasty (1030–256 B.C.). A manual codifying the rules of the art was published around A.D. 320. Today geomancy is used not only to divine the ideal place and orientation for buildings and such, but also as a means of identifying what spirits or gods should be placated when illness or disaster strikes.

The interpretation of *Feng Shui* factors requires expert knowledge and experience and every community has its master of the art. The primary tool of *Feng Shui* practitioners is a graduated astrolabe and compass (*Lo-pan*), which is used to note directions and astrological harmonies in conjunction with physical contours of the surroundings.

In addition to determining the orientation of buildings and doors, the *Feng Shui* master also counters the influence of negative cosmic breath by the use of talismans (dragons and other symbols) on buildings and other structures and charms (power words and other inscriptions) on paper scrolls or tablets. In crowded urban areas where the orientation of buildings is controlled by city codes and other factors, the primary goal of the *Feng Shui* master is to neutralize the negative forces in the area.

The first Western builders in China often ran afoul of *Feng Shui* beliefs, causing serious problems in the construction of highways, railways, and port facilities as well as office buildings.

The power and importance of these cosmic currents are not uniform to everyone. What may be regarded as harmful to one person may have no adverse effect on someone else. It is up to the *Feng Shui* master to divine these subtleties. And, of course, some Chinese, particularly those educated in the Western fashion, give no credence to such beliefs.

It is important for foreign businesspeople to be aware that their Chinese counterparts may call in a *Feng Shui* consultant on special occasions. When this happens, it should be regarded as a matter to be taken seriously.

The picturesque pagodas, a feature of the Chinese landscape for nearly two thousand years, were originally associated with Buddhist beliefs and practices, but over the generations they became associated with geomancy and were believed to bring good luck to the surrounding areas. The number of tiers in a pagoda is always uneven, and generally ranges from three to nine. The oldest pagoda in the country, on Sung Mountain in Henan, has fifteen tiers. It was built in A.D. 523.

Fortune-Telling

A great many of the ordinary, mundane acts of Chinese life are controlled by the astrological wheel of fortune, by the traditional perception of good days and bad days. What should or should not be done is prescribed in detail for each day on the Chinese calendar.

These injunctions include the best and worst days for burying the dead, getting married, signing contracts, visiting friends, exchanging gifts, traveling, and housecleaning.

The influence of these beliefs and customs varies with the individual Chinese businessperson. Some are more traditional in their beliefs and behavior than others. It can be important for the foreign businessperson to determine if any proposed action or plan might interfere with these beliefs.

Lucky Numbers

Foreign businesspeople seeking a new name for an enterprise involving the Chinese might be well advised to use the word "five" in the company name. The number five is of significant importance in Chinese civilization. There are the five elements of nature (metal, earth, fire, water, wood—which are identified with the five inner planets instead of the objects indicated). There are also five tastes (salty, pungent, bitter, sweet, sour), five colors, five atmospheric conditions, the five sacred mountains of Daoism, the classic family of five (three boys and two girls—to ensure male dominance over the female element), among other cases.

The number eight is also very important, significantly conspicuous in legends, myths, and various practices. There are the fictional "Eight Immortals," a class of superior, canonized god-fairies who represent the eight conditions of life—poverty, wealth, aristocracy, peasantry, age, youth, masculinity, and feminity; the Eight Diagrams, which form the basis for the famed "Book of Changes"; the Eight Buddhist Emblems; the Eight Treasures, and so on. The pronunciation of the number also suggests the word *prosperity*.

Hong Kong's licensing bureau raises a great deal of money for charity each year by auctioning off lucky license plate numbers.

High-climbing Day

Businesspeople planning on being in Hong Kong or elsewhere in China over the ninth day of the ninth month (approximately October 30), may wonder why so many Chinese go to the top of the Peak on Victoria Island and climb other mountains on the Kowloon side. The custom is known as "Mounting the Heights" and stems from a legend that climbing mountains on this day will help ward off disasters. In earlier centuries, the festival was primarily celebrated by members of the ruling scholar class and members of the imperial court who held chrysanthemum parties, composed poetry, and enjoyed the changing fall colors while sipping the wine of longevity.

Lucky Jade

Understanding the importance of jade in Chinese life can be of use to foreign businesspeople (if for no other reason than knowing it makes an especially prized gift to officials or business associates). Jade has been a highly prized possession in China since ancient times. Having jade on one's person is believed to ward off misfortune during life and to safeguard the body after death. Jade is primarily worn as a bracelet or earring, with some women wearing two jade bracelets—one for their own protection and the other to protect their husbands. So-called finger jade, fashioned to be constantly handled to impart good luck and longevity, is also common.

Despite popular belief, all jade is not green. Chinese jade may be clear, indigo, moss green, yellow, cinnabar red, opaque white, or lacquer black, as well as two or three other shades. Emerald green jade, often called jewel jade, is mined in Burma. Jade has a very hard surface, is not easily scratched, and "holds" droplets of water rather than letting them spread as glass does. The best grade of jade has a high luster and a "live" look, with few if any cracks. "Dead" jade, or jade without discernible luster, will sometimes come back to life as a result of contact with the human body. Pure green jade is especially prized by the Chinese, followed by lavender and red.

5

Working in a Beehive Society

*"There are four things that mark a man of superior mind.
He takes nothing for granted; he is never over-positive;
he is never inflexible, and he is never egotistical."*
—CONFUCIUS

The Chinese System

China's economic system, which continues to evolve, consists of a mixture of state-owned and -administered enterprises, a growing number of private and individual enterprises, along with a variety of other organizations that are hybrids. Many of the reforms now underway in China are designed to give government-owned enterprises more independence and responsibility in their own operation and more legal protection to private and individual enterprises. There is no indication that the government intends to change its socialist stripes—despite the fact that one survey after another proves that totally private enterprises are more productive and profitable than state-owned companies.

In Chinese terms, "a private enterprise" is a company that is operated with private funds and has eight or more employees and an "individual enterprise" is one that is privately financed and has no more than seven employees. The number of private businesses in China is approaching one million, and there are several million individual enterprises. Over 80 percent of the private companies are based in rural areas and are engaged in manufacturing and construction, while most of the individual enter-

99

prises are in cities and towns and are engaged in commerce and service trades.

Despite the growing importance of the role of private enterprises in China and the increasingly supportive policies of the Communist government, private entrepreneurs live in constant fear that government policies may change and that they will once again become the victims of official discrimination. To help offset this possibility, nearly half of all the private enterprises in China are registered as affiliates of local collectives or government enterprises, or as "nominal collectives."

The propensity for private enterprises to position themselves under the protective umbrella of a government-owned collective is known coloquially as obtaining a "red hat." In other words, a private enterprise in a "red hat" is less likely to attract the dangerous attention of ultraleftists in the government, and there are special tax breaks as well. But this protective cloak does not come free. Private entrepreneurs who affiliate themselves with collectives must share some of their profits with the government-run organizations.

There are strong critics of the red hat system. They say it cheats the central government of rightful income and confuses the legal relationship between the state and the various kinds of enterprises. Pressure is growing for the government to provide private businesspeople with the additional safeguards they need to realize their full potential, but even if the government continues moving in that direction it will no doubt be a number of years before the private sector could feel secure.

As part of its program to encourage the continuing development of private enterprises and particularly to help resolve problems between labor and management, the government advocates the establishment of company trade unions to act as mediators between workers and owners and to protect the rights of workers. As usual, however, the policy of allowing trade unions in private enterprises is on a trial basis, meaning that it can be canceled at any time.

Big Brother

In virtually every government-administered organization in China—education, commercial, scientific research, or whatever—there are two separate administrative bodies: one on the business side and the other on the political side. The top political representative in each organization is usually called the party secretary and wields as much or more power than the president or general manager of the organization. The political officer often has the final say in matters pertaining to the operation of the company or organization.

In all negotiations with foreign companies, the government is represented by these political officials who may or may not attend the actual negotiations. In cases where they do attend, they often do not present their namecards and are not introduced. In any event, virtually all contracts signed by Chinese firms or government bodies must be approved by political representatives also.

The strength and influence of party representatives assigned to companies varies greatly, as does their commitment to the party. While responsibility for promotions and other management decisions in joint-venture companies is ostensibly shared by the foreign and Chinese side, very few foreign managers can or will try to go against the wishes of their Chinese counterparts. They are very much aware that, if they insist on promoting someone against the wishes of the Chinese side, there will be trouble in the future and they will most likely end up being the loser. The only satisfaction foreign managers can get out of this situation is if the individual promoted by the Chinese side messes up. The foreign partner can then blame the Chinese and hold it over them for some future leverage.

One of the factors that makes Chinese-style personnel management especially hard for foreign managers to take is that the Chinese side—especially the political side—generally does not forget or forgive any real or imagined past transgressions by employees under their jurisdiction. Every accusation ever made against an individual and any mistake he or she may have made in the past is duly recorded in the personnel file and can be—and often is—used against the person. Since only party officials have access to these personal files, the foreign manager does not know what he is up against.

One of the primary factors in personnel management in China is that foreign managers look mostly at performance, while Chinese managers look at attitude and manner, whether or not the employee causes any waves, and at seniority. There is also often a strong political element in the attitudes and actions of Chinese personnel managers. Those who are more party-oriented base their decisions on party policies rather than the good of the company.

Linking government control with industry invariably results in abuse by profit-minded officials who utilize their political power to benefit themselves through official relationships with the companies they oversee. By the late 1980s this type of profiteering was rampant in China, leading the government to issue orders prohibiting state agencies from getting involved in the management of companies under their jurisdiction. The official circular stated that all government institutions and public officials were strictly forbidden to engage in any kind of business, and that there should be no mixing of roles and meddling in each other's affairs. The order also banned the establishment of new corporations except as private undertakings and joint ventures.

Most Chinese still are obsessed with the idea that no one, regardless of intelligence or talent, should stand out from the crowd or receive any kind of recognition for special efforts. They will generally band together to pull down anyone who demonstrates individual ambition or talent. The person who learns some English (either in China or abroad), learns how to operate a computer, gains some other valuable skill, or begins to think and behave in a "non-Chinese" way invariably faces opposition. It is still common for people who have studied abroad, including those who have knowledge of highly technical subjects, to be assigned as cooks or clerks upon their return to China. Extreme jealousy toward such people is commonplace.

There are also many who believe that work seniority takes precedence over all other considerations in management. One typical example of this attitude: the foreign director of a joint-venture firm decided to promote a forty-year-old engineer to the next highest grade. The director instructed a twenty-seven-year-old typist, who had been with the company longer than the engineer, to type up the announcement of the promotion. The secretary not only refused to type the announcement but disputed the director's right to promote the engineer, saying she should be promoted instead of him. The majority of the Chinese employees in the company backed the secretary, and the director had to rescind the promotion.

Staff Training

During the early decades of the Communist regime, young Chinese were not taught personal responsibility. Instead they were conditioned to believe it was the government's role to take care of them. They were also raised in an environment in which personal enterprise was against the law and brought sure, swift punishment, leaving them with little or no self-motivation. The first challenge facing the foreign employer is to break down the mental block that prevents employees from thinking and acting like individuals. The second challenge is to convince them that not only they but China as well will benefit if they show personal initiative and go beyond the usual "do as little as possible" attitude.

This mind-set is not as easy or as simple to break as the expatriate businessperson might think. For one, pressure on the individual to remain submerged in the crowd, to not be more aggressive or more ambitious than the next person, is very intense. As long as the individual concerned is subject to the authority of the Chinese side, both social and economic sanctions are very likely to be severe.

Training programs appear to be most effective when they cover groups that work together and individuals can be brought along at more or less the same speed. In any event, the retraining must be constant and consistent, with both the rationale and procedures repeated over and over. One of the most difficult points for a new employee to grasp is the idea of doing things promptly. The typical reaction when asked to do something is to readily agree to do it, then lay it aside indefinitely and often forget about it. This is not done to be obstructive or uncooperative but because no importance is attached to the action or the need to do it immediately. "Fortunately this reaction usually involves relatively minor things. The really big, vital things are more likely to get prompt attention," noted an expatriate manager.

Overcoming this mental block does not always mean success in retraining a new Chinese employee. One of the most sensitive areas in the foreign employer—Chinese employee relationship is pay scales. It is very difficult for many Chinese to accept the idea that a foreigner is worth from twenty to fifty times more than they are when it comes to monthly salary—even when they know the foreigner is highly skilled and contributes far more to the enterprise than they do. They are not used to thinking in those terms, and put it on a human-to-human level.

While Chinese employees generally do not confront foreign managers directly with what they perceive as an unforgivable injustice, they complain bitterly behind their backs. A few who have become more outspoken will say, "How can you expect me to work any harder or do as much as you do when you are getting paid twenty times more than I am?"

Because of this factor and others, new young Chinese employees seldom have any concept of being members of a team, particularly a team that includes foreign staff. Without long, hard training, they simply cannot see themselves as members of a special group, working hard together in a spirited fashion for the benefit of the company and themselves. Some foreign managers approach this problem head-on, repeatedly telling their employees: "You are not working for the Chinese government! You are working for 'X' Company! This company supports you and your family! Your responsibility and loyalty is to *this* company!"

Foreign managers report that it takes about six months of daily, consistent reindoctrination and on-the-job training to develop an acceptable attitude and a modicum of efficiency in the typical employee. This generally does not mean that employees can be left unsupervised, however. Probably the point most often emphasized by foreign managers is the importance of following up on every order given, on every detail of work that is supposed to be done. Some managers report that even after four years of working with the same group, the need for supervision and follow-up continues unabated.

For one thing, say these managers, their Chinese employees do not automatically think beyond the immediate question or situation. "When an office staff member or clerk in a hotel or shop is asked a question and does not know the answer, the typical response is 'I don't know,' and they go no further. It does not occur to them to ask someone else or refer the questioner to someone else," explained one manager. "It is like talking to a blank wall. You have to persist to get anything done."

The most successful foreign managers also emphasize the importance of being completely honest and forthright with Chinese employees, to let them know clearly what is expected of them and why. The last thing one should do is treat employees as if they were dumb, said one foreign manager. "Even the rawest recruits we get in here are *not* dumb. Far from it. They just have to be taught a new system of thinking and doing," the manager added.

Of course, language is often at the root of employee problems. The standard of English among Chinese employees of foreign companies is still relatively low, and despite the fact that more and more expatriate managers are able to speak Mandarin, the linguistic gap remains wide.

Said a manager in a joint-venture hotel: "When employees are left on their own they develop their own way of working, which is most often slow and seemingly without serious purpose. If an outsider comes in and tries to change the system, they will strongly resist. About the only effective approach is to identify one or more people in the group who are more open-minded, who will listen and learn and become your ally. Working through these allies, you introduce new concepts and methods very gradually, bits and pieces at a time. There will come a time when the productivity of the group has obviously increased dramatically, which is generally followed by a gradual acceptance of the new system.

"In the process of converting employees over to a new system it is important to recognize effort and success with special perks, such as giving them a little extra time for lunch or occasionally letting them go home early. Having training sessions away from the workplace is also appreciated. It is important to keep everyone in an upbeat mood, which requires a great deal of personal effort. Training sessions can be made lighthearted instead of stiff and formal."

Western companies should be wary of relying entirely on Hong Kong Chinese for their managerial staff in China. Hong Kong Chinese tend to take the authoritarian approach, something that mainland Chinese strongly resent because that is the system they are trying to eradicate from their society. A very personal approach that includes a lot of compassion will often get the manager much further. Singapore Chinese are decidedly more likely to use this approach. Austrian, German, and Swiss managers, often seen as being excessively dogmatic and having little interest in the personal lives of their employees, also come in for their share of criticism.

As is often the case, however, generalizations about Chinese workers are often wrong or unfair. While millions of Chinese do seem to sit or stand around, doing very little, millions also commute, often by bicycle, for up to four hours to and from work in all kinds of weather. The important thing is to treat each person as an individual and take their total environment into consideration.

The most successful managers say the most effective management approach is to treat employees like family—be concerned about them, take care of them, and make sure they understand and appreciate what they are supposed to do to deserve such a relationship. The least successful manager is the one who takes a harsh, critical approach and complains a lot.

Despite policies announced in 1988 making it legal for companies to get rid of undesirable employees, the procedures for firing workers are precise and cumbersome. Any company that wants to terminate an employee has to be serious about it. Employers must document the undesirable behavior of the employees for several months, warn them to mend their ways, and then consult with the labor union before initiating any action. There are several legal entities involved in the firing process, including the Labor Bureau, the local labor union, and the government administrative agency responsible for the enterprise concerned. Each of these is subject to national, provincial, and municipal laws. Each of these entities investigates the complaint against the employee, votes on whether or not to sanction action, tries to mediate between the worker and the employer, and then if they all agree that the worker should be dismissed, action is approved.

"It is all quite new to us, and both complicated and difficult," said one Chinese official, "but the situation should improve along with the economy."

One of the more upsetting characteristics that has traditionally been associated with the Chinese and is especially pertinent in today's China is their propensity to go into business for themselves whenever the slightest opportunity presents itself. A typical example of this is regularly demonstrated when companies establish central purchasing offices. It is almost axiomatic that people in the buying office will make side deals with the suppliers, getting a piece of the action. In the worst scenarios—which have happened to a number of Western companies recently—the managers of the buying offices did not maintain any office records of what was being bought or from whom, kept the names of the suppliers secret, and of course made out like bandits.

The foreigner involved in any kind of enterprise in China faces a set of new circumstances. Ilse Massenbauer, principal of Beijing's Lido Kindergarten, talked about her experiences: "There are so many highs and lows in working in China. It is exciting one moment and depressing the next. At this stage in China's evolution the foreigner has to make many sacrifices to live and work here. I was here for eight months before I was able to have a real discussion with my staff. They simply would not talk. They could not understand that I wanted to be their friend.

"Nobody sees anything they are not told to see or does anything they are not told to do. They have very little sense of time. If you change anything you have to start over again, explaining why over and over again. You have to watch everything. It is very much like dealing with children."

Massenbauer said that none of her staff would take the lead in asking questions or bringing up matters that needed to be discussed. "They almost never take an idea or problem to top management. They talk a lot among themselves but seem unable to come to a conclusion about anything, except when they oppose something.

"It took workmen four months to build a playground that could have been done in two or three weeks. They spent most of their time sitting around, talking and smoking. When I complained, they smiled. They could not understand why I was so frustrated. You need to be very honest and frank—not hold back. You also need a break every three or four months, or you burn out."

She added: "Those who fraternize with foreigners are severely criticized. There is a tremendous amount of jealousy toward both foreigners and the Chinese who associate with them."

The IBM Kingdom

The experience that IBM has had in China is especially interesting from the entrepreneurial viewpoint. Despite its size and clout, the "Kingdom of IBM" has often met its match in China. In its commitment to succeed in the Chinese market despite obstacles that have to be overcome, the computer giant has had to bend its imperial rules. On a number of occasions, its Chinese customers have signed contracts only to come back after the merchandise has already been shipped and say they don't have the money to pay for the order. They ask that part of the shipment be given to them free or that the price be reduced down to the amount of money they have—a common ploy. Rather than lose the business, IBM has both given additional discounts and withdrawn some of the less vital items from such orders.

On other occasions, IBM has battled its customers to keep them from ordering equipment they could not possibly use—and lost. In other instances, the company has been castigated by its customers for not shipping the latest technology—models that did not even exist when contracts were signed—despite the fact that they could not integrate the new technology into the systems already in place. Said an IBM staffer: "They do not trust us to advise them on what is best for their needs. Still, when something doesn't work, they blame us."

Another situation that has to be very embarrassing to giant IBM: the Chinese government exercises authority over how many personal computers the company is able to bring into Beijing for use by its head office staff, strictly limiting the number of machines well below what is normal for the company.

IBM has not lost all of its battles, however. Where its Chinese staff is concerned, it has the last word in hiring and firing as well as promoting. "The government doesn't like it but they accept it," said a spokesperson. At the same time, the company is so attractive as an employer that it reportedly gets the best and brightest of China's young technicians.

Foreigners Are Fair Game

The Chinese are not reticent about criticizing the weak points of foreigners, particularly Americans, who want to do business with them. Not surprisingly, one of the most common complaints is that Americans are too impatient—they want things to happen too fast. Probably the second most common criticism is that Americans, especially head office executives, attempt to use purely American-style strategies in their approach to the Chinese market.

Perhaps even more unsettling to the Chinese, however, is the American custom of acting as individuals instead of as members of a group, and for American companies to generally limit their activities and affiliations to one single industry. Unlike most Japanese companies, for example, American companies usually do not belong to closely affiliated groups that include banks and trading companies (as well as special agencies of the government), and therefore cannot offer the Chinese the same kind of package deals they get from other countries.

Another area where Chinese interests and foreign joint ventures often part company is in the payment packages offered to Chinese employees. Foreign companies often attempt to pay their Chinese managers significantly more than what they pay lower-ranking employees. In the Chinese context of things, this would result in friction and instability among the Chinese employees, and also act as a threat to the overall personnel policies of the Chinese government and Chinese companies.

During the first years of the Open Door policy, joint-venture companies in China were all required to hire their employees through government agencies. In these instances, wages were paid to the agencies, which then divided them among the employees the way they saw fit—keeping most of the money intended for wages. This was a key part of the government's policy to make sure no one got paid more than anyone else.

Since it is virtually impossible to have a classless society even in the broadest sense, China eventually had to relax its efforts to maintain equal pay standards for Chinese workers. The income-leveling policy (the "Big Pot" concept), instituted by the government of New China shortly after the revolution, simply was not compatible with the country's swing toward free enterprise and competition.

There is now a variety of pay scales for different jobs, and bonuses are common. This change has caused criticism by people, particularly those in universities, research institutes, and even government ministries, who do not have the same opportunities to earn as much as those who are the best paid. The result of this situation is that many academics as well as top-level bureaucrats are opting to join industry, adding to labor mobility and variations in wages.

Animal Farm Revisited

Officially there are no social class distinctions in China, but rank, among businesspeople as well as government bureaucrats, is very important. In business it is vital to know the rank of each individual you must deal with and to know how to respond to them consistent with their rank.

In the government bureaucracy, the *ganbu* or cadre (officials) are divided into twenty-four grades, each with its corresponding salary, privileges, and power. Unlike in the United States, where higher numbers denote higher rank, in China grade 24 is the lowest rank. The top leaders in the country are grade 1. The salaries of grade-one officials are said to be "about ten times" that of cadre in grade 24. Just as in the West, however, rank determines the amenities and perks of Chinese officials, notwithstanding their relatively low salaries. Old China hands say one of the most conspicuous signs of rank is the type of chair the individual has. Cadre in grades 18 and above get plain wooden chairs; those in grade 17 are eligible for cushions with their wooden chairs; those in grades 16 to 13 generally have upholstered chairs. Officials from grade 12 to 1 get leather swivel chairs. The automobiles of ranking officials are distinguishable by the red flag decal on the lower right side of the windshield.

On the business side, technicians and engineers are divided into eighteen grades; factory workers into eight. University professors are divided into twelve grades. There are sixteen grades for entertainers; even artists and writers are ranked and get paid accordingly. Chefs are ranked from four to one.

As residents of China say repeatedly, it is connections and rank that count. Connections and rank gain one access to the *te-quan* or "special privileges," meaning stores and shops that are operated for the exclusive use of ranking officials, providing them with food and other merchandise that is not available in public stores.

The perks and privileges of ranking Chinese officials (from grade 8 to grade 1) include such things as allowances for maids and servants. Military officers from company commander on up have orderlies assigned to them.

Name Cards and Seals

The personalized "name card" has a long history in China. Until around A.D. 1500, "visiting cards," as they were called, were fairly large and printed on white paper. Lui Chin, a famous eunich-regent of this period, introduced cards printed on slips of vermilion paper that were eight inches high and three inches wide. From then on, the cards for ordinary use became more colorful, while white was used by people who were in mourning.

The negative connotation of white calling cards has long since disappeared, of course, and not too many businesspeople today go around passing out larger-than-life cards in pink or red.

It is important to have your name cards in Chinese as well as in English. Some foreigners, particularly those who speak Chinese, select Chinese names for themselves, usually ones that sound like their English names. It is generally recommended, however, that foreigners should stick with Chinese transliterations of their names to avoid possible confusion. Beijing's Commercial Press (*Shangwu Yinshuguan*) publishes a huge directory of foreign names with their Chinese transliterations. Or you can ask a Chinese contact to do the conversion for you.

If you have your name cards printed in Taiwan, Hong Kong, or elsewhere, make sure the Chinese language characters used are the modern, simplified version now in use in China—not the old-fashioned characters still common outside of China.

Name seals are frequently used in China in lieu of signatures. Earlier name seals, were made of stone and were called *feng yin* or "stone seals," but they are heavy and time-consuming to carve. Present-day seals are generally made of rubber. Many official documents have to be stamped with name or company seals, which, in the case of foreigners, may be in English.

Despite the progress China has made in reducing bureaucratic barriers to business, the system remains a formidable obstacle, with the use of name seals as one of its most conspicuous elements. In a recent case in Shanghai, an application for a joint venture required the seals of 126 individuals representing four committees and nineteen bureaus. At the end of fifteen months it was still hung up somewhere in the maze of government offices. This, however, prompted the municipal government of Shanghai to transfer approval power to lower levels, eliminating a significant number of seals needed on any application—and making it possible to get approval of some projects in just one day.

Learning to Play the Game

One of the most vital and interesting aspects of doing business in China is learning to deal with the cadre or government officials, especially on the local level. In matters pertaining to joint ventures, the goodwill and support of local officials can mean the difference between success and failure. In addition to making courtesy calls on local officials on the occasion of the first visit to China, it is advisable and often essential that foreign businesspeople invite ranking cadre to their offices and/or plants on a regular basis. Some experienced expatriate managers say the more local officials are invited in for goodwill visits, the smoother things run.

There are, in fact, many situations where a matter that would ordinarily be handled on the private side outside of China must be brought to the attention of the appropriate cadre in order to get anything done. Some of the more experienced foreign managers in China have learned how to use their connections with officials as "bargaining chips" in their dealings with their own employees, suppliers, and others. One such manager said that at the first sign of trouble, he goes directly to the top official in the district. The reason for this, he said, was that lower-ranking cadre have no decision-making powers and tend to be inflexible in their attitudes and actions.

Especially knotty problems can result when a businessperson needs coordinated decisions or actions from several government bureaus or agencies. Communications between departments in the same agency can range from poor to virtually nonexistent, making cooperative effort a serious obstacle. There is also a great deal of jealousy and political skirmishing that goes on between departments and bureaus. Here again, the best approach is to identify the top cadre and get him or her on your side.

In playing the political game in China, it is essential that the foreign businessperson spend a substantial amount of time becoming acquainted with officials, finding out about their likes and dislikes, what their ambitions are, and any special talents they may have. Knowing this kind of inside information can often mean the difference between a deal and no deal. Having friendly contacts inside the various government offices can also be invaluable when it comes to finding out what is going on and where opportunities lie.

The number of instances in which local officials came to the rescue of foreign companies leaves no doubt as to where the power comes from. Of course, Chinese officials are past masters at getting benefit from the goodwill and favors they bestow, so the foreign businessperson must be willing and able to reciprocate.

Negotiating Chinese Style

As with most Asians, where ritual and personal relationships are a vital part of the smooth functioning of society, Chinese businesspeople do not rush into discussions or negotiations as Westerners are wont to do. The Chinese want to get acquainted before they do business. They also want to extend hospitality to demonstrate their respect for others and their own appreciation of the finer things in life (eating and drinking) and, as some add, to soften their visitors up.

There is usually a lot of small talk during the first full day, when the Chinese will try to learn as much as possible about the visitor and his goals. That evening during the welcoming banquet, they learn more, for it is in such casual situations that the foreign visitors are most likely to reveal themselves.

The Chinese have a highly structured style of negotiating that goes well beyond the usual Western practices. For example, the Chinese often make use of a shame technique to gain an advantage—making their adversaries feel ashamed about something and give way. They will also typically try to make the opposite side feel responsible for any problems or errors that might occur. Knowing that Westerners tend to be very impatient, they use this to their advantage, using go-slow tactics to encourage the opposite side to give away more than planned.

Experienced foreign businesspeople typically say the Chinese resort to a variety of tactics to get what they want, including using the visitors' lack of knowledge about the Chinese market, threats of taking their business elsewhere (to the Japanese, for example), and so on.

The Chinese are past masters of the "bad cop—good cop" technique of negotiating and interrogating, and they use this strategy in almost every situation imaginable, in personal as well as business situations. They are also adept at keeping people on the psychological sharp edge, as a control technique to keep them from doing anything that might have a negative impact on the Chinese system (whatever the system is at that time). By sustaining this kind of psychological pressure, adversaries or potential offenders, especially if they are inexperienced with this approach, generally develop a paranoid personality.

At the same time—and unlike the Japanese—the Chinese can be very direct and blunt in their dealings with foreigners. While claiming to operate on the principle of equality and mutual benefit, they will often point out that what may be fair to the foreigner has nothing to do with the circumstances in China. But as in Japan, the Chinese do not look at a contract as the end of negotiations and the beginning of wholehearted cooperation. To them it is just the beginning of a relationship that naturally changes from one day to the next and has to be reevaluated and renegotiated on an ongoing basis.

Until very recently, one of the main challenges facing foreign businesspeople negotiating or doing business in China was getting reliable information about China—whether it was business information or political information. For years, the Communist regime exhorted all Chinese to avoid providing foreigners with any information about the country, regardless of how trivial, making it confusing and difficult for foreigners in the country to function well in any capacity. This problem has been significantly alleviated on the highest official level, but it has not been fully accepted on lower levels and is still a handicap that often mystifies and stifles.

There are generally two distinct phases of negotiating business deals in China—the technical phase, which comes first, and the commercial phase, and generally there are two negotiating teams. The technical phase is usually the most drawn-out and detailed. If the foreign side is also represented by two teams, it can be several days before the commercial team sees any action.

If the foreign group is also divided into two teams, the commercial team is advised to attend the technical negotiating sessions as well (regardless of how long they take or how boring they might be) in order not to miss out on any aspect of the exchanges and to learn more about the process of interacting with the Chinese.

Ian Stones, a bilingual, bicultural businessman with years of experience in China, notes that Chinese negotiators often use teacups in their negotiating. They use the crockery to represent the foreign side and themselves, moving it around to graphically illustrate the points they are making. Stones laughed and said he often mused that Chinese negotiators might be tongue-tied if they didn't have their teacups.

Stones added that the days when senior negotiators readily showed their anger if things weren't going well are apparently over. "They make a serious effort to mask their feelings," he said, "but if you watch closely you often see them squeezing hell out of their chair arms."

The Right Stuff

An ideal approach for a newcomer wanting to do business in China on a large scale is to arrive with introductions from one or more people who are known and respected by as many Chinese as possible. These valued introducers may include famous political figures (like ex-presidents!), business leaders, successful overseas Chinese, government officials, and trade consultants who have been to China and are appreciated for their efforts to help the country.

Official Trade Missions

The government agency or organization that acts as the host in inviting foreign trade or company missions to China is called the *jiedai danwei* or "host unit." The host unit assumes full responsibility for getting official approval for the visit, providing documentation for visas, arranging accommodations, and establishing the schedule and the activities.

It is customary for the Chinese side to match the executive level of the foreign mission with officials from the appropriate agencies or ministries. The higher officials selected on these occasions may not participate in any of the actual negotiations. However, they will play a vital role in welcoming the visitors in ceremonial occasions and in making the final decisions concerning any business arrangements.

In setting up missions to come to China, the Chinese want to know precisely who is going to be on the mission, with a significant amount of professional as well as personal information about each individual. In addition to needing some of this information for visa and accommodation purposes, they also want to know in advance what each individual can be expected to contribute to the presentation the foreign mission will make.

The Chinese expect every business mission to China to have a leader who represents the group not only on the ceremonial side but also in any negotiations that take place. They expect other members to participate in the presentations, but not to disagree with what the leader has to say.

Generally the first meeting is just to establish the initial relationship and to feel the foreigner out. This getting-acquainted process often takes two or three trips and can take more. It is not uncommon for exchanges and negotiations to continue over a period of months or years and involve a dozen or more meetings. The foreign company wanting to do business in China must therefore make a long-term commitment to the market from the beginning.

Keqi hua or "polite talk," the casual conversation that is mandatory before any serious business is done at a meeting with Chinese, can be lengthy. In some cases, the polite talk continues throughout the meeting and seemingly nothing is accomplished. This is both a get-acquainted process and a kind of test foreign visitors are put through to see how they react.

The business meeting in China has been compared to an audience that one might have with the pope. The visitor can talk himself blue in the face and pass out all kinds of literature, while the pope listens with a smile, asks questions, and never makes any commitments.

One of the worst things the foreign businessperson can do is to try to force the Chinese to respond immediately and directly to a presentation. First of all, they consider it a serious breach of etiquette, and second they invariably do not have the authority to make any statements, or prefer to refer it to their group for a consensus decision in order to avoid any semblance of personal responsibility.

Foreign businesspeople experienced in China say that Chinese representatives they meet often behave more like messengers whose purpose is to soak up as much information as possible and then report back to their workplace.

Another grave mistake is to display any sign of anger—although the Chinese, particularly cadre, often do—because it gives the Chinese side leverage or an out. On the other hand, the Chinese themselves often put on a show of serious but controlled anger as a ploy to intimidate negotiating adversaries. The challenge, of course, is to be able to distinguish between genuine anger and role-playing.

One of the negotiating tactics of the Chinese is to get the foreign businessperson caught up in a web of friendship obligations, which they then use to their advantage. If the visitor has been to China before, or has had some other kind of connection with China, it is usually enough to earn one the status of "old friend."

Despite the natural friendliness of most Chinese, it is important for businesspeople going to China for the first time to keep in mind that it is the official policy of the Chinese government that its officials as well as private businesspeople treat foreigners with special courtesy and hospitality, so that all of the goodwill and enthusiasm demonstrated toward them is not necessarily spontaneous or personal.

The Chinese show great respect for rank and status, especially when the person of rank is someone they want something from, but their private feelings are another matter. When a possible business activity goes sour and the Chinese switch their goodwill and enthusiasm to someone else without batting an eye, the foreigner often feels that his good and great friends let him down—that they were two-faced.

Foreign businesspeople dealing with China should keep in mind that genuine friendship, if it develops, comes only after a relatively long period of proving that intentions on both sides are sincere and a solid relationship has been established. The Chinese do not start new businesses with foreigners for the sake of friendship—as is so often publicly claimed. They do business with outsiders because that is the fastest and most practical way they can develop their economy.

The Golden Goose

The foreign company wanting to take new technology into China has its work cut out for it. In the act of "introducing" the technology to the potential Chinese importer, the foreign company is expected to reveal all of its secrets. The Chinese word for such technical presentations, *jishu jiaoliu*, means "technical transfer." While they expect all of the technology to be transferred to them, they usually have nothing to give in return except their very avid attention. Further, it is common for them to schedule very long sessions during which the foreign experts are expected to perform tirelessly.

Chinese members assigned to take part in foreign technology presentations are carefully trained and selected to get as much information about the technology as possible during the presentation. If the Chinese side decides to make a deal, they will then bring in negotiators who are especially good at beating the other side down on cost and other factors. All of this may seem decidedly unfair to Americans especially, since our supreme philosophy is unequivocal fairness. It is also common for the Chinese side to systematically bring in new members of their team who just as systematically ask all or most of the same questions their predecessors asked. It is an approach the Chinese use not only to make sure everyone who might be involved is fully briefed on the technology/project, but also as a way of "training" staff in such proceedings. Being invited to participate in these presentations is also "handed out" as a favor to certain people.

The Chinese attitude is that foreign companies have a lot while they have nothing or only a little. The more they can get from the foreign company, the fairer it is for them and for China. They see each encounter with a foreign group of technology experts as a valuable learning process, regardless of whether or not the meeting results in a business deal. This is pragmatism, Chinese style. Not surprisingly, foreigners are expected to understand, appreciate, and cooperate with this approach.

Foreign businesspeople who have participated in presentations in China say that attempts to obtain technical knowledge without paying for it are often carried to extremes, and that foreigners have to be prepared to draw a line as to how much they are willing to give away. In any event, the foreign side should prepare meticulously for such show-and-tell programs and should also make sure that the Chinese fully identify all of those from their side who have been invited to attend the sessions.

Who Comes First?

Chinese business etiquette is often the reverse of what it is in the West. While the ranking foreign business executive is often preceded through doorways (into offices, factories, and restaurants, etc.) by underlings, in China it is typically the top executive who enters first (followed closely by an interpreter, if one is going to be used). They therefore often have problems in identifying the head person in groups of foreigners who enter meeting rooms at random.

Since hierarchical relationships are very important to the Chinese, seating arrangements are rigidly adhered to. The leaders of each group sit at the center of the negotiation table, facing each other, with their assistants on each side in descending order or rank and importance to the sessions.

At official banquets, the chief guest is seated at the left of the host. The traditional explanation of why the Chinese favor the left side when seating guests is very practical, and is indicative of the great age of Chinese civilization and its concern with human affairs on all levels. Since most people are right-handed and therefore wield their weapons with their right hands, seating a guest on the left side, away from the sword-hand, was seen as a very conspicuous way of expressing trust and goodwill toward the guest— since the guest would have the advantage in a fast-draw sword fight. Ancient Chinese also preferred to pass possible enemies on the side of their sword-hand when walking or riding horseback. When wheeled traffic developed, the driver was placed on the right side of the coach or wagon so his whip would not interfere with passengers seated behind him. (In China people drive on the right side.)

At formal official functions the Chinese customarily greet arriving guests with a round of applause. The proper response is to applaud back.

Negotiating Guidelines

Foreign businesspeople should approach all negotiations with the Chinese from the basis that nothing can be taken for granted, which is not to say that every Chinese they might approach is going to be untrustworthy or unscrupulous and therefore dangerous. The point is that what the foreign businessperson expects as natural or "to be expected" may not be the case at all. Having said this, another crucial point to keep in mind is that the Chinese *want* to do business. They just have a different approach.

To begin with, the hospitality and entertainment that invariably precedes and accompanies doing business in China is seen as an important part of the process of business—which is the reason the Chinese spend so much time and money at it. The purpose of this social aspect of business is to get acquainted with and "soften up" the other side—both perfectly legitimate, often fun, and equally useful to the foreign side if it takes advantage of the opportunity.

Probably the first roadblock that must be passed is that the Chinese side will attempt to get more for less than the foreign side thinks is called for or fair. The Chinese look at one aspect of this approach as natural and to be expected. It is just good business. The other aspect is that they believe the foreign side should pay more and ask for less because China is a poor, undeveloped nation trying to catch up. This is especially true of government officials in charge of the various ministries and agencies responsible for administering industry.

A second roadblock is that the Chinese are not used to and do not like to sign long complicated contracts that attempt to tie absolutely everything down. They will frequently refuse even to read a lengthy contract, insisting that it be simplified and shortened. Contracts written in English legalese may not be understood by the Chinese, since they have little or no experience with such language.

To the Chinese, a contract is a commercial agreement, not a legal document, and should not be the last word on anything. You might say that they sign contracts only as formal confirmation that they intend to do business with you, not *how* they are going to conduct the business. For one thing, the government frequently announces new laws impacting on international trade, so both businesspeople and cadre try to keep arrangements as open and flexible as possible.

The Chinese continuously emphasize that all agreements should be based on friendship and goodwill, making finely detailed contracts unnecessary. However, in any disagreement, they take a legalistic view of contracts and do not feel bound by anything that is not explicitly stated in a contract. The only choice is, again, that contracts should cover every contingency possible. This is especially important since new people who had nothing to do with negotiating the contract or any verbal side agreements will invariably become part of the picture at some future point.

Another factor is that the Chinese, particularly the cadre, are determined that all business relationships must be established on their terms and that they must be structured to conform to both the laws of the country as well as cultural practices, even when these practices lack any real justification. Generally speaking, these demands are nonnegotiable, although exceptions can sometimes be arranged through the "back door." Another official characteristic that often baffles and frustrates foreign negotiators is refusal to provide information to support their position or claims—frequently saying that it is none of the foreign company's business.

At the same time, foreign engineers and technicians generally find negotiating with their professional counterparts in China far easier than dealing with officials, since they speak the same technical language and are able to establish a common bond that transcends politics.

The position of the Chinese negotiators has been arrived at in advance, by consensus, and is not subject to revision during the course of negotiations. If pressured, about all they can do is repeat themselves. If the negotiations reach a stalemate, and they are not willing to give up, they have to go back and reach a new consensus, which can be time-consuming.

The first rule mentioned in any discussion about negotiating with the Chinese is invariably patience. Next usually comes accepting long periods of time during which nothing appears to be happening (which is another phase of patience). Then there is the admonishment to ignore much of what the Chinese say about their expectations (which is often equally applicable to foreign businesspeople). The foreign side is also warned to expect the Chinese to use some kind of shame technique as a means of gaining leverage, and to not be surprised when the Chinese accuse them of being responsible for snags or other kinds of problems.

Lack of advance preparation by foreign businesspeople is also often a major factor in creating misunderstandings with the Chinese and stretching out negotiations. For one reason or another, foreign groups often arrive in China with only the vaguest notion of how the Chinese government works or how the market functions.

When a trip and/or negotiations are over, it is customary for foreign businesspeople to invite their Chinese hosts to "thank you" dinners. In such cases, all of the Chinese who were at the welcoming banquet should be invited to the farewell party, along with anyone else the visitors feel is appropriate.

Negotiating in Three Dimensions

Americans in particular tend to see business negotiations in two dimensions—presentations and closings (followed by the smooth implementation of the contract). To the Chinese, there are three distinct stages in establishing a business relationship: the social aspect, the talks leading to the signing of a contract, and then really getting down to the give-and-take of the working relationship after the contract is signed. This latter stage is where the real problems generally arise, and where the foreign side must be especially effective in working out the differences. It is especially important that as many details and specifics as possible be included in contracts to avoid future misunderstandings, different interpretations, and disagreements.

Once again, nothing should be taken for granted. Problems invariably arise, stemming from government controls and the inability of the Chinese side to control enough factors, from differences in the way each side views its responsibilities, or from differences in cultural values.

The foreign negotiating team should be prepared for a variety of stress-causing situations, perhaps the most irritating of which is the tendency of the Chinese not to give direct, concrete answers. Not being able to measure progress and see the eventual end of the negotiations is also especially troublesome to foreign businesspeople.

Given the problems and pitfalls involved in negotiating in China, the people who represent the foreign company are of vital importance. To say the least, foreign negotiators (in addition to being thoroughly familiar with their own company and its technology, products, and markets) should be older individuals. They should have a great deal of genuine respect for the Chinese but not be blinded or mesmerized by the country. They should also have a vast store of patience and persistence in pursuing goals and have had substantial experience in cross-cultural business dealings. They should not have become cynical but in fact delight in matching their wit and experience against formidable opponents. They preferably have had some direct, recent experience with China and are secure enough in their own positions to know they are not going to be undercut or fired by impatient senior management back at the home office.

Some additional advice given by Arne J. de Keijzer, a consultant on doing business in China and president of A. J. de Keijzer & Associates Inc. and China Liaison Inc., is also especially valid. He says that foreign businesspeople going to China to negotiate business relationships should not isolate themselves from their own culture or things that are familiar to them and that help to sustain them at home. He suggests that they take along a tape deck and some of their favorite music and a VCR with some good movies if they are going to be in China for an extended period. He further suggests that businesspeople in China for drawn-out negotiating sessions engage in a daily exercise program—walking, jogging, bicycling, and so on, to dissipate stress and keep their energy level high.

The System as a Scapegoat

Difficulties in communicating and in achieving coordination and cooperation in China are compounded by rivalries between departments and agencies. The relations between many such groups has been likened to guerrilla warfare—with the hapless foreign businessperson often in the line of fire but not allowed to fire back. It is also said that some of the differences between departments or agencies are like blood feuds that are decades old.

As is typical of the bureaucratic mentality, Chinese managers often blame "the system" for many of their own shortcomings and the weaknesses of their organizations. Rather than recognize a problem for what it really is and tackle it in a practical way, they will often do nothing, saying it is impossible because of "the system." Again, this is a symptom of the take-no-responsibility syndrome and extreme reluctance to deviate from established procedures.

Because of generations of conditioning, the Chinese are inclined to see every problem as having only one solution—usually one that is "safe" because it follows established procedures. They will often not even engage in the rational consideration of alternate possibilities

When pressed to take some expedient action not specifically provided for by the system, many Chinese managers will dig their heels in and become even more literal in their interpretation of designated procedures. When this appears to be happening, it is best to draw back and take another tack. Often the most successful gambit is to take a personal approach—invite the individual out for an impressive dinner or give a gift you know will be appreciated.

With little or no experience in catering to consumers, many Chinese managers often demonstrate a lack of concern with basic efficiency, much less the quality of their products or services—all problems the foreign businessperson may have to deal with in China.

Time Stands Still

The association of precise increments of time with economic concerns is a very recent phenomenon in China, although the clock was invented there.

Clocks and watches were available in China during the 1800s, but generally no time standards were kept. The language itself was very imprecise when it came to time. "Tomorrow" did not necessarily mean the following day; more likely it meant some indefinite time in the future.

The Chinese today, even those living outside of China and thoroughly familiar with Western ways, do not automatically equate the passing of minutes or hours with the loss of money or opportunity. The foreign businessperson who tries to negotiate according to a tight time frame creates a situation that is intolerable to the Chinese. The larger or more important the deal, the more the Chinese are inclined to discuss it from every possible angle, and then some.

Experienced Chinese businesspeople and government bureaucrats take full advantage of this factor when dealing with foreigners, often deliberately delaying the proceedings simply to squeeze more concessions out of the foreign side. The only recourse for foreign businesspeople is to control their emotions and frustrations and play the game. But after a calculated interval, foreign businesspeople may have no choice but to let their Chinese counterparts know that it is *not* a life or death issue, that they too have other options and can walk away from the bargaining table.

Just as time is less sacred to the Chinese than it is to most Westerners, the days of the week may also be regarded differently—which sometimes results in confusion for the uninitiated. Employees of many *danwei* "units" work six days a week on staggered schedules. Their day off is called Sunday regardless of which calendar day it actually falls on. The next day is Monday, and so on. This means that many individual Chinese are following different "days of the week," making it essential to verify what people are actually talking about when they mention a specific day.

Using Interpreters

Interpreting on a professional level is one of the most difficult of all arts, particularly when widely diverse cultures are concerned. Interpreting to and from Chinese is said to be one of the most difficult challenges of all, not only because of the extraordinary cultural subtleties of the language but also because of the political connotations of words and the fact that both the vocabulary and nuances of words are changing rapidly.

Since most business, a well as political affairs between China and the rest of the world, must go through interpreters, it would seem that the profession of interpreter would have high prestige and pay extremely well. Generally speaking, such is not the case. Too many people on both sides continue to regard interpreting as a mechanical function—input Chinese and out comes English or some other language.

Good interpreters must be both bilingual *and* bicultural to a very high degree. They must be extraordinarily sensitive to myriad nuances of the languages they are using, as well as to the relationship between the two speakers, the political climate, and the personalities (and even the moods) of the speakers. They must be actors in the strongest sense of the word— self-confident and aggressive when the occasion demands.

There have been many recorded cases in which mistakes in cross-cultural interpretation resulted in serious aftermaths. The number of unrecorded cases is probably too large to express in numerical terms.

English is now widely taught in China, and the number of people going on to specialized language training is growing rapidly. More and more Westerners are also taking up the study of Mandarin as a professional skill. But good interpreters are still scarce and mostly underpaid and mistreated. Most Chinese interpreters often have had limited or no experience outside of China, are not familiar with the latest technical vocabulary, and have only a general idea of the business concerned.

Foreign businesspeople using interpreters, whether they are Chinese or foreign, should do everything possible to help them. They should carefully brief them in advance and give them as much written material as possible. They should not overload them with long blocks of comment when speaking and not expect them to go on for more than two hours at a time. If a presentation is to last all day and, especially if it is to go on for several days, more than one interpreter should be engaged. In situations where a great deal of sensitive matter has to be transmitted, it is wise to have a backup interpreter as a monitor.

Obviously having to work through interpreters lengthens the amount of time any business conversation or negotiation takes. Because interpreting generally requires frequent explanations, particularly when dealing with Chinese officials and business managers, a good rule is to allow three times longer than would be expected if only one language were being used. The amount of time needed in any such meeting can be significantly reduced by having most of the points you want to make translated into Chinese in advance and passed out to your Chinese counterparts prior to the meeting.

Another obvious point is that you will be much better served if you have your own interpreter instead of relying on someone provided by the Chinese side. It can be difficult enough without prejudicing your case by using a go-between whose primary interest and loyalty lies with the opposite team.

Foreign businesspeople should also keep in mind that it is a matter of courtesy and professionalism to look at the person being addressed, not at the interpreter (a common failing when people have not been briefed on this kind of protocol or had sufficient experience with it). It goes without saying that businesspeople using interpreters should avoid esoteric references, obtuse vocabulary, and complicated phraseology.

Among the industrialized nations, the United States is probably on the bottom of the totem pole when it comes to the appreciation and training of interpreters, particularly where Asian languages are concerned. The American businessperson who does not want to depend on Chinese counterparts for providing interpreters should begin preparing early.

Holding on to Power

One of the more common complaints lodged against many Chinese business managers is their almost paranoid reluctance to delegate authority. Managers typically insist on approving every action or transaction, no matter how trivial, which results in misuse of their time as well as reduction in efficiency and slows down the process of business. Often, as much time is spent maintaining this system of management as in actually accomplishing work.

One of the reasons for this attitude and approach, say expatriate businesspeople, is what appears to be inability or failure to distinguish degrees of importance in actions or considerations. Something that is very important will habitually get no more attention or concern than something that is of very little importance. Managers often seem to be incapable of viewing the overall picture.

Another aspect of the problem of delegating authority, which must be based on confidence and trust, is the common Chinese practice of giving responsibility to people who have no authority, and vice versa. Probably the primary reason for this dichotomy is that the traditional Chinese social system did not foster trust or confidence in anyone outside of family members who were under absolute control of the father.

This is also the reason why the Chinese traditionally rely on family members and close family friends and tend to form tightly knit family-type organizations in virtually all of their endeavors. Generally, every Chinese company is run exclusively by one powerful father-figure.

A further result of this type of management is that it works against innovation and enthusiasm and makes it difficult or impossible for employees in different sections or departments to cooperate with each other. Not being members of the "immediately family," they are not trusted.

The Buck Never Stops

Another manifestation of this reluctance to delegate authority and accept responsibility is the practice of passing the buck. Even when someone has authority, he or she will frequently pass the buck to avoid responsibility. One of the most common examples of this syndrome is when someone is asked for permission to do something or for approval of something for which there is no well-established precedent. The typical reaction is to refuse the request. No one wants to accept responsibility for having made a decision about something new.

To emphasize the problem of how far buck-passing can go, one Chinese official listed the "travel route" for a simple request in a city office. The request was first put into the form of a written draft and then routed upward to the following: department head, assistant manager, manager, assistant general manager, general manager, place for receiving documents (in-tray), all departments concerned, all department heads, supervisor, vice-director, director, secretary, and mayor. Once the mayor took action, the document was returned to the sender by the same route.

The overall result of this attitude is that typical Chinese employees will not do anything they have not specifically been told to do by a higher-up. The rationale is that they will not gain anything by doing more than they were told to do even though it turns out to be highly desirable. They will definitely be subject to criticism and possibly even termination if the action is viewed as undesirable for any reason.

The don't-rock-the-boat syndrome also affects the quality of the information that is passed on to top management by employees. Not wanting to upset anyone or create any kind of problem, employees tend to report only positive things and to gloss over negative things—or ignore them altogether. The boss is therefore often in some degree of darkness about what is going on in the company. By the same token, managers will commonly withhold information from employees, individually and as a group, either to avoid dealing with unpleasant things and save face or because of lack of information.

These attitudes greatly limit the overall potential of any group or company. When employees in general are not willing to make suggestions, to do anything more than narrowly defined tasks, or to take any new responsibility, it leaves virtually all of the burden for innovation and growth to the top person. When employees are not kept fully informed, they are not in a position to contribute to management.

At the same time, outsiders, particularly foreign visitors, should beware of giving advice to Chinese managers even when asked for it. It is customary for the Chinese to ask visitors for suggestions on how they can improve their operation, but this is more flattery than anything else. People asking for advice are probably doing the best they can under the circumstances, are aware at least to some extent of the weaknesses of the operation, and will consider it presumptuous if not rude for a guest to actually tell them how they "should" be running their business.

Rather than sincerely wanting advice from an outsider, the Chinese businessperson is more likely behaving in typical Chinese fashion, expecting praise instead of suggestions for improvement.

Maintaining face is another facet of this situation. The Chinese will typically go to extremes to avoid losing face or causing a friend to lose face. This greatly reduces the role of honesty and frankness in personal as well as professional relationships. Both the incompetent employee and incompetent manager may go on presuming they are doing a good job and that everyone is pleased.

Because of the sensitivity of individual Chinese to saving face and to respectful treatment, it is not common for Chinese managers, especially in bureaucratic organizations, to single out high-performance individuals for praise. They are treated very much the same as those doing inferior work. This has a detrimental influence on those with more ability and ambition, and they often lose incentive to do their best.

Another common aspect of buck-passing is for clerks and others to shift responsibility by saying they are too busy to do something, or that something can't be done, or something isn't available. This type of reaction is frequently encountered when one attempts to buy bus or train tickets or walks into a hotel and tries to get a room on the spot. Clerks will often, almost automatically it seems, state that no tickets or rooms are available. If you politely persist, however, you will often get what you want.

In this and many other cases the Chinese often express the negative to foreigners in sign language, by waving their right hand in front of their face—meaning "no, I don't have any, there aren't any, you can't do it, I don't want any," or any other version of a negative response.

Clerks in many hotels will tell people who telephone asking for reservations that there are no vacancies when there are in fact rooms available. The clerks simply fail to explain to the callers that the hotel does not accept call-in reservations made only a few days ahead of time.

Working Hours

Because all of China is in one time zone, and because there are differences in regional customs and the availability of transportation, official working hours vary. (Daylight Savings Time goes into effect on the second Sunday of April and ends on the second Sunday of September.)

Beijing area	8 A.M.–12; 1:30 P.M.–5:30 P.M.
Chinghai area	9:30 A.M.–1 P.M.; 3:30 P.M.–7:30 P.M.
Fujian area	8 A.M.–12; 3 P.M.–6 P.M.
Guangzhou area	8:30 A.M.–12:30 P.M.; 3 P.M.–6 P.M.
Hunan area	8 A.M.–11:30 A.M.; 3P.M.–6:30 P.M.
Nanjing area	8 A.M.–12; 2 P.M.–6 P.M.
Northeast area	8 A.M.–12; 1 P.M.–5 P.M.

Shanghai area	9 A.M.–12; 1 P.M.–6 P.M.
Sichuan area	8 A.M.–12; 2:30 P.M.–6:30 P.M.
Tianjian area	8:30 A.M.–12; 1:30 P.M.–6 P.M.
Yunan area	8:30 A.M.–12:30 P.M.; 3 P.M.–7 P.M.

While these are the official hours published by the municipal and provincial authorities, there are variations. In Beijing, for example, the employees of many government offices begin their lunch break at 11.30 A.M., and from August 1 to 15 many quit working as early as 3 P.M. Because of the variations in the hours of government offices in Beijing and many of the outlying provinces, especially during the summer months, communication between them and the capital is reduced to around two hours in the morning and two hours in the afternoon.

Titles

President	Jongchi (*jhong-chee*)
Vice President	Fu Jongchi (*fuu jhong-chee*)
Director	Jongjen (*jhong-jen*)
General Manager	Jong Qingli (*jhong-cheeng-lee*)
Manager	Qingli (*cheeng-lee*)
Assistant Manager	Fu Qingli (*fuu cheeng-lee*)
Executive/Officer	Juren (*juu-wren*)

6

New Rules and Guidelines

"Make loyalty and sincerity your guiding principles in life. Have no friends who are not as good as you. When you have erred, do not hesitate to rectify your mistake. Aim not only for success but to be of value to your fellow men."

—CONFUCIUS

When in China

It is vital that foreign businesspeople in China be especially sensitive to changes that are going on at all times within the government and in society in general and be both adaptable and imaginative in response to these changes. The present contract system, under which managers of state-owned enterprises sign contracts with the government to operate the businesses more or less as private enterprises, continues to evolve. As originally applied, the contract management system specified how much revenue in taxes each enterprise would deliver to the government on an annual basis—one idea being that the system would provide more motivation for efficiency and productivity. Fully private enterprises are continuing to appear like so many mushrooms.

Foreign businesspeople must keep in mind that the personal contacts they make are often the only guarantees they have in pursuing business goals, and that these contacts must be continuously nurtured. While the rules of surface protocol are set and fairly strictly observed, there are no specific rules that can be prescribed for dealing with Chinese businesspeople and bureaucrats in every case.

It goes without saying that you should be well informed about your own company and its goals and as knowledgeable as possible about who your counterparts are and what they want. But each situation is usually different enough that it requires its own strategy, devised as you go along. The universal rules that always apply are to be patient and calm, **never** speak in absolutes or ultimatums, and maintain a cooperative stance.

Given the nature of the Chinese system, success in any endeavor is determined more by individual character, personality, and personal situation than by genuine merit of a project or product, justice, or the common good. For this reason, people on every level automatically think in terms of connections and "going through the back door" when they want to accomplish something.

Probably the advice given most often about doing business in China is the obvious—that to succeed you must learn how to operate within the system and do as the Chinese do. This includes being patient, using connections, taking advantage of opportunities, and being imaginative and clever. American businesspeople dealing with China often find themselves at an especially serious disadvantage in taking the "back door," however, since they cannot be as free with gifts and other types of inducements that are customarily used to oil the back-door system. In such circumstances, there is often no choice but to come up with some kind of creative approach that satisfies everybody.

Expatriate businesspeople in China say that before any strategy can be devised for a joint venture it is important to get well enough acquainted with the factory managers and local government officials concerned to find out how each one of them reacts to the possibility of working with a foreign company. It is also important, they say, to find out how effective local managers are in dealing with officials in charge of their area of industry.

The First Contact

Solicitating business in China directly, particularly with personal visits, can be extraordinarily time-consuming and costly. No doubt the ideal situation is to make your company and products known to the "right" Chinese indirectly and encourage them to make the first approach. One of the prime reasons for this is that it is difficult to measure the degree of interest on the Chinese side during the usually long period they take to consider a possible project. There is also the factor that they see an opportunity to pump a foreign businessperson seeking to do business in China for knowledge as part of their on-the-job training, when they actually may not be serious about the product or project.

Foreigners must accommodate themselves to the fact that establishing a personal relationship comes before business in China. The Chinese are conditioned to be wary of strangers and not to get involved with them. They do not make "friends" instantly, as Americans in particular are accustomed to doing. Their position is that since business is a give-and-take process, and it can be successful in the long run only if there is trust and confidence between the parties, the relationship must be on a personal basis. The more personal contact there is, the more familiar each side is with the other, the more likely that differences can be resolved and that the enterprise will succeed.

Another sign of the personal, often arbitrary, nature of business in China is the fact that demands and prices often vary with the nationality of the foreign businessperson. On the personal as well as the businessperson side, there is often one price structure for Chinese and another for foreigners.

Sending in an Advance Party

It is highly recommended that any large business mission to China be preceded, by three or four days, by an advance person. This person makes sure that all of the arrangements have been made, including such simple things as hotel reservations and travel itineraries or special preparations, such as audiovisual equipment. Of course, the company with an agent in China can usually delegate this responsibility.

While details such as this frequently slip through the cracks, the Chinese are famous for their personal treatment of official guests. In their wooing of foreign investors, they have gone so far as to have special lounges at airports for rent to host organizations for receiving and welcoming their foreign guests. Usually, the welcoming ceremonies at the airport are relatively brief, since the Chinese are genuinely solicitous about the comfort and convenience of guests who often have been en route for many hours.

Unit-to-Unit Business

The bureaucratic administrative system in China is set up to deal only with organizations, not with individuals. For the most part, you cannot do things as an individual. You must do them as a representative of your company or organization, and when approaching a government office you must have a letter or other document from your "unit" authorizing you to do whatever it is you are trying to do.

After the Contract

It is often noted by foreign businesspeople experienced in China that the real negotiating begins after a contract is signed. Most of the problems that do occur result from the fact that officials have limited authority and naturally tend to interpret the provisions of contracts from their own cultural, political and economic viewpoints.

It is especially important that foreign businesspeople who sign contracts in China make careful arrangements for ongoing follow-up. The larger and more important the contract, the more valuable it is to have your own person or an agent on the spot. Despite the obvious advantages to the foreign side, however, the Chinese do not like to deal with local agents. They will often do their best to convince foreign partners to dispense with them, or they will attempt to circumvent them.

Another factor in signing contracts in China is the role of the Ministry of Supervision, which was established in 1987 to "check" all contracts signed with foreign interests for any indications of "corruption"—from failure to provide for compensation within legal limits to undercover arrangements that amount to bribery. This would include foreign businesspeople agreeing to act as sponsors for the children or relatives of Chinese officials to study abroad. In the first year of activity, the ministry reportedly went over 300,000 contracts, found that more than eight hundred of them were "faulty," and recouped $30 million that otherwise would have been lost to the government.

The "ministry of honesty in foreign contracts" operates offices and bureaus in other ministries, commissions, and administrations that are under the jurisdiction of the State Council, the supreme administrative body of the government. To avoid problems with the Ministry of Supervision, local governments also review contracts signed with foreign enterprises.

More on Negotiating

"Chinese negotiators are famed for their shrewdness. Their representatives in important commercial negotiations are well trained in the art of positioning, posturing, pricing, psychology, and effective use of timing; and they operate from the position of knowing their adversary's strengths and weaknesses well enough to obtain maximum advantage to their side," writes Thomas D. Gorman in *China* (Euromoney Publications, Hong Kong, 1986). President and publisher of China Consultants International (Hong Kong), Gorman goes on to emphasize that Western businesspeople dealing with the Chinese sometimes mistakenly associate the cultural traits generally attributed to the Chinese ("subtlety, indirectness, soft-spokenness, avoidance of conflict") with their character and behavior in negotiations.

The Western businesspeople would be much better off, Gorman says, to look at negotiating with the Chinese as a sporting event in which the play can get pretty rough, and while each side does its best to win, the end result should be something that both sides can live with. He adds that Chinese business protocol is closer to that of the West than to Japan's, and that the primary difference between Chinese and Western protocol is the Chinese emphasis on rank, maintaining proper hierarchical order, and depending on one individual to act as spokesperson for the group.

One challenge facing foreign businesspeople going into a negotiating session with Chinese is to determine the rank of the individual Chinese members, since it is not always obvious from their titles. The best approach is simply to ask the Chinese side in advance to provide you with a list of their negotiators, denoting the rank of each. This advance determination of rank is also important for seating arrangements in any lunch or dinner banquet hosted by the foreign side.

In larger gatherings, the Chinese (just like Westerners) use place cards to designate where individuals are to sit. This is always an option even for smaller groups, but it is important to have the ranking members in the right place—and you may want to confirm this in advance with a lower-ranking member of the Chinese delegation.

Another point to keep in mind is that the Chinese do not like surprises. They should be briefed in advance about the subject to be discussed, and the agenda should be followed as far as possible. If it is not, be prepared for lengthy delays while the Chinese discuss the new points at their convenience. The Chinese side generally expects the foreign group to make its presentation first, which in some respects gives them an advantage.

Where protocol is concerned, many foreign businesspeople tend to be intimidated by the rigid ritual of Chinese banquets and business meetings. While it is very helpful for the visitor to know something about Chinese etiquette in advance and therefore feel more at ease in following it, the Chinese are not so ignorant or naive to expect all foreigners to be skilled in their manners and are tolerant. The main thing is for foreign visitors to remain polite and cooperate and to demonstrate goodwill by following local customs as well as they can. When you are the guest of Chinese, let them take the lead and direct you. If in doubt in any situation, following Western rules of etiquette that you would exhibit toward a respected and valued guest will do nicely—and you do not have to apologize for "barbarian (non-Chinese) manners."

Should the CEO Go?

Generally speaking, the chief executive officer of a major foreign company should not go on the first mission to China unless the mission has been invited by an organization headed by someone of equal rank and it has been made clear that the chief executive of the organization will meet the foreign

CEO. The Chinese normally assign negotiating duties to lower-ranking managers and staff members, and bring in the higher or highest executives for the signing of a contract or the opening of a new plant. At the same time, the higher the rank of the foreign mission leader, the more obvious it is to the Chinese that the mission is important to the foreign side and the more likely they are to assign it higher priority. But if it is a first-time visit and there is no "friendship" involved, they cannot be expected to involve the highest officials.

A main point to keep in mind is that once a relationship has been established the Chinese are meticulous about matching rank with rank in their dealings with foreigners. The visitors should not overplay a hand by trying to outrank the other side in any kind of meeting.

Role of Host Organizations

From the beginning of its Open Door policy, the Chinese government required that all foreign business missions to China be invited by "host" organizations" as a form of control. When new laws made it possible for foreign companies to open their own offices in China, this system was applied to them as well. It was made necessary for each foreign company to have a Chinese organization as its "host" or "sponsor" to accept responsibility for the actions of the foreign company.

This requirement is not exactly a popular one, since the interests of the Chinese sponsor and the foreign company may not always coincide. In the event of any problem involving the foreign company, the first recourse of the government or any Chinese organization concerned is to go to the host or sponsor for satisfaction, a serious responsibility to say the least.

Of course, many of the sponsors are active participants in the business of their foreign affiliates and their involvement is voluntary. In other cases, the Chinese side is more or less forced by the government to assume the role of sponsor, creating a situation in which friction is likely to develop.

Dealing with Unwritten Rules

The laws governing foreign operations in China are complicated enough, but there is another factor that can make doing business in China more complicated than it appears to be. This factor is the tendency of Chinese officials to apply "unwritten rules" in their reaction to approaches by foreign companies and in their administration of foreign firms operating in China. These unwritten rules reflect a variety of influences. Some are based on precedents or other model arrangements. Others derive from special guidelines that legally apply only to the Special Economic Zones, while still others are based on "future" laws or regulations that are being considered.

This approach by the Chinese, particularly where "future laws" are concerned, is not necessarily insidious. For the most part, officials and company managers are simply trying to anticipate what is likely to happen in the future and to structure a relationship that will still be workable when these new laws do come into effect.

One of the major advantages of using the services of a law firm with extensive current experience in China is the fact that they have model contracts for use in negotiating virtually any kind of arrangement. Much of the wording of these contracts has already been approved by the Ministry of Foreign Economic Relations and Trade (MOFERT) and can, therefore, greatly simplify and shorten the process.

In forging a final contract, it is better to stick to your guns and make it as detailed and as specific as possible, not only to avoid future problems but also because it is customary for the Chinese to use past contracts as models for future use. If you agree to one contract without really approving of it, there is a chance it will come back to haunt you in the future.

Hiring and Firing

As of 1986, it became legal to hire (and fire) most workers under a "competitive contract" system, which also stipulated that workers were to sign individual labor contracts with their employers. Both regulations and practices differ regionally, however, and the labor issue remains one of the more challenging aspects of doing business in China.

The Chinese partner in some joint ventures prefers to sign a collective labor contract with the venture, notes Jamie P. Horsley, a member of the international law firm of Paul, Weiss, Rifkind, Wharton, and Garrison, based in Hong Kong. A specialist in the legal issues of doing business in China, Horsley adds that many joint-venture managers prefer this kind of arrangement. It means the Chinese side assumes all responsibility for recruiting and supervising the labor force in a package deal, making it possible to fix the cost of labor for a predetermined period of time.

Horsley adds that others disagree with this approach, however, believing that joint responsibility for hiring and supervising makes it easier to introduce Western concepts into management, enhance productivity and quality control, and build greater loyalty among the workforce. Recruiting in particular requires extensive knowledge of international as well as domestic regulations and evolving practices. Firing employees can be even more of a challenge. Newcomers are advised to engage the services of an expert in the field.

Beijing's Foreign Enterprise Service Corporation (FESCO), founded in

1979 as the exclusive employment agency for foreign companies operating in the city, began to reduce its monopoly in 1988, allowing foreign companies to hire new personnel directly, without its approval, in accordance with new labor laws passed that year. One of the biggest complaints about the old system was that employees provided by FESCO were often incompetent and companies ended up being stuck with them. Another complaint was that all salaries were paid directly to FESCO, which then arbitrarily decided how much individual workers were to receive, creating low morale among the workers and stifling incentive.

Under the new system, foreign companies have more say-so in the employees they do accept from FESCO and have the right to return workers to the employment agency after a two- or three-month trial period if they are not satisfactory. As a further improvement in its services, FESCO also began placing Help Wanted advertising jointly with foreign companies seeking new employees. (And perhaps seeing the day when its services would no longer be required by foreign enterprises, FESCO also started offering classes in Mandarin, calligraphy, painting, piano, martial arts, and cooking.)

Similar organizations, such as the Diplomatic Service Bureau and the Foreign Translation Company, have respective monopolies on providing Chinese employees to embassies in Beijing and providing translation services to foreign businesses.

Another far-reaching development in the recruiting and employment system in Beijing was the establishment of the Beijing Talent and Technological Information Exchange Market in 1988, in cooperation with the China Scientific and Technological Information Research Institute. The purpose of the labor exchange market was to give newly graduated technicians, as well as those already employed in industry, more choice in jobs and to give companies and government agencies in suburban and rural areas an opportunity to recruit professional talent from Beijing.

The exchange market is staged several times a month in different locations, sometimes for specific areas or groups of enterprises. Graduating students, as well as others, are eligible to register with the exchange for interviews with companies seeking new employees. While judged an outstanding success, the labor exchange "fairs" have not had completely smooth sailing. Some companies and state-run agencies have refused to release workers who want to change jobs. Others say that employees who quit must reimburse the company for any training fees involved and give up any housing the company helped them obtain. Some employers have refused to hand over the personnel files of workers who quit.

In the spring of 1988, state-owned and -managed commercial enterprises and service companies in Beijing began implementing a new employment system called "Optimum Seeking." Under this system, managers have some say-so in the choice of workers, and workers are able to express their preference for managers. The system also allows for a ''reasonable flow'' of workers, meaning that employees have the right to quit their jobs, and managers are permitted more leeway in firing unwanted workers. Both managers and workers sign employment contracts under the "Optimum Seeking" system.

Mergers: The Way to Go

Introduction of the contract responsibility system in 1984 led to the first takeovers and mergers among Chinese enterprises, starting a trend that grew rapidly and is now described as a ''third wave'' in the country's ongoing business reforms. Many of the country's most progressive reformers see buyouts of inefficient companies and mergers not only as a desirable but an essential ''cleaning process'' in the transformation of the economy.

Exchanging Experts

Another factor in the economic revolution now going on in China are the personnel exchanges between Chinese and foreign enterprises, joint ventures, organizations, and individuals. Beginning in 1985, the China Association for International Exchanges of Personnel (CAIEP) and its subsidiary, the China Foundation for International Exchange of Personnel (CFIEP), have invited more than two thousand foreign experts each year to China to work with and counsel Chinese companies. Some of these foreign experts have received shareholding positions in the companies where they serve as technical advisers. The China Foundation for International Exchange of Personnel has permanent representative offices in Japan, Germany, the United States, and Hong Kong.

Beware of Economic Crimes

Foreign traders and investors in China must be especially wary of economic crimes in their business dealings, warns Mitchell A. Silk, an attorney with the international law firm of Hughes, Hubbard, and Reed and research consultant to the East Asian Legal Studies program at the University of Maryland Law School. Silk, who spent several years in China working, researching, and teaching law at Beijing University, notes that economic crime has proliferated in China since the early 1980s.

Writing in *The China Business Review* Silk listed the major categories of economic crimes in China as smuggling, bribery, speculation, swindling, diverting foreign exchange, trademark counterfeiting, and tax evasion. He emphasizes that scores of foreign importers have suffered losses because their Chinese suppliers did not have the necessary quota or did not obtain the necessary documents, resulting in the goods being confiscated and destroyed. Importers should insist upon documentation from the seller and relevant agencies to certify that all of the required steps have been taken.

Foreign businesspeople exporting to China must also confirm that their buyers, including both the buying unit and the trading agent, have the authority to buy such items and the foreign exchange to pay for them, Silk warns. He adds that foreign businesspeople stationed in China must always be aware that various categories of trade information may be considered confidential by the Chinese and asking for it or having it in one's possession may contravene the law.

Silk goes on to say that China has no law comparable to the U.S. Fifth Amendment against self-incrimination. Anyone who is questioned about an alleged infraction and does not fully answer every question is regarded as guilty and is subject to punishment. This, explains Silk, reflects the ancient Chinese tradition that those who confess are treated leniently, while those who resist are punished severely. He adds that foreign businesspeople who are unfortunate enough to be called in for questioning must be very careful about their responses and avoid giving officials any indication of being uncooperative.

There is the further danger, Silk goes on, that government officials will confuse what is actually legal according to law with what they believe is undesirable. He gives as an example cases in which tax officials have judged that the "legal" avoidance of taxes was wrong and therefore punishable.

The "Understanding" Cop-Out

One of the fundamental reasons why Westerners often have difficulty in understanding and dealing effectively with the Chinese (and Japanese and other people of the Confucian sphere of Asia) is the widely held stereotype that theirs is a cooperative society and that they live by compromise and consensus. However, the harmony that appears on the surface of life in China—and so deeply impresses many Westerners—is in fact only a surface phenomenon that hides a cauldron of discontent.

The harmony that is seen by outsiders is not the result of voluntary behavior deriving from an enlightened level of goodwill. It is and always has been enforced by all the sanctions available to a despotic government. Those without recourse to a higher or countervailing power generally have no choice but to suppress their dislikes and differences of opinion or to channel them in some other direction.

People in hierarchical, despotic societies like China tend to form small groups or factions which then defend their own turf and attempt to force their will on others who are in weaker positions. This is always done with the rationale that the outsider must "understand and accept" their attitudes and behavior as something that is either right or cannot be helped. This has always been the social structure and psychology of the Chinese and is the source of much of the stress and inefficiency in the country. The natural tendency of each faction is to behave arbitrarily, stretching the limits of its actions as far as possible. When criticized or confronted, these factions and their members either deny wrongdoing in the first place or ask for "understanding" of their situation—which includes accepting or tolerating the situation regardless of what it is.

Social critics in today's China say that the word "understand" is one of the most used and abused words in the language. Parents use it with children, students use it with teachers, tradespeople use it with their customers, bureaucrats use it with the public—invariably to excuse behavior that is irrational, self-serving at the expense of others, irritating, immoral, damaging, or illegal. Understanding that this system exists does not necessarily mean that one can eliminate it or get around it, but it should help relieve some of the stress in putting up with it.

(As those who are intimately familiar with Japan know, the Japanese have also traditionally used this psychological ploy not only in their personal affairs but also as government policy, particularly in their international relations.)

China faces a growing problem of corruption. Corruption among government officials is said to be especially serious in Guangdong Province, which adjoins Hong Kong. Graft there is so common that local authorities have a special policy of allowing officials to accept up to $540 in "financial incentives" without charges being filed against them. The People's Criminal Investigation Department of the province operates a twenty-four-hour hotline for citizens to report corruption.

Most of the "financial incentives" that go beyond this limit are generally difficult to pin down and prove, and only a very small fraction of them are ever called into question. When caught, however, big league grafters are subject to being shot.

Bribery remains pervasive throughout Chinese society, but it is generally illegal only when the person receiving the bribe is a government employee. Not only is the person receiving the bribe subject to punishment, so also are the person giving the bribe and any go-between who may be involved.

Trademark counterfeiting in China remains a serious threat to both Chinese and foreign companies, resulting in substantial economic losses. Despite strict laws against trademark counterfeiting, enforcement is complicated by many factors, including conflicts of interest between agencies responsible for enforcing the laws, a hostile environment, especially when foreign companies are concerned, and an almost completely inadequate system of restitution when counterfeiting is proven.

The Apology Syndrome

If there is one thing that will set Chinese authority figures off and bring out the worst in them, it is when someone who is known or presumed to be guilty of some offense refuses to acknowledge guilt and apologize.

It has traditionally been the way of Chinese officialdom to deal very harshly with people who resist authority and the idea of being "rehabilitated" (the assumption being, of course, that they are guilty of something), or being punished when the official believes they deserve it.

Part of this old attitude came from the fact that in denying an accusation and resisting punishment, individuals caused inconvenience and trouble for the system. This might result in the government representatives themselves being criticized (for failure to keep peace and harmony in their districts).

The key point to keep in mind in any conflict with the law in China is that right or wrong is circumstantial and is based on Chinese interpretations of the situation. Trying to use logic and epistemology to "explain" is likely to get you in deeper.

When foreigners in China get into any kind of trouble—guilty or not— the best thing to do first is to apologize to everybody for causing a disturbance and then get someone else to present your case for you. If you prefer to represent yourself or are questioned, it is very important to remain dispassionate about your *rights* and to take care not to anger anyone. Loud protestations and an apparent uncooperative attitude are likely to be taken as arrogance toward China and its laws and customs.

Payment Problems

One of the more bothersome of the ongoing problems facing foreign companies in China is dealing with the labor laws. China's labor laws specify that foreign firms pay their Chinese managers on the same level as their expatriate managers, resulting in a huge disparity between what the Chinese managers in foreign companies receive and what other Chinese managers receive. The law is based on equal pay for equal work, but it has been the cause of a great deal of trouble.

Because of the problems resulting from the law, government officials in the mid-1980s began showing some flexibility, allowing the wages of Chinese managers to be based on prevailing Hong Kong standards.

Many employees working for foreign-managed joint ventures in China are paid more than double the amount received by other Chinese. In an effort to mitigate this disparity, some Chinese companies are legally permitted to pay their employees from 20 to 50 percent above the national level—all of which is the source of a great deal of envy and criticism from people still caught up in the "Big Pot" syndrome. A reflection of this situation is that more and more young people, especially those just finishing college, prefer to work for foreign-funded enterprises.

One pay peculiarity that foreign businesspeople in Beijing should keep in mind is that when the temperature soars to 40° C, the law requires that people who work outside receive an extra five yuan per day. (This outside category includes hotel doormen.) To get around this law, however, the government-controlled weather bureau will report the temperature as 38° C or 39° C even though it is 40° C or above by their own thermometers. When the temperature has stayed at 40° C or above for several days, the weather bureau has been known to report the temperatures as below 40° C for the first three or four days, before finally acknowledging the actual temperature.

Added one experienced expatriate: "Reality is whatever the Chinese government says it is, whether it's the temperature or something else, and this is a lesson foreigners have to learn in negotiating with the Chinese."

Arbitration in Disputes

As the volume and complexity of Sino-foreign joint ventures increase, so too do disputes between partners. In the early years, most foreign companies generally took such disputes to the appropriate government offices, often with unhappy results. Now both parties are more likely to take their conflicts to the Foreign Economic and Trade Arbitration Commission (FETAC), an agency of the China Council for the Promotion of International Trade (CCIPT).

Dating from 1952 and still the only commercial arbitration body in China, the commission saw little action until 1983, when the pace of China's international involvement picked up dramatically. The commission now receives an average of over one hundred disputes a year and has a substantial backlog of cases.

Some 75 percent of the cases brought before the commission are trade disputes involving the quality of goods or late arrivals and payments. Most of the quality disputes are lodged by the Chinese side, while most of the complaints about late payments are made by the foreign side. Another 15 percent of the disputes concerns such things as insufficient financing, poor management, and arbitrary changes in both workers and management by the Chinese side. Other disputes involve labor and construction contracts, real estate, copyrights, and patents.

The biggest case arbitrated to date involved a joint Chinese-British hotel project valued at twenty million yuan. The Chinese side accused the British of not bringing in enough money to finish the construction. The British countered that the Chinese had squandered the original budget. Both sides asked for nine million yuan in losses. Eventually, the Chinese interests bought the British out for eighteen million yuan.

The commission has cooperation contracts with arbitration organizations in several foreign countries, including Japan, Sweden, France, and Italy, and working relations with similar organizations in Hong Kong and Canada.

Dealing with the "Old School"

The firing of an American manager of a joint venture in Chongqing, Sichuan Province, is indicative of the conflicts that arise regularly in such enterprises in China. In this case, the conflict arose because the American insisted on managing the enterprise as efficiently as possible, keeping control of expenditures and making the company profitable.

The Chinese board of directors and upper-level Chinese management, however, continuously bypassed the foreigner in hiring, firing, and transferring personnel without his knowledge (described by local residents as "a common practice in China"), by running up personal expenses and charging them to the company, and otherwise undermining his efforts to properly manage the firm. When the foreigner complained to the board about their interference, they accused him of "lack of knowledge of Chinese conditions," and justified his termination by saying he had made "mistakes" in his management.

A Chinese commentator who criticized the dumping of the foreign manager said one of the "mistakes" he made was firing several sons and daughters of upper-level government officials who had been given jobs at the company but were inefficient in their work. The commentator added that foreign businesspeople in China ignore such "Chinese conditions" at their own peril. He warned that it is traditional for the Chinese to strike back at anyone they feel has slighted them or done them a disservice. He said this was "policy" followed by many ordinary people as well as officials, and that they applied it against foreign bosses as well as higher-ranking Chinese managers or cadre.

Other examples of "resistance against foreign management practices" include stories of how factory workers take time out of work-hours to sleep or play poker, posting guards to signal them when foreign managers approach the work areas.

China's vernacular *Economic Daily* regularly carries commentary about clashes between Chinese and foreign managers, primarily centering on low work efficiency. Says *Economic Daily:* "Foreign investors meet with many ideological contradictions when dealing with their Chinese cooperators. Many officials know little about the outside world and are likely to judge the rights and wrongs of foreign enterprises using their own outmoded ideas. They try to make foreign businessmen agree to backward management methods and put up administrative interference when the latter express different opinions."

The *ED* editorial adds that practical regulations and systems should be introduced to guarantee the rights of foreign managers involved in cooperatives so that "old ideas will not influence the business of foreign enterprises."

The behavior of some Chinese officials sometimes goes beyond "misunderstandings" with foreign managers and includes an element of arrogance, particularly in the conduct of meetings and negotiations, when they may give insufficient consideration to the foreign side. At the same time, not all behavior that may be perceived as arrogant is actually intended. In many cases this kind of treatment occurs because the people involved do not know any other way of conducting themselves and are behaving naturally. Perhaps one point for which some Chinese may be faulted is that they expect foreign businesspeople to be humble and subservient—reminiscent of past ages when foreign delegations were treated as supplicants. As usual, the best response to this type of behavior is to remain calm, patient, and diplomatically persistent.

Quality-Control Problems

China's cultural similarity to Japan often breaks down completely when it comes to quality control. Instead of Total Quality Control, to which Japanese dedication verges on obsession, ordinary workers in the provincial areas of China either never think about quality control as anything special or important or look at it as something extra that management is trying to force on them for no justifiable reason.

The experience of Katharyne Mitchell, assigned to a caviar factory in northern Heilungjiang as a quality-control engineer, is instructive. As she recounted in *The China Business Review,* Mitchell was several days late in arriving at the factory because of flooding and delays in getting a residence permit. The canning season had already started when she got there so she had to reject all of the caviar that had been canned without prior inspection. This made the factory manager very angry, and his resentment toward an outsider trying to tell him how to run the plant was intensified.

Sanitary conditions at the factory were terrible. Realizing that she had to do something to overcome the impasse with the manager, Mitchell went out of her way to establish friendly relations with the workers. They were sympathetic toward her because they realized she was just trying to follow her orders, and also because she pitched in and worked with them to clean the place up as much as possible. At the same time, she adds, the workers themselves were often the cause of the problems because they had no concept of the importance of sanitation.

Eventually, Mitchell says, she was able to develop a working relationship with the manager based on mutual compromise and a degree of understanding, but they did not become friends. On one occasion when she discovered a very serious problem that the manager would not allow her or any of the workers to correct, she and two of her most trusted worker-friends surreptitiously corrected the problem during the manager's rest period.

Mitchell said she used to dream about her American boss suddenly arriving on the premises to arbitrate some of the disputes that arose, but that when he did show up midway through the caviar season he created more problems than he solved. The American manager began to demand additional changes in the processing and canning. The interpreter assigned to him was incompetent and made many mistakes. His translations were often either meaningless or offensive to the Chinese. All the goodwill that Mitchell had managed to build up with the manager was lost, making her assignment more difficult than ever for the rest of the time she was there.

Among the things Mitchell said her experience taught her was that the level of business sophistication diminishes in direct relation to the distance you get away from China's major cities and that any foreign representative assigned to a remote area in China must have absolute authority to represent the company. She also learned that the Chinese partner should agree in advance as to the nature and extent of the foreign representative's authority, and that the judgment of the foreign representative on the spot should take precedence over the opinions of visiting managers. Mitchell summed up by saying that the only thing that made it possible for her to do as much as she did was the fact that she spoke Chinese.

The Five *P*'s

The success of a foreign investment project in China is invariably determined by how well the investor follows the five "*P*" principles, say Samuel X. Zhang and Jeffrey L. Snyder, attorneys in the Washington, D.C., law firm of Graham and James. After observing both successful and unsuccessful foreign investment projects in China, Zhang and Snyder came up with an

investor checklist for venture planning and execution that involves five P's—
project, partner, pattern, profitability, and protection.

Expounding on their five "P" principles in *The China Business Review,*
Zhang and Snyder note the following:

1. If the project is compatible with China's planning goals, the chances of
    it being approved are greatly enhanced, and if it falls into a priority sector
    of the economy the chances of success are even better.
2. The partner chosen must be authorized to participate in such an invest-
    ment project; all of the potential partner's strengths and weaknesses
    must be taken into account, along with whether or not any other official
    organization has to be involved in the project.
3. The type of investment structure that would be best for the project must
    be carefully determined.
4. A thorough examination must be made of the project's anticipated market
    share, what form profits will take, and the various restrictions that apply
    to the use and repatriation of foreign exchange.
5. The foreign company must determine clearly the type and extent of
    protection Chinese law affords such an investment, and a process for
    settling disputes must be worked out in advance.

Zhang and Snyder add the obvious: that there are many variables in all
of these "P" areas and that careful planning and implementation are essential no mater how attractive or desirable the project. The greater contribution
a project will make to China's advancement, the more support it will get
from key officials. For example, a project aimed solely at capturing a share
of the domestic market has much less chance of approval than one that would
improve China's export picture.

One of the most demanding tasks, they add, is choosing the best partner.
This means taking the time to examine all personal partners very carefully.
Part of this consideration should be the location of the candidates, since
incentives, tax benefits, land-use rates, and other factors vary significantly
in different areas. Once a candidate is chosen, they go on, the negotiation
process presents another challenge: it is normal for the Chinese side to
include representatives from half a dozen or more different organizations,
some of which have no direct relationship with each other but all of which
play some role in foreign investments.

The pattern, or structure, of the investment is a critical element, Zhang
and Snyder add, and should be determined only after extensive research and
expert advice. As for protection, Zhang and Snyder say that the best approach is to make sure that the documentation creating the enterprise and
delineating its operation conforms absolutely with Chinese law and is officially approved by every authority with any pertinent jurisdiction, so that
in the event of a dispute the foreign side not only will have maximum legal

protection but may also be able to accept Chinese arbitration without fear of unfair or illegal treatment.

Promoting Private Enterprises

In still another move to strengthen business in China, the State Council in 1988 passed legislation confirming the legal status of companies and detailing their legal rights. All enterprises, including state-run, collective, joint-venture, foreign-financed, and private businesses, are required by the legislation to register with the State Administration of Industry and Commerce (SAIC).

All firms properly registered are legally empowered to sign contracts, open bank accounts, use seals and stamps, and conduct any other kind of legal activity. Companies that go out of business are required to apply to the SAIC for cancellation of their registration and license.

Also in 1988, the State Administration for Industry and Commerce passed a law specifically aimed at turning more of the nation's hundreds of thousands of small collectives into private enterprises. The law applies to companies in which the assets belong to the individuals involved and which have more than eight employees. Besides giving proprietors the same legal rights as state-run enterprises, the law makes it possible for the owners to bequeath the companies to their heirs.

Cutting Red Tape

Government bureaus responsible for approving and regulating foreign ventures in China, particularly those in Beijing, continue working earnestly to reduce the amount and complexity of the red tape involved in doing business. The Beijing Administration for Industry and Commerce, for example, in 1988 set up a service center where all of the procedures for foreign investment can be completed at one "window." There is also a "special window" at Customs for expediting import-export documentation.

The Beijing Economic Commission monitors complaints from foreign businesspeople in the city and, once the cause of the complaints is determined, seeks to "break" barriers and "lower the threshold of difficulties" encountered by foreign firms.

In an effort to reassert itself as China's business capital, Shanghai in 1988 established the Shanghai Foreign Investment Working Commission to cut red tape and speed up the process of bringing in foreign capital. The commission, which has jurisdiction over any investment worth more than US$5 million, operates under the principle of "one organization, one window, one stamp," as a means of simplifying the investment process.

In addition to reducing the red tape involved in the application and approval process, the commission also provides potential investors with various research and administrative services, including background on the investment climate, finding qualified Chinese partners, and consulting on China's policies and laws. At the same time, the city took several steps to improve its notoriously bad taxi service.

Getting the Right Certification

Some foreign investors choose to take advantage of Chinese laws passed in 1986 and 1987 providing special incentives for export-oriented and technologically advanced investments. Pitman B. Potter, resident attorney in Beijing for Graham and James International Consultants (Washington, D.C.), says that obtaining such certification is not always as easy as it may sound. One of the qualifications for an export-oriented certification, for example, is determined by the level of production and exports, while definitions of what is technologically advanced vary.

Maintaining export-oriented certification may also be more difficult than it sounds and involves making all production and export records, as well as pricing records, available to the proper authorities each year. The process of annual renewal can become a trial. Potter notes that while the benefits to foreign companies obtaining either of these preferential statuses are real and worthwhile, obtaining the status and keeping it requires a thorough knowledge of the intent of the Chinese laws and a willingness to work cooperatively with the appropriate supervising authorities.

Public Relations

American-style public relations has found a home in China. The Chinese have an unquenchable thirst for information and are conditioned to put great faith in the printed word and to depend upon third parties, introductions, and connections. They love staged events, such as receptions, openings, and trade shows, which are virtually guaranteed huge press turnouts—all of which contributed to the rapid growth of public relations activity in New China.

At the same time, leaders in the PR industry say they do not just copy the Western approach. Public relations in China must have some Chinese characteristics in order to succeed in the long run, according to the Beijing PR Society.

One of the splashiest PR successes in New China was textbook American. Jixin Teng, director of a deficit-ridden chemical plant in Shashi City, Hubei Province, began looking for a new idea to stave off bankruptcy. At a Guangzhou (Canton) trade fair, he met a trader from Hong Kong who was looking for a mainland source of washing powder. In just twenty-eight days. Teng and his research staff came up with a new detergent that had up to four times the strength of ordinary washing powder. They dubbed the new detergent Power 28, and began exporting it to Hong Kong, where it was called "King of Detergents."

Power 28 was a success in Hong Kong but the market was too small to give Teng the volume he needed to make it profitable. He began distributing the detergent in China, simultaneously launching a major advertising campaign, using television, radio, and newspapers. But the product did not take off. Realizing he had to do more to attract attention, Teng put up a 700,000 yuan building on Shashi City's busiest commercial street. He then signed a contract to sponsor the province's struggling soccer team, which was renamed the *Hubei Power 28 Soccer Team,* and staged the first "Power 28 Soccer Match" at the city stadium.

The sponsorship was a rousing success. The fortunes of both Power 28 and the soccer team shot upward. Sales of Power 28 went from eight thousand to eighty thousand tons in two years, and the soccer team went from nowhere to fourth place in the National Games. Teng then contracted to finance the Shashi Han Opera Troupe and launched a new line of Power cosmetics. The company now has several joint factories in the Special Economic Zones of Hainan and Zhuhai and is expanding into overseas markets.

More on Gift-Giving

Just as in Japan, gift-giving in China has a long history with its own rules based on different social levels and the occasion. Since gift-giving on a large, costly scale may be construed as bribery, it is important that such implications be considered. Chinese law states clearly that individual gifts from foreigners are not to be accepted, but in actual practice it is illegal only for government officials to accept gifts. The law does not distinguish between a small, inexpensive gift and an expensive one. In the eyes of the law it is the gesture, not the value. However, the law overlooks the giving and receiving of small token gifts.

It is still common for executives of larger companies to give major household appliances and electronic equipment as gifts to top officials and high-ranking company managers, despite the fact that occasionally someone is brought to trial and punished for accepting such beneficence.

In any event, gifts given should suit the individual and the occasion.

Lower-ranking people receive correspondingly less expensive items. Some things that are popular now are elaborate appointment books, pen sets, calculators, colorful calendars, travel books in full color, and subscriptions to well-known magazines like *National Geographic* and *Arizona Highways*. Some insiders advise that personal gifts to individuals should be small enough that they can be pocketed and taken home without attracting any attention, and that they should be given discreetly when you are alone with the individual.

IBM is one of the few foreign companies with enough clout to break the circle of gift-giving, limiting it to the two main annual gift-giving occasions— National Day on October 1 and Chinese New Year's in February.

It is frequently noted that people with political power in China do not need money. Officials are in fact paid relatively low salaries, but many manage to live as if they were very affluent. In addition to a variety of real gifts, they receive numerous benefits in kind from people and companies who want their goodwill and/or their cooperation. These benefits run the gamut from free trips, medical attention, and hard-to-get repair services to entry into prestigious schools for their children.

A leading economic newspaper in Beijing recently ran a cartoon depicting the gift-giving circle that exists in virtually all areas of Chinese life. The drawing showed cakes and liquor being passed around in an unending circle, which included people wanting to travel abroad, people seeking housing, parents wanting their child in a good school, and so on. (Many people who receive liquor as a gift never drink it. They pass it on to someone else.)

Person-to-Person Communication

One point that new as well as old China hands repeatedly emphasize is the importance of person-to-person communication in doing business in China. They point out that unless the Chinese know you personally and have acknowledged your existence, you do not exist, and no amount of letter writing, telexing, or faxing will do any good.

The Chinese political system does not favor its citizens making friends with foreigners, either for specific business purposes or for social reasons. From the government viewpoint, all relationships with foreigners should be limited to those between offices, companies, and other organizations, and not be put on a personal level. And all those wonderful toasts to friendship cannot be taken too personally—except perhaps for billionaire businesspeople and ex-government leaders who have established an enduring rapport with the highest levels of Chinese officials.

Of course, the government's attitude toward relationships between ordinary people is virtually impossible to enforce, but it does tend to put a damper on the social life of foreign businesspeople in China.

What to Translate

Generally, the more of your material you can translate into Chinese the better off you will be from the viewpoint of clear communication and time. When translations are left to the Chinese side, you lose a lot of control, and it usually takes a long time because the translation sections of the various ministries and organizations are invariably overloaded with work.

Taking Group Rosters

It is a good idea for business groups to prepare rosters of their members, including pertinent biographical and professional information about each member. You should send these to China in advance and take along ample copies to pass out to appropriate officials and managers not on the mailing list.

Taking Your Own Plugs

If you are going to be using any kind of audiovisual or other type of electrical equipment during your visit to China, especially in outlying provincial cities, it is a good idea to carry with you an assortment of adaptors and electrical plugs, since sockets are not always standard. International hotels can usually be depended upon for transformers and adaptors.

The Workload and Punctuality

Business groups invited to China should be prepared for a full, heavy schedule. The Chinese appreciate evening banquets, brief side trips for sightseeing (usually on Sundays) during business trips, and short rest breaks, but they do their best to get as much as possible out of every encounter.

Another point to keep in mind is that the Chinese are sticklers for punctuality. They expect people to be on time or early for appointments and meetings. Being late is regarded as lacking in sincerity and concern for others.

Chinese Versus Japanese

A Chinese attorney-friend in Beijing repeated a popular story about the reaction of foreign businesspeople to Chinese as compared to Japanese. The foreigner, the attorney said, does not have to be afraid of a one-on-one situation with a Japanese because individually the Japanese tend to be weak and easily intimidated by their foreign counterparts. The situation is reversed, however, when foreign businesspeople are faced by two Japanese because they "team up" and are therefore able to outlast and outmaneuver them, he continued.

On the other hand, the attorney went on, foreign businesspeople have learned to be cautious in dealing with a single Chinese because he or she functions best alone. Put two Chinese (of equal status) together, however, and you have an instant conflict. They will disagree and argue and present a divided front, weakening their bargaining powers, he said.

The attorney also reemphasized that patience and persistence, coupled with the age-old practice of "buying" cooperation through doing favors and giving gifts, is still an essential ingredient in doing business in China. He illustrated the point: "On your first visit to a government official it is very unlikely that he will do anything on your behalf. If you remain polite and deferential and leave some kind of desirable gift (which the official will repeatedly tell you he cannot accept), and then go back a second and probably a third time, continuing to nurture the relationship, chances are the official will eventually say, 'What can I do for you?' and then proceed to do it.''

In another scenario comparing one of the differences between Western and Japanese businesspeople in China, the attorney said a Japanese will go to an office for some kind of official action or help that he needs, be put off with some excuse and told to come back again—maybe two or three days or even a week or more later. The Japanese will quietly accept the situation and come back when he is told to.

Western businesspeople, however, and particularly Americans, are very likely to point out that they are going to be in China for only a certain number of days, that it is costing them enormous amounts of money to stay there, that what they are trying to do will benefit China, and so on. This reaction generally has no positive effect at all on the Chinese. In fact, it is very likely to make the Chinese cadre even less cooperative. When the Chinese repeats what he or she said the first time, foreigners often say that they cannot possibly stay several more days or whatever. To which the typical response from the Chinese is "suit yourself."

Japanese Success in China

Japan has the largest share of China's world trade despite the very real presence of anti-Japanese feelings among the Chinese. Arne J. de Keijzer, one of the foremost authorities on doing business in China, attributes this success to the carefully calculated way the Japanese approach the Chinese market. He delineates this approach into several categories:

1. The Japanese saturate the country, not just Beijing, with technical, sales, and support people (whereas American and European companies generally send in only one or two people).
2. The Japanese aggressively discount their prices until they get the market, then make their profits from spare parts and services.
3. The Japanese offer package deals, even bringing in competing firms, to cover virtually every aspect of the venture.
4. The Japanese readily accept compensation in trade arrangements, a type of trade in which they lead the world.
5. Sharing the same cultural experience as the Chinese, the Japanese are masters at using the Chinese system of connections and gift-giving and taking advantage of the similarity of written Japanese and Chinese. Most Japanese executives assigned to China have also studied Mandarin, giving them an overwhelming advantage.
6. The Japanese government makes low-cost loans available to Chinese who agree to buy equipment made in Japan.

Foreign businesspeople, as well as foreign governments, can learn something from the Japanese approach.

Injecting a Cultural Element

Foreign businesspeople who are eager to demonstrate their diligence, integrity, trustworthiness, and social responsibility to the Chinese can help their cause by incorporating cultural and educational elements into their business relationships. Like Japanese and Koreans, the cultural component in the Chinese value scale is very strong and close to their heart. They are also strongly committed to raising China's educational level and react positively to long-term programs designed to contribute to that goal.

In all dealings with the Chinese, it is vital to keep in mind that the very foundations of American business—profit-making, promotions based on accomplishments, competition on an individual level, independent thought and action, individual responsibility—are still new to the Chinese and, in some cases, either socially and/or politically unacceptable or illegal. This difference is of course compounded by the fact that the Chinese committee system based on a hierarchical arrangement of government bureaucrats makes any kind of understanding and cooperative effort challenging to the mind, spirit, and stamina.

At best it is going to take one or two decades for the Chinese to assimilate the broad themes of economic and social change that have already been introduced. In the meantime, the lot of many of the country's millions of private and individual enterprise operators is far from rosy. The following are among their long list of complaints: they had to grease palms to get permits to start their businesses in the first place; they have to work harder and longer hours than state employees, while taking much greater risks; government-run companies frequently refuse to do business with them; prejudice toward private enterprise is still strong and disrupting; laws pertaining to private enterprise do not provide sufficient protection; and their children do not have access to kindergartens subsidized by state-run agencies.

Growing Successes

Despite appearances, the growing number of foreign businesspeople who are succeeding in China is proof that the problems are not overwhelming. Also of vital importance is that the Chinese are rapidly filing off the rough edges of their system, making it more and more responsive to both the domestic and foreign marketplaces. As long as there is common interest and goodwill, virtually any problem can eventually be resolved with common sense, courtesy, and patience.

"There are many absolutely brilliant men and women in China, wonderfully sophisticated and international in their thinking, and if you look carefully at what they are trying to do for China you cannot help but be impressed, even awed, considering the obstacles they must overcome," said a British expatriate.

"Now is an exciting time in the history of China, and it is especially important for everyone, particularly educators, writers, and other mind-molders to act responsibly. The attitude of the Chinese government and the people in general is that they must learn as much as possible from other countries but be very selective in the process, taking only what will be beneficial to China in the long run," he added.

In any event, foreign businesspeople must learn how to manipulate their Chinese employees and use the traditional system of connections or go home, said one veteran expatriate. He added a warning to foreign businesspeople preparing to move to China: "Don't come with a marriage problem, a health problem, or a psychological problem! China will make them worse and probably destroy you.

"The foreigner in China lives in a goldfish bowl. Whatever insecurities or problems you have will be made worse. Just surviving is an emotional drain. Expatriates must recognize this China syndrome in their friends and colleagues and help them as much as possible. People who do not recognize the symptoms of the syndrome and do not share the problems are the ones who don't make it—and when they break no one will help them. To succeed here you must have extraordinary staying power—which often means that the best person for the job is not necessarily the most capable or the most brilliant. Anyone who lasts for four years in China and remains healthy in mind and spirit is a remarkable individual.''

Ongoing hassles facing foreign businesspeople in China are dealing with air or rail transportation to provincial cities and making sure that hotel accommodations are in order. Travel agents regularly buy up large blocks of seats between major destinations, leaving few for businesspeople, especially on short notice.

It is generally not recommended that foreigners drive in China, but more and more of them do so because the only other viable choice is taxis. The chances of an accident are very high, and under Chinese law the driver is held accountable for the accident regardless of who was at fault. Where foreigners are concerned, this can require a very high compensation to any Chinese victim or the surviving family. The amount of compensation is determined by the driver's ability to pay or the ability of his company to pay. Representatives of large, presumably wealthy, companies are fined accordingly. Generally, foreigners who are involved in traffic fatalities are expected to leave the country as soon as they have paid whatever fines were levied.

A sinister aspect of traffic accidents involving foreigners is that some of the people killed appear to have been deliberate victims. Local informants say the practice is fairly common. An elderly member of a family in dire straits will deliberately rush into the path of an oncoming vehicle, knowing that the surviving family will receive substantial compensation.

Another point to consider is whether or not overseas Chinese make good managers in China. According to some, the Chinese do not like overseas Chinese on a personal basis, particularly those from Hong Kong and Singapore. They often clash in ways that are far more subtle and important than the friction that is common between Chinese and Caucasian Westerners. Third parties say the overseas Chinese look down on mainland Chinese and are frequently arrogant in their behavior. One reason for this, say others, is that most of the Singapore and Hong Kong Chinese who come to China do so strictly for the money so they can buy citizenship in Australia, Canada, or the United States, and get out of Asia as quickly as possible.

At the same time, there are many who say Chinese from Singapore and Hong Kong make ideal managers in China, not only because they generally speak Mandarin, but also because they are not hesitant about being frank and persistent in dealing with employees. They are therefore able to get things done whereas Caucasian managers often hold back for fear of irreparably offending anyone.

Overseas Chinese who have returned to China as expatriate businesspeople are often put in untenable positions by their relatives who can be relentless in their demands for help, financial and otherwise. The Chinese in general, and especially bureaucrats and officials, also expect more and demand more from overseas Chinese, laying a much heavier burden on them to work for and sacrifice for the motherland. The double bind on overseas Chinese sometimes is serious enough to burn them out in two or three years.

The Legal Maze

One expatriate businessman who had the great fortune to start his career in China as a Mandarin language scholar warned that foreign businesspeople should not take China's ongoing economic reforms, usually announced in the form of new laws, too literally too soon. He explained: "Chinese laws are written in very vague terms, in some cases to the degree that they are almost useless. Just about every new law pertaining to business also includes what amounts to a disclaimer, such as: 'It is preferred that you continue doing business the same way you have been doing it but if you cannot, then you may follow this new law, but to do so you must obtain official permission.' In other words, you have to negotiate for the right to make use of new laws.

"Resident foreign businessmen often get copies of new laws before the Chinese do, and there is usually a hassle to convince the Chinese that it is all right to take advantage of the laws. They are invariably reluctant to change anything, even when there is legal foundation for the change. One reason for this attitude and behavior is the pressure that government ministries put on them to conform to the already established ways."

He added that the situation had improved considerably, however, after Chinese lawyers were authorized to provide legal counsel to foreign firms.

Being able to read as well as speak Mandarin, this businessman is able to monitor events in China far more comprehensively and effectively than most expatriates. He is very optimistic about the reforms now taking place in China but again cautions that it is still a dedicated Communist regime that runs the country.

"The government cannot go too far in its reforms," he said. "It must maintain its legitimacy, and the only way it can do that is by creating and maintaining a mythology of its right to govern. When you pin the top leaders down, their ultimate response is the party line, no matter how unreal it might sound. I do not see the system changing fundamentally for many years. The Communist party has too much invested in it. It would be too painful for them to make the political decisions necessary to really establish a democratic system."

Commenting on some of the more significant improvements that have impacted on his life in China, this observer noted: "A heightened sense of time and money; greater efficiency; a vastly improved telecommunications system that is continuing to improve; and a significant reduction in the number of meetings necessary to do business. The Chinese now will even come to you."

The Non-Confucian View

A growing number of Chinese have become very critical of the continuing influence of the teachings of Confucius on the nation's political and economic systems. They now say Confucianism was one of the primary reasons China remained virtually stagnant for nearly two thousand years, and still today is more of a hindrance than a help. They say that the economic success of Japan, South Korea, Taiwan, Hong Kong, and Singapore resulted because they adopted Western educational, legal, political, and economic systems. They add that social changes already well advanced in these successful Asian countries clearly reveal that Confucian values are incompatible with individualism, democracy, and free enterprise.

Sociologists in Taiwan and Hong Kong buttress this judgment, noting that Confucian values are being rapidly eroded in their areas, and the gap between Confucian ethics and "modern people" is widening still. They also note that where Confucianism and capitalism coexist, the Confucian system suffers in comparison and is often a totally negative influence.

Corruption and the abuse of power, both of which were traditional in Confucian China, are ranked by the government as among the biggest threats to its reform programs. Official party publications are filled with stories exposing cadre for using their positions to get rich quick. They also warn that if those who are guilty are not severely punished the standards of social conduct in general will continue to deteriorate.

Government spokespeople say that the more there is to steal, the larger the cancer of corruption grows. Foreign businesspeople add that government officials who used to be satisfied with just gifts may now ask for foreign currency. One of the techniques used by officials to extract gifts from foreigners was to say they needed more *yen jiu* or "study time" before a business proposal could be approved. In the northern Chinese dialect, *yen jiu* also means "tobacco and liquor," and is used as a euphemism for gifts.

In its efforts to curb the spread of corruption, the Chinese government encourages foreign businesspeople to report officials who attempt to use their positions to enrich themselves. In August 1988, China's new Ministry of Supervision established a network of "Corruption Report Centers" designed to encourage people—both resident foreign businesspeople and Chinese—to "supervise the work of government officials" and to make it easier for them to expose all abuses of government power. The Corruption Report Center in Beijing has a 24-hour telephone line. The number to call is 202-5391.

Cultural Weaknesses

Other weaknesses of traditional Chinese culture, particularly when compared to Western culture, are the subject of heated discussion and debate among Chinese intellectual circles. One school of thought says that the Chinese have no morality of their own because total immersion in Confucianism made it impossible for them to have personal opinions and that all they could do was to adapt to the judgments of others regardless of how ludicrous those judgments might be.

This same school adds that since the Chinese have been conditioned to be dependent and obedient, both their personality and ego were impaired or destroyed completely. This, they add, was not conducive to the development of logical thought or science and puts China at a serious disadvantage in competing with advanced nations. Social commentator Xiaoda Fan says that the Chinese people must make a complete break with their old culture and create a new national character for themselves—one based on freedom of thought and activity in which the individual's personal qualities can be developed to their fullest.

Sidestepping Socialism

More and more social scientists in China are also repudiating socialism as unrealistic and unworkable and are openly advocating "capitalistic competition." Says Honglin Li: "Since a socialist society cannot eliminate competition, the only way out is to face up to the reality and let competition work." He adds that normal competition works at its best only in an environment of personal freedom, openness, and a commitment to equality. The challenge, he continues, is to utilize part of the wealth created by the capitalistic system to remedy the social ills that accompany it.

Political Conflicts

There are obvious serious political conflicts in today's China that go well beyond Chinese and foreigners dancing with each other. For some four thousand years, the people were steeped in the tenets of feudal autocracy. Following the establishment of New China in 1949, communism became the new religion, grafted onto the age-old feudal system. The present political policy is designed to create a democratic socialist country, with strongly capitalistic overtones. But since there has been no education or experience in socialism, democracy, or capitalism, the process is something like the traditional blind committee making an elephant.

What exists at this time is a mishmash of communism, socialism, and capitalism still grafted onto the huge autocratic feudal trunk. The feudalistic roots and limbs of virtually every system in society, in the government, and in business are clearly visible. Chances are this feudalistic facet will remain the primary element in life and work in China for at least the next two or three generations.

Generally speaking, the top people in a ministry, state office, or enterprise are still viewed by the people below them as a supreme authority, as a modern-day Mandarin with all the rights and prerogatives exercised by these dynastic feudal lords. The people do not expect them to share any of their power, and the tendency is to leave all decisions up to them. In most cases, whether they want to or not, they are forced to make all decisions, including minor ones.

Never having lived in a country of laws, the Chinese are conditioned to expect that policies and procedures will change every time the top person changes. Their relationship is therefore with that person and not the company or the institution. This has profound consequences when it comes to their attitude and behavior toward the company that employs them and the office or department where they work. Maintaining the proper relationship with the boss, as seen from the feudalistic Chinese viewpoint, takes precedence over their work. Joint-venture managers face a real problem in reorienting the thinking and behavior of their employees, to get them to understand that doing their job right and well is their primary responsibility—and the *only* way to please the boss.

The official policy of the government is that China is to learn from the West and incorporate all that is good and beneficial from capitalism into the Chinese system. But there is an enormous gap between such pronouncements and the reality of the workplace. China's millions of cadre and business managers are more or less on their own when it comes to interpreting and implementing government policy. And they do so to a great extent on the basis of their own feudalistic views and experience.

Yet there are rays of hope that the practical nature of the Chinese will help lead them out of the present political maze. Well-known economist Dalin Tong, formerly vice-minister of China's State Commission for Restructuring the Economy and later head of an economic research group, says that the teachings of Marx and Lenin regarding the evils of capitalism are no longer valid and that capitalism today is quite different from what it was in their time. He adds that there are certain facets of capitalism, such as the market-oriented economy, that are a matter of "common economic law" and should not be labeled with any of the "isms." He says that no country, regardless of its political structure, can develop its economy unless it follows the basic economic laws.

The most dangerous problem faced by Chinese leaders is coordinating the conversion of the economy from state control to free market control while preventing runaway inflation and satisfying the still powerful Marxist-Leninist faction that is determined to perpetuate the communist system. Communist ideologues are now pitted against homegrown economists. China's future hinges on the outcome of the struggle.

China's Educational Hang-Up

Like many other countries that put a high premium on academic credentials as opposed to innovative thinking and practical experience, China's headlong rush to modernize itself is often hampered by laws and customs that give precedence to people with diplomas rather than ability. Complaints about this sort of discrimination are especially common because so many Chinese with degrees have only theoretical knowledge without ever having had the opportunity to put it to practical use.

Social critics point to another "problem" the Chinese must overcome before they will be able to create a rational society, with their values "in the right place." These critics single out the traditional Chinese obsession with the pursuit of perfection, and how this results in all sorts of irrational behavior that often ends up destroying the very perfection they seek.

Ren Si, writing in *Liberation Daily*, quoted the ancient chinese writer Xun Lu in describing this particular mentality. Lu wrote: "If you are not born a saint, hero, or genius, then don't get born. If your book is not an immortal masterpiece, then don't write it. If a reform cannot make the world a paradise overnight, or at least result in immediate benefits, then forget it."

This attitude, Si says, is still visible in China today, and is dangerous because it leads to a dead end.

Yet the government is making heroic efforts to help overcome the scarcity of technically educated and professionally trained people in all areas of administration and industry. In the early 1980s, state-run technical schools and colleges all over the country opened their doors to millions of adults in their thirties and forties who had missed out on education because of the Cultural Revolution. The government also initiated nationwide retraining of millions of employees in state-run enterprises, both to increase efficiency and to move them into new, more worthwhile jobs.

Reinventing the Great Exams

Unable and unwilling to cut too many ties with the past, the Chinese government in 1988 reinstated the national competitive examination system for civil servants—something that had set the character and tone of both government and society of Imperial China for nearly two thousand years.

Under the new system, all employees of ministries and agencies, including international bodies, as well as some provincial and city officials, must pass examinations that are open to all. As part of the system, the government has set up a national and several local colleges of administration where people wanting to enter government service can go for specialized study.

By opening up civil service to anyone who is qualified according to today's standards, the new system is expected to have a dramatic effect in reestablishing confidence in the government that was lost due to the Cultural Revolution (1966–1976).

Where Is China Going?

Foreign businesspeople in China must always be aware of the cultural element of both the principles and practices of business. Business cannot be separated from society and all its cultural complexities, as is the tendency in the West. Foreign businesspeople must also be constantly aware of and deal with the fact that relations with their Chinese counterparts are held together by personal factors that transcend material things and profits. To the foreigner whose loyalties in business are more likely to be determined by the bottom line, this can be a Catch-22 situation.

The typical Chinese is a bundle of complex beliefs that are ages old and are often opposed to both the social and economic changes occurring in China today. No matter how sincerely he may want to see the country modernized, he cannot easily or quickly cast aside the things that make him Chinese. When these conflicts and contradictions are mixed with the ancient Chinese habit of viewing things in terms of decades and generations, the Chinese face formidable handicaps in dealing with the West on any terms other than their own. There are important implications in this point.

Deep down, the Chinese, just like the Japanese, have a visceral dread of foreigners taking over their country economically and politically if they relax their guard. They also feel strongly that culturally they are the superior nation and once they have overcome the technological gap, relationships between China and the rest of the world will assume their natural order.

Just like the Japanese, the Chinese *do not want permanent relationships with foreign businesspeople*. Despite declarations of eternal friendship, the Chinese want close cooperative relationships with foreigners for only as long as it takes them to learn all they can, and then they will go on their own. Just as the Japanese severed all relationships with American and European importers and set up their own importing and distribution systems in the West as soon as they became strong enough to do so, the Chinese will naturally follow the same formula.

In the minds of the Chinese, the rest of the world is there to serve China, and eventually to learn from China. This mentality is not unique to Japan or China. Every great nation of the past, including the United States, has been motivated by this belief in its imperial destiny. The world is already acutely aware of where this drive has taken Japan—a country that is miniscule in size and potential when compared to China. This should be given some thought by the world at large.

The prevailing mood of much of China today is one of discontent. Virtually everybody wants more than they have and are frustrated that they cannot get it quickly. This feeling is manifested in many ways, including the way many people greet each other. Greetings are often negative. They feel so misused and abused, so left out, it colors their view of everything. They have been made suspicious of the outside world and from long and painful experience do not trust their own government. A significant percentage of those who work in foreign-affiliated firms and get a taste of what life is like for other people develop an overwhelming compulsion to get out of China.

For the typical foreigner, living and working in China is both a challenge and a sacrifice. Except in Beijing, good housing as well as office space is still scarce and what does exist is expensive. Many companies as well as their managers are still housed in hotel rooms. The biggest boon to the foreign community in Beijing has been the large hotel complexes that include residential, commercial office, and recreational facilities, pioneered by Holiday Inn Lido, a joint venture between the well-known hotel chain and Chinese interests.

The success of the Holiday Inn Lido complex inspired a number of similar office-residential-recreational complexes, most on a much smaller scale, and turned it into a model for growing foreign communities in other parts of China.

Outside of the Lido and other large international hotels in Beijing and the equivalent hotel facilities in other cities, recreational opportunities for foreigners, other than sightseeing and bicycling, are rare. Even sightseeing in China has its downside. Transportation is scarce. Land travel is both scarce and basic in its amenities. Destinations are crowded. For those whose taste for Chinese food has been developed in the world's Chinatowns, or Tokyo, Taipei, Hong Kong, or Singapore, the fare served in most Chinese restaurants may not qualify as edible. About the only expatriates who choose to spend their holidays and leaves in China are those with a masochistic streak.

Family members (of foreign businesspeople stationed in China) who do not speak Chinese, especially if they are there for the first time, often spend most of the time holed up in their apartment, "living in total fear," as one put it. Their fear covers everything—not knowing, not being able to communicate, not being able to help themselves. It is something like suddenly being struck both deaf and dumb and not knowing sign language.

Other than this kind of culture shock, there is very little if anything to fear in China. There is no sense of tension or danger in the country. Despite recent reports, China is far from being a police state. One seldom sees police officers. The ones you do see are not armed. People come and go freely. There are simply too many people, both Chinese and foreign, coming and going for even the most efficient security apparatus to keep record of them. Old-time residents say it was never really as bad in the early 1980s as some stories made it out to be, and that much of the reaction was just paranoia.

Be that as it may, one's privacy is still subject to being breached. One foreign lady recounted that when she came out of the shower one day (in 1988) there were five Chinese women in her living room, going through her personal things. She said she also knew of other cases in which apartments were searched.

There is also a general belief among foreign residents that "bugs" are still common in foreign offices and residences, but no one offered any proof. "If they do exist," said one, "it would take an army of multilingual, multicultural listeners to make any sense of it. It just doesn't *make* any sense, so I don't worry about it."

One of the greatest luxuries for the bulk of all Chinese is the opportunity to take a hot shower. Some foreign residents make a practice of inviting their closer Chinese friends in to use their showers.

Compared to its major cities, life in much of rural China has stood still. The people live and work much as they have since the early 1900s. A typical town of one thousand inhabitants has no running water, only one community bath, and one washing facility. Businesspeople who have traveled to factories and industrial sites in the hinterlands say that conditions are often primitive, and employees effectively work only two or three hours a day.

In advising newcomers on the pitfalls as well as pleasures of living and working in China, old-timers regularly note that Beijing is not China; that while there are basic similarities in business etiquette and ethics throughout the country, there are just as many if not more differences. In generalizing, they say that the biggest handicap for businesspeople in Beijing is the excessive bureaucracy; that Shanghai businesspeople, who are famed for their skill in negotiating and getting the best possible deal, get so caught up in negotiating that it takes forever to get a contract signed; and that businesspeople in Guangzhou are anxious to make a fast buck and go into contracts so quickly that you have to be extra careful about their deals falling through.

One veteran British businessman said that it was probably more difficult to do business in Beijing than anywhere else in China because the various ministries are always looking over your shoulder. "The red tape is redder in Beijing," he said.

While there are distinctive cultural differences among the Chinese in each of the major geographic divisions of China, the primary factors affecting business, and making the conduct of business different, are not cultural but political. All of the open cities, counties, and provinces have their own business regulations and requirements, along with different attitudes about dealing with foreign companies. Generally speaking, they are more liberal and more cooperative than what one experiences in Beijing.

In Beijing the control that some state offices were exercising over joint ventures as late as 1989 included such things as the color of new buildings and their wallpaper, the size of windows, and the number of employees the company had to hire.

Letting the Hair Down

The standard scenario of business entertainment by the Chinese, besides the famous dinner banquets, includes escorted sightseeing trips, invitations to cultural events, and help with shopping trips. The foreign side, particularly if it is made up of a group of negotiators, is expected to reciprocate only on the dinner. A very encouraging development in the mid-1980s was the growing willingness of many Chinese businesspeople and some officials to accept invitations by foreigners to informal lunches or dinners at hotels and elsewhere.

Western-style bars had made a comeback in New China by the end of the 1980s, particularly in Guangdong Province and not only in major cities and the Shenzhen Special Economic Zone but in smaller cities as well. The better of the bars are attractively decorated and feature full-course meals prepared by experienced cooks—some of them hired from Macao and Hong Kong. Some of the pioneering proprietors also had experience operating bars in Hong Kong and elsewhere outside China. Most of the bars have taped light music and popular songs. In some cities, discos are popular as are rooftop restaurants that appear in the summer.

Another type of nightspot that began proliferating in the mid-1980s were "Kala OK" bars, which were a takeoff on the *Karaoke* (kah-rah-oh-kay) or "Empty Orchestra" bars of Japan. These are bars with microphones and sound systems that encourage patrons to get up and sing their favorite songs, just like professional entertainers. The name comes from the fact that the taped music gives one the impression of singing before a live orchestra. According to newspaper reports, a number of people with extraordinary talent have been "discovered" in the *Kala OK* bars and have gone on to become successful professionals.

Elsewhere, recreational facilities for the Chinese in general continue to increase in variety and volume, from public swimming pools to billiards, snooker, dancehalls, discos, and *qigong* deep-breathing exercise parlors. The Zhubo Swimming Pool in Tianjin complex covers eighteen thousand square meters, and boasts a multilaned fifty-meter water slide.

While Western-style nightlife in China is growing gradually, it is still rare and tame by standards that exist in the rest of Asia. In addition to casual meetings in hotel lounges and recreational facilities, the most common opportunity foreign businesspeople have to associate with their Chinese counterparts is at banquet-style meals and afternoon receptions. Despite the ceremonial formality at Chinese banquets, which primarily has to do with seating by rank, the parties usually become quite informal as they proceed, with casual conversation, funny stories, and jokes just as common in China as anywhere else. It is generally advisable, however, to refrain from the more risque jokes and comments that are typical of such gatherings in the West.

Chinese businessmen and government officials seldom if ever involve their wives in their "business" banquets or receptions. If you are invited to a businessman's home, his wife will generally not join in any conversation, and except when serving something, will remain in the kitchen or elsewhere in the house. Exceptions occur, of course, when the wife has become Westernized.

Rules for Working in China

A growing number of foreigners now employed in China first went there as students or as dependents of diplomatic or commercial entrants stationed there. Employment regulations for foreign students and for other foreigners without residence permits are the same (and cover those who are in China with class F, L, G, or C visas, along with those whose residence permits have been withdrawn because of changes in their visa status).

Foreigners under any of the above visas cannot apply for a job in China unless they are over the age of eighteen, hold valid passports and visas, and have a skill or specialized knowledge that is vital for the jobs they are applying for (if the work they are proposing to do is really needed by the potential employer and cannot be done by an available Chinese).

If these conditions are met, the individual applies to the local Labor and Personnel Bureau for a work license, following which a contract for one year may be signed with the employer. The employed foreigner must then go to the local Public Security office within ten days to apply for a change of status and a residence permit. The employment license, a work contract, and a health certificate must be presented to the Public Security department. At present, employment licenses for people in these categories may be extended only once.

Summary Reminders

Expect Chinese negotiators to question everything, repeatedly, ad infinitum, and to come up with cost factors that are well above what you imagined they would be. Also be cautious about accepting anything at face value. Negotiators often report that things are going well when they are not. Factory managers do the same thing. It is important to keep your antenna up and your feelers out.

Be cautious of grand-sounding commitments made by officials, especially if you are asked to spend a lot of up-front money. They have a habit of not fully explaining their projects or goals and have been known to lead enthusiastic foreign investors astray. What you see is often not what you are going to get. Many of the joint ventures that are now operating successfully, and receiving positive publicity, were achieved only after years of painful and costly experiences and often then only after intercession by top Chinese leaders to avoid serious negative publicity.

The Chinese do not resolve issues or make decisions at the negotiating table. These are done after and in between meetings. It is also customary for them to informally and unofficially drop hints and make inquiries outside of the meeting rooms, during breaks, and at night.

The Western method of doing things is the straightforward cause-and-effect approach. The Chinese method might be called a grid or web approach, involving many other considerations, some of which appear to have little if any relationship with the matter at hand. Their attitudes and behavior are therefore often incomprehensible to the Westerner.

When things are not going well, the Chinese will often deliberately delay the proceedings by using all kinds of tactics, without explanation, rather than admit it isn't working out. If the problems are not eventually resolved, the whole project finally just dwindles and dies.

As soon as foreign expatriates learn something about the Chinese and begin to express the Chinese viewpoint to their head office—as part of their efforts to explain a situation—they are in danger of being accused of going over to the enemy, of no longer properly representing their own company. They are thus confronted with having to deal with cultural gaps in front of them as well as behind them.

Foreign expatriates in China are subject to acute attacks of paranoia—paralyzing feelings that the Chinese are doing everything possible to not only defeat them but to bring themselves down as well. An extraordinary effort, plus support from the home office, family, and friends, is necessary for them to transcend this feeling, see the big picture, and hang in.

Policy changes are likely to occur overnight, without warning. It is therefore essential that foreign businesspeople keep a very open and flexible mind, and stay light on their feet.

The cross-cultural strain of working with the Chinese cannot be ignored. It is real and it is serious. And it is accumulative. A lot of little things over a period of time can break the strongest expatriate's back.

In evaluating possible candidates for assignments in China, choosing someone just because they have spent time there can be a costly mistake. Many foreigners who have spent years in China may know a lot of surface things about the country but have no skill at all in cross-cultural communicating and dealing effectively with the Chinese. In this case, cross-cultural expertise, which may have been obtained in some other country, is the most important qualification.

Learning Some New Skills

First-time visitors to Hong Kong, China, and other areas in Southeast Asia where there are large Chinese populations are seldom there for more than a day before they come across one or more Chinese engaging in a form of graceful, outside exercise that resembles a slow-motion dance. The individual or individuals engaging in the exercise may be on a rooftop, in a small park, on a dock, or just in some small secluded spot off the street. Wherever they are, the participants appear to be in a world of their own.

This distinctive Chinese practice, usually an early morning activity starting at sunrise, is sometimes called "Chinese shadowboxing" by foreigners— more and more of whom are being attracted to the exercise. In Chinese it is known as *Dai Ji Juan* or "Great Ultimate Fist."

Legend has it that the practice of *Dai Ji Juan* was originated during the Tang Dynasty about a thousand years ago by one Hsu Hsien-p'ing, but Sanfeng Chang, apparently a disciple, is credited with conceiving the theory behind the exercise after watching a fight between a large bird and a snake. The snake avoided attack after attack just by moving its body in a carefully controlled manner. Finally, the bird tired, misjudged its timing, and became the victim of a lightning strike by the snake.

Dai Ji Juan consists of thirteen movements, eight with the arms and five with the legs, all performed slowly and with perfect balance, so that all the nerves and muscles of the body are brought into play. It stimulates the body and calms it at the same time, thereby promoting health and longevity. The exercise is said to be especially helpful in eliminating and preventing headaches, digestive problems, and rheumatism, and to be ideal for all ages, since it requires neither strength nor stamina. The movements of the arms are all circular as the body is gradually turned to eight points on the compass, which figuratively denote the cyclical changes in the cosmos and the evolution of nature.

Later disciples of *Dai Ji Juan* developed it into a martial art for use in fighting. The principle is to always retreat in the face of an attack and then to counterattack when the enemy overreaches himself. The body movements of the *Dai Ji Juan* fighter emulate those of the snake, keeping the adversary puzzled and denying any opportunity to strike a decisive blow.

Chinese practitioners of *Dai Ji Juan* are always willing to teach the exercise portion of the art. In fact, many people, foreigners included, are first initiated simply by showing up at a spot used by Chinese, taking a position a few yards away, and imitating the actions of the more skilled performers.

Foreign visitors in China (as well as Taiwan, Hong Kong, and Singapore) might take advantage of the opportunity to get some personal instruction in *Dai Ji Juan*—something that could well enhance both their mental and physical health and help establish lifelong relationships with Chinese.

Acupuncture

The businessperson in China who comes down with some kind of physical complaint might also take advantage of the opportunity to try acupuncture. This form of treatment originated in China at least 2,500 years ago and is available in all modern Chinese hospitals today.

Acupuncture is based on inserting thin needles (now often stimulated with an electrical current) into "energy channels" on various places of the body to alter the flow and distribution of the energy—to cure ailments as well as prevent them. There are said to be over 650 such "meridian points" on the body but only about a hundred of them are regularly used.

At this point, Western medical authorities dispute the Chinese belief of "energy flow" in the body and the relationship of this flow with the health of the various body organs. Some Western doctors say, however, that acupuncture does appear to act as a painkiller. Acupuncture treatment generally consists of several sessions, depending on the nature and seriousness of the illness.

Deep Breathing

Another skill that foreign visitors in China might find interesting is known as *qigong* (chi-gung) or "deep breathing." It is an ancient technique that is said to dramatically improve one's peace of mind, health, and longevity.

Qigong is also promoted as a technique for helping obese patients lose weight and thereby reduce high blood pressure.

Qigong dates from the period of Ze Dao in the seventh century B.C. *Qi* refers to the vital energy or "force" of life, which might be compared with electricity. Just as electricity gives "life" to a piece of mechanical or electronic equipment, *qi* does the same for the human body. Chinese scientists say they have not been able to explain *qi* through biological science, but that they believe it is in fact a special form of energy.

Over the centuries, people who mastered the use of *qi* were able to achieve extraordinary mental and physical feats that go well beyond what is recognized or explainable by modern-day science—to the extent that during different ages, masters of the art were accused of being practitioners of black magic.

Effort is now under way to establish a scientific basis for the ancient practice of *qigong*, directed by the China Qigong Science Research Center in Beijing. A staff of *qigong* masters and scientists are working to develop the art into an independent science.

The leading advocates of *qigong* today are scientists, engineers, and medical doctors, instead of monks as in the old days. One such group of professionals in Beijing founded the private China Qigong Training (or Refresher) College, which is devoted to training *qigong* teachers. The college also sponsored the research and writing of ten textbooks covering the history, theory, and practice of *qigong*. With an annual enrollment of some three hundred, the college already has several thousand graduates who have set up schools in their own districts. Administrators at the college say they regard *qigong* as a national treasure and believe it will be at the forefront of the life sciences in the twenty-first century. An estimated fifty million Chinese now practice *qigong* daily, and the numbers are growing rapidly.

7

Other Cultural Factors Affecting Business

Limits of Chinese Etiquette

The Chinese long ago made etiquette a key element in the foundation of their culture and turned the learning and following of graceful manners into a life-long discipline. Formal, as well as informal behavior, was built around specific rituals that symbolized the hierarchical relationships between people.

The rituals of etiquette were not just surface manifestations of good behavior. They embodied the Chinese concept of cosmology, ethics, morality, and the law, and applied to everyone. Despite the great economic and social gap between the elite of China and the great mass of peasants, their manners and ethics were based on the same philosophical principles, with the same or similar symbols and rituals.

There were so many rituals, and many of them were so complex that on the higher levels of society ritual masters were required to advise on when and how to follow them. Failure to perform a ritual or making a mistake in its performance was a serious matter.

A precise etiquette, as opposed to laws, thus became the basis for the structure and cohesiveness of Chinese society. Viewed from the inside, the logic of the system was impeccable. However, it did not prevent all friction or violence, and in fact was the source of much of the disorder that has traditionally afflicted China because it forced people into unnatural patterns of behavior and made most of them subject to the arbitrary rule of a tiny minority.

Still today, like most other Asians, the Chinese are famous for their politeness and protocol in formal and personal situations. But generally speaking, Chinese politeness pertains only to family, friends, and acquaintances. Strangers are beyond their circle of social responsibility.

There has never been a universal "good Samaritan" syndrome in China that went beyond one's own personal circle or group. For one thing, people have always had more than they could do just trying to look out for themselves. This, plus the exclusive nature of the family and group system, traditionally conditioned the Chinese to avoid unnecessary contact and involvement with other individuals and groups.

Chinese are not inherently antagonistic toward others unless they are in competition. They are just indifferent. When competition is present, however, they are quick to take action, including resorting to violence when they feel threatened or want to make a point.

As the Chinese become more and more mobile and the "caste" nature of the group system weakens, the self-imposed social walls separating them are gradually being lowered. All of these walls, however, are not likely to disappear in the foreseeable future.

In addition to group-orientation dividing the Chinese, there is also a deep-seated compulsion to avoid interacting with other people simply because there are so many of them. People packed together in situations where they have no private space and no way to escape literally *have* to withdraw into themselves and ignore those who are around them, in order to keep mentally balanced.

This tendency for people to withdraw into their own worlds when surrounded by others is not an exclusive Chinese trait. It is apparently universal and kicks in automatically within a short time when one is exposed to crowding. But it is a lot more conspicuous in China because it is combined with an equally deep-seated fear of endangering one's livelihood and survival, resulting in a callous disregard of nongroup members and their problems, as well as public things in general.

The compartmented behavior of the Chinese not only offends the sensibilities of most newcomers, but also has a direct, negative impact on business. It either totally prevents or greatly limits communication between different departments in the same company or government bureau and is one of the reasons why it generally takes an unreasonable amount of time to accomplish things in China.

Generally speaking, a Chinese in one part of a larger company cannot call up or visit someone in another department and ask for information or assistance without going through the whole routine of establishing a personal relationship with that person and creating a mutual obligation situation— something they are conditioned to avoid unless it is for their own personal benefit.

Introduction Protocol

When you introduce yourself or are introduced to the Chinese, it is polite protocol to shake hands first, then proffer your name card, using both hands. You should also say your name, surname first, with the usual "I am pleased to meet you" (or *Ni hao* / hello). It is also good Chinese manners to use both hands when accepting the other person's name card, demonstrating that you are aware of Chinese etiquette and respect their ways and sensitivities.

If you sit down at any kind of table after being introduced, it is both polite and practical to place the card or cards that you have just received on the table in front of you so you can refer to them. If several people are involved in the meeting, it pays to arrange the cards in the order in which the people are sitting so you can keep track of who is who.

The traditional custom in informal situations in China is to introduce the oldest person first. In formal situations, the most senior person should be introduced first, regardless of the age.

In formal sittings you should refer to your own colleagues and to the Chinese participants as Mr., Ms., or Mrs. It is also very acceptable to refer to senior Chinese participants by their professional title plus surname, such as President Chang, Vice-President Chang, or Chief Engineer Chang.

More and more Chinese businesspeople, especially those educated abroad, are adopting Western first names and welcome their use. However, they should not be used in formal sittings that include others who are not old, close friends.

You may meet new people who are obviously not Westernized but have nevertheless adopted Western first names for business convenience. It is generally wise not to use the first names until you have met the person several times and established a relationship, in order to avoid appearing shallow.

To traditional Chinese, the use of first names is rare and implies a degree of personal intimacy that can be misleading to both sides. If there is any doubt about what form of address to use, stick to the surname with the appropriate honorific (Mr., Ms., or Mrs.).

The Inscrutable Face

One of the Chinese traits that evolved from the need to protect face is the deeply ingrained habit of being indirect rather than direct in their verbal responses. They ask questions rather than make comments, modify or qualify everything they say, and often just remain silent.

There is no quick and easy way to change this aspect of Chinese behavior, so the challenge is to learn how to work with and around it. Patience, calm persistence, approaching the problem from different angles, and creativity devised on the spot are advised.

Favor, Face, and Fate

Contemporary Chinese philosopher Lin Yu-tang very succinctly summed up the traditional Chinese way as "favor, face, and fate." By this, he meant getting things done because of obligations that people owe you and doing things for others as favors for which you expect something in return. It also includes doing everything possible to protect your face and the face of family and friends and stoically accepting the natural and manmade vicissitudes of life as things that cannot be avoided.

This characterization, written in the 1930s, is still valid for some 90 percent or more of the one billion-plus mainland Chinese and will not change significantly anytime soon. In Taiwan, however, the changes in the attitudes and behavior of the people have been dramatic.

The New Taiwan Chinese

Despite the growing variety and volume of relationships between Taiwan and China proper, the Taiwanese are at least one and maybe two generations ahead of mainland Chinese in their evolution into free-thinking, free-speaking, free-spending practitioners of market economics.

In Taiwan, the Confucian-oriented beliefs and attitudes that sustained Chinese civilization for more than two thousand years have been watered down and mixed with a melange of Western values and consumption habits. This has created a new East-West hybrid culture that is, no doubt, a portent of what will eventually happen in mainland China as well.

The emerging Taiwan Chinese are not likely to retain any of the cultural aspects of traditional China that interfere with individualism, independence, the pursuit of profits or any attempt to give full vent to these new and previously alien concepts.

The only aspects of China's traditional culture that the Taiwan Chinese are likely to keep are those that contribute directly to their newfound goals. Since immorality and distrust are ever present, family ties, all the way down to third and fourth cousins, are a valuable asset in business and will remain an essential part of the Taiwan-Chinese character.

Virtually absolute rule by the top person in an organization, with practically no delegation of authority, will also remain a common characteristic of Taiwan Chinese business because it will be a long time before founders or owners can develop the confidence and trust necessary to do business any other way.

The refined tastes in art, food, clothing, and sexual pleasures have been an integral part of upper-class Chinese culture for millennia. Since they contribute to, rather than detract from, success in business, they too will remain a part of the new Taiwan Chinese world.

As far as the post-1970 Taiwan Chinese are concerned, the very bedrock of the Confucian way has turned into dust. It consisted of blind obedience to government officials and paying respect to people and institutions that did not deserve it.

Hereafter, the continuity of the Taiwan Chinese family will not be guaranteed by worshipping and sacrificing oneself to the past, but by achieving the survival power and options that come with having wealth.

Chinese Time

Few Chinese have been conditioned to equate time with money. When foreign businesspeople arrive in China at the end of a long journey, most Chinese do not expect them to immediately rush into business. Their first priority is to get the visitors settled into their hotels and give them an opportunity to rest up. And generally they will politely but firmly reject any attempt by visitors to alter this routine.

Chinese who are involved in international business are generally familiar with the Western "time is money" concept. However, they do not automatically relate it to the pace of business, particularly to first meetings and negotiations, before business actually starts. Since there often appears to be no set time frame for the length or extent of negotiations, they use that to their advantage in dealing with foreigners.

One tactic that the foreign side can use to help limit negotiation time is to announce up front that, because of economic or other circumstances that cannot be changed, there is a deadline. These circumstances should be explained in detail to avoid any suspicion that the tactic is nothing more than that. Given the Chinese mind-set and business environment, however, any deadline should be reasonably long and flexible enough to prevent it from eliminating the possibility of success.

Despite having invented clocks (for astronomical purposes, not to impose controls on personal behavior), the Chinese never defined or segmented time as was done in the West. To most Chinese today, time simply flows from one day to the next. If a job isn't done today, maybe it will be done the next day or the next. It takes a substantial amount of reconditioning to program the Chinese to pattern their work and productivity on the Western time frame.

Another aspect of traditional Chinese behavior that clashes with the Western way is their custom of giving precedence to the form and process of doing things rather than actually doing them. This generally adds to the amount of time it takes to do things and is a habit that is difficult for the Chinese to break. In an office or factory setting, the only way to work through this problem is to create a well-defined work procedure that can be explained and demonstrated. It is also helpful to be patient and persistent in retraining your employees.

Sharing the Rewards of Labor

There is no tradition in China of automatically linking personal effort or productivity in an office or factory with income or with the success or failure of a company. The Communist regime, which took over the country in 1949, further reinforced the concept that everyone should be treated the same and get the same no matter how much or how little they worked. They got away with it because government-run enterprises did not have to make a profit to survive.

This belief and behavior is still the norm in most government enterprises and remains a significant factor in independent enterprises as well. Foreign-affiliated firms have learned that the only way to contend with this problem is to reprogram the thinking of employees, that is, to convince them that all employees are responsible for doing their share of the work.

Facts Versus Opinions

Since the Chinese do not automatically distinguish between facts and opinions, it is important to be careful about what one says. Because something said as a throwaway remark or in jest can also be taken as a fact, casual comments and attempts at cross-cultural humor can backfire.

At the same time, the Chinese have a broad and sophisticated sense of humor. Once you know your counterparts and have established rapport with them, humor is very much in order and can be used to bridge gaps and help solidify relationships.

Going Overboard in Drinking

Establishing a relationship and doing business in China requires an inordinate number of meetings and a lot of eating and drinking. Regular meetings in bars, clubs, and restaurants are an important part of the business culture.

This calls for a word of caution. Drinking is a skill the Chinese have been honing for several thousand years and visiting businessmen are strongly advised not to try to outdrink them or even match them glass for glass. People who like to drink, can "hold their liquor," and do not suffer hangovers or any diminishing of their abilities, may choose to play the drinking game.

However, it is wise even for those with iron stomachs and heads to pace themselves when jousting with Chinese.

For everyone else, drinking modestly or not at all is the best course no matter how forceful the Chinese host might be. And they, and the situation, can be very intimidating. Explaining firmly that you cannot drink for some reason or that you can drink only a little is acceptable, however, and allows you to ask for juice or some other nonalcoholic drink.

When Your Host Isn't Your Host

The Chinese are generous hosts, often to the point that it is unreasonable if not impossible for foreign visitors to reciprocate. But it is important for you to be aware that the cost of some of the luxurious facilities and services arranged by your hosts may be put on *your* bill.

Chinese hosts frequently make hotel, transportation, and other arrangements for expected visitors without any advance consultation or approval. It is, therefore, often impossible to tell where their hospitality ends and the visitor's responsibility begins. The only safe recourse is for visitors to politely but clearly inquire about the cost of everything that has been arranged for them, from limousines and interpreters to lunches for government officials.

This inquiry can be prefaced by stating that, since you are on a tight budget, you need to know exactly what you are expected to pay for and approximately how much it will be. Failure to find out in advance what you are going to be charged for can be a shock. If you make a fuss after the fact, your Chinese ''hosts'' will be upset and angered, and you will off to a rocky start.

Visiting businesspeople are routinely hosted at regular meals and banquets by their Chinese hosts, but it is expected that the visitor will host at least one dinner party before leaving. And this is something that should be planned with your Chinese counterparts in advance, as a specific part of the overall agenda. One rule of thumb is that the Chinese host the visitor the first or second night, depending on the arrival time and events of the day, and the visitor may host a dinner the following night.

Depending on the circumstances (who initiated the visit, who will be the major beneficiary, or which side is the largest and the richest) the visitor may also want to, or be expected to, host a farewell dinner at the end of the visit. The main point to keep in mind is not to leave things unplanned or unsettled. The Chinese expect and appreciate very specific agendas that cover every detail. If the visitor does not come forward with an agenda or make contributions to a joint agenda, the Chinese will presume it is all being left up to them.

Geographical Differences

One of the most conspicuous things about China is its diversity, not only geographically, but also racially, ethnically and socially. Even more conspicuous is the fact that all Chinese do not speak the same language. Mandarin, Cantonese, Shanghaiese, and Fukienese are not just dialects, as they have often been described in the past. They are different languages.

While Westerners are in the habit of lumping all Chinese together, culturally and otherwise, the Chinese themselves have always been acutely aware of their differences. Traditionally there was even a well-known saying among the major Han group that people who lived just ten *li* (about 6 miles) away were foreigners.

Until the Communist takeover of China in 1949, the huge landmass was a country only in a general political sense. Racially and culturally speaking, the large minority groups were countries within themselves—a situation that still exists today.

There were also fundamental regional differences. Today, most of the regional differences in business behavior are superficial, and they quickly become obvious to the outsider or are very quickly explained by the local businesspeople themselves, usually with a great deal of pride.

Further, most of the people classified as Chinese share many cultural traits derived from common beliefs in Buddhism, Taoism, and Confucianism and the enormous influence of the common system of writing.

The Uncreative Society

Throughout China's history, most learning has been by imitation and rote memory. The educated person was one who conformed to established etiquette, was able to read and write at least five thousand of the extremely complicated Chinese ideograms, was knowledgeable about classic writings, and, if exceptionally accomplished, wrote passable poetry and calligraphy.

The whole thrust of China's educational system was on "polishing the jade"—mastering the arts, crafts and philosophies of the past. Any thought of doing things differently or introducing new ideas was met with unyielding resistance, and often punishment if the perpetrator persisted.

In this atmosphere, creativity, even in playful pursuits, was extremely rare. This was so not only because it went against the grain of Chinese culture but also because the people were consumed by the demands of the existing life-style. Very few common people had the time or resources to do anything but strive for survival. The educated elite were dedicated to preserving the traditional system, rather than proposing or experimenting with new systems.

Present-day China has not yet succeeded in breaking this stifling approach to education. Children, from about the age of 18 months, are physically and mentally conditioned to conform, to obey, and to passively absorb whatever is offered to them. Mavericks who break away from this culture molding are still rare and still face daunting obstacles in their efforts to introduce originality into their views and pursuits.

But there is one very bright side to the Chinese educational process that, although unplanned, mitigates many of the negative elements of the overall process: the demands put on children to learn how to read and write Chinese.

Memorizing the three to four thousand complicated ideograms now required for a basic education and developing acceptable skill in "drawing" them imbues every Chinese with a high degree of physical and mental skills. This makes them stand out in other pursuits calling for exceptional memories, manual dexterity, and the ability to persevere in seemingly unending and unrewarding tasks.

Having spent several years becoming proficient in reading and drawing several thousand ideograms is obviously one of the reasons why many Chinese excel in mathematics, engineering, and other subjects requiring the absorption of enormous amounts of detailed information. This is also one of the reasons why the Chinese are so adept at copying things created by others.

Until the Chinese introduce more freedom and individuality into their nurseries and classrooms, they will continue to stifle the curiosity and experimentation that is essential for creativity. But the combination of traditional and modern skills the Chinese routinely learn today enhances their ability to copy, and sometimes improve, foreign technology. It also makes them a formidable people and may be just the right combination for this stage of China's development.

Dos and Don'ts

There is no way to anticipate or avoid all of the problems of dealing with Chinese businesspeople and bureaucrats, but there are a number of common-sense guidelines, learned the hard way by pioneers in the country. They should help to minimize the problems and significantly enhance the possibilities of success. Here is a list of dos and don'ts that front-line business veterans are quick to share with newcomers:

1. Know your own company and its products inside and out.
2. At the beginning of a relationship with a Chinese company or government bureau make a special point of emphasizing that your own company follows high ethical standards, that you are bound by those stan-

dards, and that they specifically prohibit under-the-table payments. In order to make this pill go down a little easier it pays to emphasize how everyone on both sides of the table will benefit from a successful business relationship, appealing to the nationalistic pride of the Chinese. I recommend that this statement of your company's ethical standards be in written form and printed on impressive stationery.

3. Know everything possible about the Chinese company or agency you are going to be dealing with, including personal details about the managers and executives you will be meeting. If necessary, engage the services of an investigative agency to get behind the facade of the organization. Make sure that whatever investigation is done covers the "corruption rating" of the company or bureau concerned. If you are going to do business in China through an agent, take special pains to ensure that the agent is not one of the many that rely primarily on bribes in dealing with the bureaucracy and suppliers. If you are asked for a bribe, do not show any anger. Apologize sincerely and present a copy of your company's ethical guidelines, adding that if you agree to any kind of unauthorized payment you will be fired. (If you need an escape from this position, you can always agree to try to arrange some kind of authorized consideration.)

4. If you are going to have employees in China, prepare a formal written code of conduct and require that all new employees sign the code as part of their employment contract.

5. Be as informed as possible about current social, economic, and political aspects of China. One of the best ways to accomplish this is to interview other foreign businesspeople who are stationed in China and have been there for several years.

6. Know as much as possible about the Chinese market as it relates to your products and goals. Again, the insights of foreign businesspeople on the scene can be invaluable.

7. Keep in mind that there is a social and political as well as economic content to business in China and that you will have to be knowledgeable enough and flexible enough to adapt to the Chinese environment.

8. Make sure your presentations are specific, comprehensive, and clear.

9. If you are using your own interpreter, make sure you qualify him or her in advance. Also make sure he or she has studied your presentation before your meetings.

10. Prepare summary copies of your presentation, preferably in English and Chinese, and pass them out at the beginning of the meeting.

11. Take an open, friendly, sincere stance in your presentation. Say some nice things about China (but don't overdo it) *and* about your own country, adding that you believe a successful relationship will contribute to both countries.

12. Be totally honest and frank in your responses to questions, proposals, or criticisms. If anything is amiss, if there is any kind of misunderstanding, cover it immediately. If you let it go by, it will likely come back to haunt you because the Chinese will assume that you approve or have no objections.

13. Exude sincerity and goodwill, but be firm and consistent in making your points and position clear.

14. Do not expect fast agreement from the Chinese side. Do expect a seemingly endless litany of questions, requests for more information, and a variety of demands.

15. Be prepared to give a little on some points where you have leeway, but always get something in return.

16. Do not put yourself in a position where you have to have an answer or a contract in three days or any other short time-frame. It also pays to not put all of your eggs into someone else's basket.

17. Keep in mind that the Chinese are generous in their use of time. They know that in most cases it is on their side and they will take the fullest possible advantage of it. Put yourself in a position where you can be patient and not suffer.

18. Stay friendly, stay firm, stay unflustered. Let the Chinese know that, if you cannot reach an agreement within a reasonable period of time for any reason beyond their control or your control, you are prepared to do business with someone else.

19. If you do not have powerful connections in China, get some help from friends and or other connections and make them.

20. Emphasize that the relationship must be mutually beneficial—a relatively new concept in Chinese thinking. (The traditional and still generally automatic reaction is that, in any foreign relationship, the Chinese side should benefit first and foremost. Part of this reaction is a holdover from the generations when foreigners were expected to bring gifts to demonstrate friendship and recognition of China as the supreme power. Nowadays, part of it is based on the concept that China's needs take precedence over the foreigner's desires to make what are typically perceived of as excessive profits.)

8

Other Special Points to Remember

In addition to the points of Chinese etiquette and ethics already mentioned, many other traditional attitudes, customs and their variations impact directly and forcefully on foreigners living and working in China. Here are a number of the more important ones.

Making Foreigners Pay

The Chinese believe foreigners should pay handsomely for the privilege of being in China and doing business there. They see no contradiction in charging everything the market will bear. Their rationale is that foreigners are there for their own selfish motives, to make a profit, and can leave if they don't want to pay the price.

Not Dry Behind the Ears

Foreign companies sending representatives to China should keep in mind that the Chinese do not regard people as mature adults until they are about forty years old. It is common for people in their thirties to be treated like teenagers who still need the guidance of parents and older mentors.

Part of this cultural behavior is that role-playing and responsibility in China have traditionally been based on social relationships in which children remain children in the eyes of their parents, regardless of their age. In the outside business and political worlds, older officials and executives tend to play the role of parents when dealing with younger people. This helps explain the tendency of people in their thirties and forties to assume a childlike stance when dealing with older people in positions of authority.

177

Truth Is a Relative Thing

One of the most important elements in understanding and dealing with Chinese attitudes and behavior is that the Chinese generally do not think or behave from the viewpoint of absolute truths or principles. Everything is relative; everything is based on the prevailing circumstances. In effect, Chinese-style truth, fairness, and reciprocity are created anew for each situation.

The Chinese concepts of responsibility and guilt, for example, are generally arbitrary, especially when they are applied to foreigners. A popular example of this tells of a Chinese bicyclist who runs into a foreigner's car that is parked or is stopped at an intersection. The police may charge the foreigner for being partially responsible for the accident, noting that if he had not been in China the accident would not have occurred.

The Use of Low Blows

When there is a difference of opinion or disagreement of any kind between Chinese and foreigners, one of the characteristic responses is for the Chinese to accuse the foreigners of not knowing China. The Chinese typically use cultural differences as ploys, weapons, and excuses in their dealings with foreigners. They play foreign businesses and countries off against each other with military-type strategies and tactics developed over the centuries.

Playing the Cultural Card

National and cultural pride in China often outranks any other consideration and often results in irrational attitudes and behavior that confuse and frustrate foreigners.

At the same time, many foreign visitors are so impressed and intimidated by China's long history and cultural achievements that they suspend some of their critical faculties when dealing with the Chinese, thereby lowering both their standards and expectations. The Chinese are masters at playing this card to win.

Another important factor to keep in mind is that the Chinese take extraordinary pride in cultural accomplishments, particularly knowledge of literature and the fine arts. They frequently use their own knowledge of these things to show foreigners up and put them down. Knowing something about several of China's most famous poets and being able to quote a few well-known lines can get you a lot of mileage.

Finding the Right Person

There is almost always some individual in charge of every process or thing in China, from forms to be filled out, copying machines and faxes, to tools or whatever. It is usually necessary to go through this person to get or make use of whatever is concerned. The first challenge is to identify the responsible person. If that person is not available, you often have to wait until he or she returns.

The second challenge is to establish and maintain friendly, cooperative relationships with these key people. This is often difficult because some of them invariably have unpleasant personalities and systematically abuse their positions, either out of spite or to gain some advantage.

Speak Now or . . .

If you do not immediately protest any undesirable situation, the Chinese tend to believe that you have accepted it and will not complain later. The only effective recourse is to bring the matter up immediately, and continuously if necessary, in a controlled but determined manner, until it is resolved.

Importance of a Humble Mode

Humility and an overtly humble behavior are keys to getting along in China. By Western standards, the Chinese go overboard in putting on a humble mien. They do this, of course, to avoid friction and enhance harmony since bragging and self-promotion are generally taboo.

While the Chinese have been conditioned to accept authoritarian behavior from government officials and company managers, this behavior must also include a "humble" side as an acknowledgement that the higher-ups are still human. Higher-ups are also expected to accept responsibility for the safety and welfare of the people below them.

Protecting Your Privacy

Once you have established a close friendship with Chinese, there is virtually no end to how far they will go in taking advantage of the relationship, whether it is taking up your time in social situations or seeking special favors.

It is difficult for traditional Chinese to understand the idea that anyone would want to be totally alone for any extended period of time. Most Chinese feel secure only when they are with others, and happiness is being surrounded by one's family and friends.

The Chinese also often appear to have little or no built-in sense of restraint when it comes to asking favors of people whom they regard as having more than what they need. Foreigners who work in China, including teachers and especially overseas Chinese who return for visits to relatives, are customarily besieged with requests for favors or gifts of some kind.

Extracting oneself from these situations without leaving a lot of hard feelings is a serious challenge and sometimes practically impossible. About the only recourse is to repeatedly apologize and explain that what is asked of you is "inconvenient."

Keeping a Low Profile

One of the more frustrating aspects of dealing with Chinese in general, and lower-ranking bureaucrats or employees in particular, is that they generally cannot be depended upon to take the initiative or be innovative. The Chinese have been conditioned for centuries to keep a low profile, to make no changes, and to leave everything to higher-ups. The other side of this coin, of course, is that those in positions of authority in China generally do not delegate any authority and do not share knowledge or information with those below them.

Not having any authority and not clearly knowing the policies and goals of higher-ups, which are always subject to change without warning, the average Chinese worker does everything possible to play it safe.

Passing the Buck

In negotiating with Chinese businesspeople, the foreign side must keep in mind that the Chinese are generally not free to make purely economic decisions. Their responses must be within the guidelines of both written and unwritten laws, some of which are so vague that they are subject to any number of interpretations.

Foreign businesspeople should also keep in mind that their Chinese counterparts generally cannot change their conditions or goals in midstream. They must report to and get the approval of several layers of higher-ups, including in some cases a dozen or more government officials.

Contracts as Symbols

While Western businesspeople tend to be detail-oriented, the Chinese are more interested in the big picture. Their goal is to establish a solid relationship within which details will be worked out on a case-by-case basis as the need arises.

All too often, the foreign side concentrates on getting a detailed contract that is as binding as possible, while downplaying the importance of developing personal ties with their Chinese counterparts and appropriate government officials.

To the circumstantial-minded Chinese, the signing of a contract is little more than a symbol that the two parties intend to work together to pursue mutually beneficial goals. They see the rights and responsibilities of both parties as constantly changing and impossible to pin down in a contract.

Business relationships in China also have social as well as economic values, and the Chinese approach them with a different mind-set and different expectations. As a result, they generally do not rush into new situations.

Face Versus Efficiency

Face is often far more important to the Chinese than performance, and contributes enormously to the inefficiency and apparent incompetency that plagues business and government offices. People will typically not admit an error or ignorance because they would lose face, often compounding what would otherwise could be a fairly minor problem.

It is vital that outsiders keep in mind that typical Chinese behavior is not based on universal principles of fairness, logic, or personal and individual integrity. Instead, it is based on maintaining face and harmony in their relational society. Generally speaking, harmony is more important to the Chinese than efficiency or results.

In their efforts to maintain harmony, the Chinese must exercise extraordinary caution in everything they do and say. In this world of precisely balanced positives and negatives, being too passive can be just as dangerous and disadvantageous as being too aggressive.

Two + Two Does Not = Four

In China, as in other parts of Asia, one often gets inconsistent and contradictory answers to the same questions because the "right" answer depends on who is asking the question and who is answering it. The Chinese do not see the world in terms of two plus two always equals four and fashion their responses according to the circumstances, including their mood at that particular time.

When one gets an answer that does not sound rational or possible, chances are it is neither. But a direct confrontation with the individual concerned generally makes matters worse. Among the choices one has under these circumstances is to have a third party who has a good relationship with the individual ask the same question indirectly, offer the person some kind of bribe, or ask to see his or her superior.

Getting angry, shouting and making threats does not work. Usually the best approach is to get someone who has some influence over the individual to act on your behalf.

Limiting Your Obligations

The Chinese expect a lot from Westerners. And their expectations are often beyond the realm of possibility. When this occurs, the best response is not to give a long-winded, detailed story of why you can't do it, but to simply say, with a strained look on your face, "It is inconvenient," and let it go at that. (This is the equivalent of the Japanese saying, "It is difficult.")

In addition to the Chinese using "inconvenient" as a face-saving "no," both Japanese and Chinese use the ploy "It is under study" as a polite rejection.

In negotiating business relationships with Chinese, particularly where technology is concerned, limits must be set on what technology will be transferred. These limitations should be strictly observed, or the Chinese will expect to get everything you have.

Apologies and Revenge

Because Chinese manners and ethics are based on personal relationships rather than principles, the Chinese are easily offended. A slightly off tone of voice, a disapproving facial expression, the hint of criticism, a tinge of superiority or arrogance may have made an enemy who will never forget. They also may not forgive if you don't become aware of your transgression, humble yourself, and apologize.

The apology is an especially vital part of interpersonal relationships in China because the Chinese take offense so easily. If they believe they have been slighted and do not get a quick, acceptable apology, they must have revenge. And, unlike Westerners who are conditioned to take their revenge instantly and openly, the Chinese prefer to wait and do it in a subtle way so their targets never know what hit them. By the same token, the Chinese have equally long memories when someone does them a favor, and the more time that passes the more strongly they feel compelled to return favors.

Masked Emotions

Since the Chinese do not "wear their emotions on their faces" to the extent that Westerners are wont to do it is more difficult to judge their state of mind. The demands of their etiquette require that they develop considerable skill in acting, however. They are masters at using body language as an aide to achieving their goals.

Another Chinese cultural trait that misleads and frustrates Westerners is their habit of smiling or laughing when they do not understand or are embarrassed. The person who smiles at your question or request may not be turning on a friendly face. He or she may not understand what you are talking about, so unless you get a clearly positive response, it may be advisable to belabor the point a bit.

Showing Respect

When you are visited by Chinese businesspeople or government officials toward whom you want to show appreciation or respect, you should at least accompany them to the elevator (if there is one) when they leave. You should go all the way to the front door of the building if their goodwill is important to you. This very conspicuous gesture is an institutionalized part of Chinese etiquette, and whether or not you follow the custom tells the Chinese a lot about you.

Criticizing Indirectly

The Chinese do not take direct criticism well. They are more likely to take it as arrogance and insulting, not only to them but to all Chinese. Rather than result in a change for the better, the response to direct criticism is usually the opposite—in addition to which you have very likely made an enemy. As in so many other instances, the best way to make your point is indirectly.

Dress and Punctuality

Because apparel was so intimately linked with class and rank for so many centuries in China, proper dress, as well as punctuality, remain very important. In the Chinese context, both of these things are intimately related to one's educational level, morality, integrity, and dependability.

The Chinese rationale is that if people are not punctual for meetings and do not dress properly, they cannot be trusted to be good business partners. People who dress in a flamboyant style are looked upon as undependable mavericks at best and immoral at worst.

Restaurant Bill Taboos

It is not polite to study a restaurant bill in front of your guests, and it is especially damaging to make a public fuss about it. The proper way to pay such bills is to slip away from the table a few minutes before the party breaks up and pay them behind the scene.

Projects That Have the Best Chance

Fred Schneiter notes in his humorously insightful *Getting Along with the Chinese for Fun and Profit* that one of the first challenges facing the outsider wanting to do business in China is determining the nature and level of the interest shown by potential agents, partners or representatives.

Speaking rather broadly, there are five levels of interest the newcomer to China may encounter. The first and most common is what Schneiter calls "polite interest." Virtually every private or government organization in China will show some interest in any business proposal because they would like to increase their size, power, and/or profitability, and don't want to miss any opportunity. This doesn't mean that they can, or will, do anything about it, but they can mislead naive newcomers and waste a lot of their time and resources by talking about it and studying it for months on end.

The second level of interest is the interest of one or a few individuals in a particular organization who see some personal advantage for themselves. The third level of interest involves a whole organization, the fourth level includes the community, and the fifth level is something that is of national interest. Projects that are the most likely to get off the ground floor are those that involve the third, fourth, and fifth levels of interest.

Keeping Your Guard Up

The business environment in China is almost always friendly at first, with copious drinking, eating, and expressions of goodwill. But this should not be taken as a sign that doing business with the Chinese is easy.

As strained as it might sound, it is probably best to treat all of your Chinese business contacts as friendly enemies who will cut you off at the knees if you give them the opportunity. Generally, when Chinese businesspeople and officials are nice to you, it is because they want something from you—not because they like you or enjoy your company.

Friendship between Chinese and foreign businesspeople is like that of boxers who are friends outside of the ring but once in the ring fight to win—*and there are no referees to make sure the fights are fair.*

The one overriding principle in Chinese behavior is that they will generally do whatever it takes to succeed in business. They are the ultimate pragmatists, and are under no moral or philosophical obligations to play fair. Their only obligation and goal is to win.

The Chinese also unabashedly attempt to use every shame tactic in the book to win negotiating encounters with foreigners. One of their most used ploys is to accuse the foreign side of being selfish and anti-Chinese.

Power Plays

Not unlike their Western counterparts, Chinese who want to induce you to do business with or through them will exaggerate the power of their high-level government contacts.

Structuring the Workplace

The informal, casual approach to management favored by many Westerners, particularly Americans, generally leaves the Chinese confused and unable to function to their fullest ability. Most Chinese still expect and need a strong figure to exercise authority and enforce discipline. They work best in a precisely structured environment.

Expanding the Chinese Mind

The Chinese have traditionally been conditioned to believe there is only one correct way to do things and only one correct answer to any question. Getting traditional Chinese to open up their minds and think and behave in a new way ranges from difficult and frustrating to impossible.

Using the Strategies of War

In China, where neither personal nor business relations are based on principles of equality, reciprocity, or any other aspect of fairness, it should not be surprising that the same strategems that have traditionally been applied to war are also often used in business.

Generals and scholars of ancient China wrote extensively about the strategies and tactics of warfare because fighting was such an important part of the country's history. (Another possible reason is that, over the first three thousand years of the history of the Han Chinese, they exhausted virtually every other topic of interest that could be written about!)

As the centuries passed, the more durable of the many insights into conquering or destroying one's enemies were distilled into thirty-six strategies. The first mention of these strategems appeared in a history of the Southern Qi Dynasty (479–502 A.D.). The first known book on the stratagems, privately printed by hand and secretly distributed to a select few, appeared during the latter years of the Ming Dynasty (1368–1644 A.D.).

It was not until 1941 that the first public and commercial publication of the book took place, and it has since become a sort of bible to the Chinese, its lessons applicable to almost any kind of situation. Long before this, however, the reasoning and ruses making up the stratagems were known to practically all educated Chinese.

The stratagems were distilled down to thirty-six because of the relationship of this number to the hexagram that represents yin/earth in the famous *Book of Changes*. The hexagram consists of six lines, each of which is divided into six segments.

The primary theme of the thirty-six stratagems is knowledge of yourself, knowledge of your enemy (in contemporary business terms, your competitors and markets), detailed planning, and deception. This means fooling your adversaries or competitors into believing you are doing one thing while you are actually doing something else, causing them to relax their guard and giving you an advantage.

The stratagems themselves generally occur in six circumstances: (a) when you are in a superior position, (b) when you confront an adversary, (c) when you attack an adversary, (d) when you want to turn a confusing situation to your advantage, (e) when you want to gain ground in the face of an enemy, and (f) when your situation is desperate.

Here is the military essence of each of the thirty-six stratagems:

1. Make use of camouflage. Induce your enemies to weaken their position by conducting your disguised machinations out in the open.
2. Be patient. Let your enemies make mistakes and become divided. Then attack them aggressively when they are retreating.
3. Let someone else do your dirty work. Sow distrust and discord in your enemies' headquarters. Discover your enemies' plans and use them to your advantage.
4. Be patient. Induce your enemies to use up their resources. Provoke them but do not attack until you have a clear advantage.
5. Wait until your enemies are in so much trouble they can't defend themselves; then attack.

6. Confuse your adversary by taking a variety of deceptive actions, then attack.

7. Put up a false front. Mislead or bluff your adversaries. Attack when they are too confused to defend themselves properly.

8. Reveal one strategy to your adversaries but have a secret plan that will catch them off guard and give you an advantage.

9. When there is dissension in the ranks of the enemy, be patient. Let them weaken themselves; then attack.

10. Make your adversaries think you are their friend; then strike when their guard is down.

11. Let the enemy win where they are the strongest, but utilize your own strongest forces to defeat them where they are weak.

12. Watch your enemy closely to discern any weakness; then, exploit that weakness to the fullest.

13. Find out everything possible about an adversary before taking any action; then, act quickly and decisively.

14. Conquer or use weaker opponents to achieve your goals.

15. Use various ruses to get your adversary into your territory on your terms.

16. Harass your enemies by repeated attacks and withdrawals. This will sap their strength and lower their morale. When they are weakened, attack in earnest.

17. Lull your enemies into thinking they are in good shape; then, spring a surprise attack on them.

18. Destroy or discredit the leader, and the followers will give up the battle and be easier to conquer.

19. Find the adversaries' weakest points and keep plugging away at them until they are drained of strength.

20. Take advantage of internal strife to further weaken and confuse your enemy; then, attack quickly and decisively.

21. Avoid making your adversary suspicious by appearing to do one thing while secretly maneuvering to withdraw.

22. Show no mercy when you have an adversary at a disadvantage.

23. Conquer your neighbors first; then, target distant adversaries.

24. Make yourself the protector of small states in order to guarantee their loyalty and cooperation.

25. Take clandestine action to disrupt the strength of your adversaries; then attack.

26. Threaten small states with destruction if they don't join you in bringing larger states to heel.

27. Mislead your enemies by making them think you are weak and foolish; then, when their guard is down, destroy them.

28. Entice your adversaries into a trap by pretending to be weak; then, close ranks and destroy them.

29. Make your enemies think you are stronger than you really are; then, take swift advantage before they discover the truth.
30. Treat your adversaries as guests; then, exploit their weaknesses to destroy them.
31. Fix your adversaries up with beautiful women. This will keep them occupied and demoralize their troops, making them vulnerable to your attack.
32. Play the injured bird. When your enemy relaxes, attack.
33. Spy on your enemies, and feed their spies false information.
34. Contrive to injure yourself or have someone else injure you in order to gain the trust of the enemy; then, exploit that trust to destroy them.
35. Create plots to get your enemies to destroy each other.
36. Do not attempt to take on an enemy more powerful than you. Run away and live to fight another day.

To the Western businessperson, applying these concepts to modern-day management may seem like another side of the "inscrutable" Oriental face. The secret is to look at business as another form of warfare, as the Chinese are wont to do, and extrapolate from Sun Tzu's concepts to business situations.

In this context, the lessons to be learned from Sun Tzu include (a) self-knowledge, (b) discipline, (c) knowledge of your markets and competitors, (d) planning, (e) the exercising of authority, (f) the organization of your company, (g) managing employees, (h) having well-thought-out policies, (i) handling internal "politics" among your employees, (j) managing information, (k) developing business strategies, and (l) implementing those business strategies.

It goes without saying that businesspeople are unlikely to achieve their goals if they do not know themselves, their own company and its product lines, including all of the attendant strengths and weaknesses (a).

Knowing all there is to know about yourself and your company may not ensure success if you do not have the necessary discipline to take advantage of your strengths and keep your weaknesses under control. Sun Tzu singled out the strengths that a commander/CEO should cultivate as wisdom, sincerity, benevolence, courage, and strictness. The weaknesses to be avoided were recklessness, cowardice, quick temper, excessive sensitivity, and excessive compassion (b).

Knowledge of your markets and competitors is essential to ensure long-term success (and it is amazing how often businesspeople wanting to do business in China give this factor very low priority) (c).

Sun Tzu emphasized over and over again that no matter how strong or how many advantages a commander may have, it is still vital to have a detailed plan to ensure victory (d).

Another of Sun Tzu's keys to victory in war/business is the ability to command the respect and loyalty of "soldiers." It is, therefore, necessary to know how to train people, how to motivate them, and how to keep them satisfied. Sun Tzu compared a good commander with the hub of a wheel, noting that the strength of the wheel was determined by both the hub and the spokes (e).

Organization is another key to success. All other factors in a company may be positive—knowledge, foresight, discipline, planning and so on—but the company may fail if it is not well organized (f).

The best organized company in the world may fail if management is not up to the task. Managers must know how to work with and treat employees to get the most out of them. Sun Tzu emphasized the importance of a fair system of rewards for those who made conspicuous contributions. He also said that commanders must beware of treating their people with too much compassion, as that could lead to defeat (g).

In war or in business, having clear, precise policies that the majority supports is essential for victory (h).

In any group of people or companies, there is bound to be "internal politics." The successful commander recognizes this and is able to make it a strength rather than a weakness. Sun Tzu advises the commander to lead by example, demonstrating the "five fundamental factors," wisdom, sincerity, benevolence, courage, and strictness, to avoid showing favoritism, and to know what is going on behind the scenes (i).

Sun Tzu made a special point of the importance of managing information, since the best intelligence is wasted if not properly used (j).

Sun Tzu held that one of the keys to developing and implementing successful strategies was flexibility—being able to anticipate changing circumstances and adapt to them on a day-to-day basis. To do this, he noted that it was essential to have a (corporate) mission, to be able to accurately appraise one's own organization as well as the external environment (market-place), and to set objectives. (One of the reasons why the Chinese are uncomfortable with detailed contracts is that they hinder or prevent flexibility in relationships and activities.) (k)

Sun Tzu ranked determination, the will to win, as one of the most important strategies for success. He was very much aware that having superior weapons, being better trained, having a good plan of attack, and superior intelligence, could all go for nought if the will to use all of one's advantages was not present (l).

Dealing with Your Head Office

Finally, as is the case everywhere in Asia, the ultimate challenge facing foreign businesspeople in China is not learning how to deal with the Chinese, but the need to continuously educate their home offices to accept the idea that in China some things are done differently, and that they must adapt their approach to fit the local circumstances.

9

The World of Hong Kong

"Likes and dislikes should not affect our judgment. We should be on the side of what is right and against what is wrong."
—CONFUCIUS

Training Ground for China

Hong Kong, China's main gateway to the rest of the world, has been styled by writer Melanie Leslie-Finn as the nation's "capitalist classroom," where Chinese businesspeople as well as government officials are learning how to wheel and deal in the heady atmosphere of one of the world's primary financial centers. Several thousand Chinese companies in Hong Kong are also learning the more mundane lessons of operating capitalist enterprises, from basic manufacturing procedures to management, as well as how to cope with foreign cultures and languages.

Leslie-Finn also noted that Hong Kong is the ideal training ground for foreign companies with an eye on inland China, giving them an opportunity to get a toehold in the China trade with fewer risks. It is much less expensive and easier for foreign companies to set up shop in Hong Kong and invite the Chinese to come there to see them, she added. As both a gateway and a bridge, Hong Kong offers foreign companies the opportunity to do business in the three Chinese economies—mainland China, Taiwan and Hong Kong itself—with the least amount of investment and the most liberal business conditions.

Today's Hong Kong is indeed one of the most remarkable examples of capitalistic enterprise ever seen. From a tiny trading post, whose early growth was primarily based on flogging "foreign mud" (opium) in China, Hong Kong has become an economic powerhouse whose influence is felt around

191

the world. Its success, most obvious in the jampacked forests of high-rise office buildings and apartments that line its waterways, is a magnificent monument to the spirit and ambitions of its crowded population of Chinese residents, refugees, and leavening of expatriate Westerners.

The story of Hong Kong's incredible growth since the 1950s is mostly one of luck, stupidity, and hard work. When the Communist forces of Zedong Mao took over China in 1949, the United States quickly imposed an embargo on Chinese-made imports. Many of these goods were just as quickly diverted to Hong Kong where they were miraculously provided with Made in Hong Kong certificates and then shipped to the United States. To take even more advantage of the rich American market, new factories began appearing in Hong Kong like mushrooms.

When the conflict in Vietnam was made into an American war, Hong Kong became a major supplier for the U.S. armed forces. Equally as important were the hundreds of thousands of members of the American armed forces who poured into Hong Kong on R&R (rest & recreation) leaves from Vietnam. There they spent millions of dollars a month in the shops, restaurants, bars, and redlight districts. The "colony" also became a shopping mecca for the burgeoning tourist trade.

Despite its lingering Crown Colony image, Hong Kong is Chinese, heart and soul. Its spirit, its energy, its stunning economic, cultural, and social accomplishments are Chinese. Basically, the British role was one of creating a political environment where Chinese businesspeople were free to exercise their abilities and ambitions. The paramount spiritual, cultural, and social life of Hong Kong, the family ties, the family gatherings, the rituals and ceremonies of daily life, the annual festivals . . . all are traditional Chinese. In some respects they are even more so than inland China itself where traditionalism was dealt a grevious blow by the Cultural Revolution.

In his very perceptive *Insider's Guide to Hong Kong*, novelist Derek Maitland notes that, generally speaking, the foreign and Chinese elements of Hong Kong come together in only two areas—business and sports—because of many fundamental reasons. One of the more obvious ones is that most Westerners living in Hong Kong do not regard it as their permanent home and are therefore not inclined to develop ties with the Chinese. Another far more interesting reason, adds Maitland, is that the mutual superiority complex of Westerners and Chinese tends to keep them apart. He says the historical British and Western social and economic supremacy and their colonial superiority (with very strong racist elements) is matched if not surpassed by the traditional Chinese feeling that they are the superior people, and to mix with foreigners on an equal footing is too much to expect. He adds that the only common language is business and the common religion is profit—obviously a pretty solid foundation for cooperation and mutual benefit.

Maitland boils the primary spiritual and philosophical beliefs of the Chinese down to just three key things: health, happiness, and good luck—a creed that Americans in particular can accept without any strain at all.

Arrival of the Chinese

China began investing heavily in Hong Kong in 1985, with the number of Hong Kong firms having Chinese interests jumping from 215 to 536 in just two years. The number has since been multiplied many times.

Local businesspeople say the Chinese are rapidly learning how business is done in the region, but still have a long way to go. They say that three levels of Chinese managerial ability are clearly discernible. Managers with the least amount of experience are those representing firms controlled by the central government. Next are those heading up firms under provincial jurisdiction, and at the top are those representing private, unregulated firms.

Managers of state-owned and operated firms tend to be extra conservative, while the others are more aggressive to varying degrees. Managers of state-owned enterprises are, of course, usually political appointees. Very few of the thousands of Chinese sent abroad for study end up in Hong Kong, and the Chinese-owned firms there are pretty much left on their own since neither the provincial governments nor the central government are qualified to direct them. Because of this situation, many Chinese managers dispatched to Hong Kong from Beijing, Shanghai, and elsewhere see it as an ideal opportunity to line their own pockets. Said one observer of the scene: "The only rule is 'Don't get caught!' " He added: "There are no laws in mainland China, just policies, and they are subject to change."

The Best and the Worst

Hong Kong probably represents the best and worst aspects of Chinese etiquette and ethics in business. Every extreme possible exists in varying degrees of abundance, from the most hidebound traditionalists to modern business sages who reflect the Confucian idea of the perfect gentleperson—compassionate, temperate, rational, wise, whose every thought and action is in harmony with humans and the cosmos—to the most unscrupulous, conniving scoundrels imaginable.

Rather than acting as a melting pot for Chinese and Western influences, Hong Kong is more like an international crossroads marketplace where widely diverse influences have intermingled but have not mixed sufficiently to create a single new way of doing business. In no other area of Asia are generalizations about business morality or business styles more likely to be wrong than in Hong Kong. And yet within the ethnic Chinese community, whether or not the individuals concerned are native-born Chinese or descendants of overseas Chinese, there is a thread of commonality that helps to identify and tie the community together.

Where any particular Hong Kong Chinese businessperson fits within this framework of traditional, nontraditional, ethical, or nonethical is determined more by personal and business circumstances than by cultural factors. Experiences and conversations with typical representatives of Hong Kong's Chinese businesspeople reflect this diversity.

An executive of an advertising agency announces: "There is still a big difference between how the East and West do business, and these days only a mix of the two can be successful. Chinese have never learned to delegate anything, authority or responsibility. It is difficult to figure out whether that comes from a lack of ability or lack of interest. But because of it, Hong Kong will never be able to govern itself and the current style of business will have to change or die."

He claims that for the most part business methods in Hong Kong have not changed that much in the past 140 years. "The typical Chinese-run office is still a total autocracy, with stacks of 25-year-old box files the only link to daily dealings. This style of management thrives in an environment where a few qualified people are able to control everything, but markets have become too sophisticated and competitors too plentiful.

"Chinese are passionately devoted to their families and friends. They cannot cut anybody. For generations it has been the way things are done— one sharp individual and a bunch of low-paid family members who made the clothes or pushed the paper. Chinese do not like to change things that work. The old superstition that you are inviting bad luck if you change things that are working is still very strong."

On the other end of the scale are the Chinese businesspeople who have adapted Confucian ethics with modern computerized technology and management procedures. In some ways, for the time and place, they are often more successful than their foreign counterparts. "The Chinese are still among the hardest working people in the world and they hate to be beaten. If there is a profit to be made they will somehow make it," the ad executive added.

The ad exec continues that he can almost always predict whether or not foreign businesspeople are going to be successful in Hong Kong or China shortly after meeting them. "If they do not recognize and understand that there *is* a basic difference in the way the Chinese do business, and if they cannot or do not commit themselves to a long-term approach of developing the necessary contacts, laying the essential groundwork and persevering in the face of obstacles and competition, chances are they will not make it.

"Probably one of the most important things the foreign business executive can learn about doing business with the Chinese is that the bottom line is not how much profit you and they can make but the quality of the relationship you establish with them and how earnestly and loyally you maintain this relationship. If you do not have a solid relationship with the Chinese they are very unforgiving. They do not ordinarily give anyone a second chance.''

In describing Chinese attitudes toward work and business, another Hong Kong Chinese referred to the old proverb that a company is like a boat at sea with a single captain. All remain afloat and prosper under the command of one person, or they sink together. He pointed out, however, that this kind of loyalty to a company is no longer the rule in Hong Kong—that so great is the desire to make more than a bare living, to provide some security for their future, that Hong Kong Chinese on the lower rungs have a compulsion to start their own companies. ''They work for a company for a few years, learn the business and then start their own. Today if a worker is offered $10 a month more by a factory next door, it's goodbye.''

The Shopkeeper Mentality

Said another: ''The traditional Chinese business system is based on the shopkeeper mentality, in which the owner-boss makes all of the decisions, oversees everything, collects all of the money and pays all of the bills. The owner/presidents of good-sized companies may insist on signing all of the payroll checks themselves so they can keep up with who is working for them and how much they are earning.

''Hong Kong's Chinese prefer to do business face-to-face. Whether it is a multi-million dollar deal or a very small transaction, the personal contact is a vital aspect of the business relationship. This is part of the personally oriented approach to life that is characteristic of the Chinese. While dealings begin on a group-to-group or company-to-company basis, all interactions thereafter are on a person-to-person basis. The Chinese must like and trust the other party to do business with them. Unlike business in the U.S. and elsewhere in the West, where intercompany dealings are often totally imper-sonal—oftentimes handled by computer without any personal touch—the Chinese want and need the face-to-face contact.

''In the Chinese concept, a business relationship is not based only on supply and demand or the bottom line. It is a personal relationship first and a business relationship second. And generally speaking, the personal relationship has to come first and thereafter takes precedence over all other considerations. The Chinese do business on the basis of trust and knowing that the other party will follow the rules and not let them down,'' he added.

Hong Kong is probably the most competitive economy in the world and there is no sympathy for unrelated companies that have problems. ''Two of the most important rules among Chinese businessmen here," said one, "is that you don't make mistakes and you don't cheat. If you do either of these, your credibility is shot. And another thing: Chinese companies do not share information."

A top Chinese executive in one of Hong Kong's largest companies said one of the primary differences in the Chinese and Western way of doing business could be traced to the fact that, in the West, business developed its own culture, separate from private or personal culture, with a different set of rules and a character of its own. This separation, he continued, resulted in the development of a different morality for companies, one that depersonalized management and workers.

"In the Chinese context there is no separate morality for business. There are no separate rules that divide the conduct of business from that of personal affairs, in which the key factor is proper human relations. And, of course, proper human relations in Chinese terms means personal relations primarily based on Confucianism. A successful business relationship between Chinese companies begins with the establishment of a personal bond between the principal managers of the companies and is based thereafter on the careful maintenance of these personal ties.

"Within the Chinese-run company, good managers also know that the happiness of employees is as important to the company as profits. If they are treated properly and are happy, you can count on their loyalty and productivity. Of course, Hong Kong Chinese are very entrepreneurial minded, so you are naturally going to lose a certain number of employees regardless of how you treat them. The overriding concern of Chinese is future security."

Continued the executive: "Generally speaking, Western businessmen do not do business on the basis of personal trust, personal commitments or obligations. They emphasize product, price, profit and service, which have very little to do with their personal character or beliefs. When they come to Hong Kong they often have a difficult time because they have never had to truly depend upon anyone else."

Starting Small and Working Up

Ordinarily Hong Kong Chinese do not make big deals immediately upon establishing a relationship with a company. "We prefer to give the relationship time to develop, to create friendship and trust, and only after we feel secure in the relationship do we go for big deals. If a customer feels he will not be taken advantage of, he will buy confidently and recommend freely," said one.

Despite all these factors, dealings with Hong Kong Chinese do not have to be the long drawn-out affairs that are typical of the Japanese. In fact, businesspeople in Hong Kong probably make quicker decisions than anywhere else in the world. Here the competition is so intense they cannot afford to delay things.

The bureaucratic restraints of the People's Republic of China contrast sharply with the quicksilver entrepreneurial methods of Hong Kong and Taiwan, says Albert Cheng, Asian representative of a Canadian gold marketer. "You are dealing with a government agency. You know you cannot get a decision from a single individual, and you are often not sure if you are talking to the right man or the top man."

Cheng says business in Hong Kong is done in a dozen different styles. "The typical family style of business is still common but things are changing fast despite the objections of the older generation. The reasons for these changes are as varied as the places they come from. I think the greatest contributor to change in the way business is done in Hong Kong is the United States. American influence here is becoming stronger and stronger, and I think change is good as long as it comes naturally. Look at many of the Japanese companies that have come here. They are totally insular and have very little contact with anyone else. They don't seem to trust any non-Japanese. Their style is not a healthy mix. It is more parasitic. Yet it is causing change here."

The Chinese concept of stability is different from that in the West, Cheng said. History has proven to the Chinese over millenniums that if they don't take care of their own families, no one else will. This feeling of absolute responsibility includes the next generation as well, not just the present one.

One of the hallmarks of business in Hong Kong is the degree of service provided by most companies. In a business community where pressure from competitors and potential competitors is a constant threat to one's survival, service often makes the difference. "As a general rule, the policy is to 'over-serve' rather than 'under-serve,' " said one.

Banking is one area where the differences between Chinese and Western concepts are clearly distinguishable, says Hong Kong banker John Man. "Although the banking systems in China and the West serve the same purpose, they are very different in nature," Man said. "The West cherishes the preciseness of financial statements, while the Chinese put more faith in the virtue of the individual. In the West it is statistics, records and cash-flow. You put the values into a computer and press a button. In China the focus is on the individual. If the relationship between people is strong, money is usually secondary. Developing this degree of trust is complicated and slow, but it is the Chinese way.

"In the U.S. in particular, success is generally measured in individual financial terms. In China success is more likely measured in terms of individual relationships, and in improving one's own economic station through close cooperation and interaction with others. The most successful firms in Hong Kong are those that combine Chinese and Western concepts—the Chinese way of building relationships, and the Western way of management. By itself the Chinese way of doing business is often impractical, while the Western way is generally superficial. Taking the best parts from both is a slow process but it seems to work well.''

Service is especially important in the banking business in Hong Kong, and John Man personifies the Chinese approach. "The most important thing for me to always remember is that if I cannot help a customer, I am not doing my job. It is my job to provide customers with what they want or find someone else who can. The Chinese expect that kind of service, and if they don't get it they won't do business with you if there is any other choice.''

Understanding Chinese Motives

Said a foreign business executive stationed in Hong Kong: "You cannot stereotype all Chinese businessmen, but if you can understand their love of money and their desire to provide the best security for their families and their companies, you can do business with them.

"Most Western businessmen I talk to say the Chinese are the worst liars in the world, and will change prices, quality and other commitments from one day to the next. But you rarely see or hear of this kind of thing among Chinese companies. It generally only happens to foreigners who come here to make quick money, without doing things in the proper way. In a way, foreigners are considered fair game. They aren't part of the family.

"It is typical of Western businessmen to jump at bargains or at what appear to be bargains, often at the expense of established relationships. That kind of behavior creates distrust among the Chinese, and gives them another reason for being wary of Western businessmen. To the Chinese, protecting one's business relationships is a primary rule of the game.''

Another area in which Hong Kong's Chinese businesspeople and foreign businessmen often part company is in "paying" for introductions and connections that lead to business. There are exceptions, but Hong Kong Chinese generally expect to be paid commissions on such business. While foreign businesspeople generally do not expect to be paid directly for such favors, they gladly accept payment in kind—either in the form of meals and entertainment, gifts, trips, or other favors.

Probably the best approach to doing business with Hong Kong Chinese, said an experienced Westerner, is to never take anything for granted. "As a foreigner you are never truly accepted by the Chinese because you cannot *become* Chinese, but if you follow the rules and prove yourself worthy of their trust there are no people in the world who are better to do business with. Their loyalty to you even transcends time and is passed on from one generation to the next.''

Hong Kong Spirits

There are said to be some one hundred geomancers still practicing the ancient art of *feng shui* in Hong Kong. While most of the more Westernized Chinese may choose to ignore the ancient belief, many others will not take any fundamental action without calling in a geomancer, whether the action is something as ordinary as arranging furniture or taking a trip. Old-timers in Hong Kong delight in pointing out buildings that have their front doors where Westerners would expect the back doors to be and mirrors strategically placed to confuse spirits and keep them out of buildings.

Believers say the proper alignment of walls, doors, desks, even beds, is essential if people are to stay in balance with the eight elements of nature and the forces of yin and yang that control the world.

Hong Kong Cantonese are also especially sensitive to numbers, which accounts for the popularity of three, eight, and nine. Three sounds like the word for ''life'' in Cantonese; eight sounds like ''prosperity''; and nine suggests ''eternity.'' Each year the Hong Kong government takes in several million dollars extra (for charity) by auctioning off combinations of lucky license plate numbers.

A Little Cantonese Lesson

The principal Chinese language of Hong Kong, Macao, and the surrounding region is Cantonese, which has nine tones. Since it has five more than Mandarin, it is said to be more difficult to learn. It is certainly a ''noisier'' language. Foreigners first exposed to Cantonese often believe the speakers are engaged in a serious shouting match. Apparently having to enunciate the different tones clearly makes it necessary to emphasize them loudly. Here are a few useful words and numbers (which you do not have to shout out to be understood!).

Good morning	Jo san (*Joe sahn*)
Good night	Jo tau (*Joe tah-uu*)
Goodbye	Joy geen (*Joy gheen*)
Thank you (for service)	M'goy (*Mm-goy*)
Thank you (for gift)	Doh jay (*dor chay*)
Yes	Hai (*Hie*)
No	M'hai (*Mm-hie*)

Please (for service)	M'goy (*Mm-goy*)
Please (invitation)	Cheng
How much?	Gay daw cheen?
I'm sorry (excuse me)	Doy-m-jay
Hello (on the phone)	Way!
Today	Gum yat (*Goom yhat*)
Tomorrow	Ting yat (*Ting yaht*)
Where?	Been doh?
When?	Gay see hai? (*Gay-see-hie*)
How far?	Gay yuen? (*Gay yuu-inn*)
A menu, please	Tsan pai, m'goy (*T'sahn pie, mm-goy*)
The bill, please	Mai dan, m'goy (*My dahn, mm-goy*)
Coffee	Kahfey
Beer	Bayjau (*Bay-jauh*)
House maid	Amah (*Ah-mah*)
Bottoms Up!	Yam Seng (*Yahm Sing!*)

1 yaht	12 sahp yee	23 yee sahp sahm
2 yee	13 sahp sahm	24 yee sahp say
3 sahm	14 sahp say	25 yee sahp ng
4 say	15 sahp ng (*sahp nng*)	30 sahm sahp
5 ng (*nng*)	16 sahp luk	40 say sahp
6 luk	17 sahp chat	50 ng sahp (*nng sahp*)
7 chat	18 sahp baht	100 yaht bahk
8 baht	19 sahp gau (*sahp gow*)	200 yee bahk
9 gau (*gow*)	20 yee sahp	300 sahm bahk
10 sahp	21 yee sahp yaht	400 say bahk
11 sahp yaht	22 yee sahp yee	500 ng bahk (*nng bahk*)

Place Names in Hong Kong

Aberdeen	Heung Gong Chai (*He-ung Gong Chie*)
Causeway Bay	Tung Lo Wan (*Tung Low Wahn*)
Central District	Chung Waan (*Choong Wah-ahn*)
Hong Kong	Heung Gong (*He-ung Gong*)
Kai Tak Airport	Kai Tak Gei Cheung (*Kie Tahk Gay Chee-ung*)
Kowloon	Gau Lung (*Gow Loong*)
Macao Ferry Pier	O Moon Ma Tau (*Oh Moon Mah Tauh*)
New Territories	San Gaai (*Sahn Gah-aye*)

Ocean Park	Hoi Yeung Kung Yuen (*Hoy Ye-ung Koong Yuu-inn*)
Outlying Districts Services Pier	Gong Noy Sin Ma Tau (Gong Noy Sin Ma Tou)
The Peak	Saan Deng (*Saahn Deng*)
Repulse Bay	Chin Sui Wan (*Cheen Swee Wahn*)
Star Ferry Hong Kong side	Tin Sing Ma Tau (*Teen Sing Mah Tauh*)
Star Ferry Kowloon side	Jim Sa Jui Ma Tau (*Jeem-sah Juu-ee Mah Tauh*)
Stanley	Chik Chue (*Cheek Chway*)
Tsim Sha Tsui	Jim Sa Jui (*Jeem Sah Juu-ee*)
Wanchai	Waan Chai (*Won-chie*)

10

Eating and Drinking Etiquette

"For the people, food is heaven."
—A CHINESE PROVERB

Mystery and Mystique of Chinese Food

Eating together has traditionally been next to sex in shared human experiences. Inviting someone to be your guest at a meal is one of the strongest expressions one person can make to another—and nowhere is this more so than in China. In fact, one of the best and easiest ways the foreign businessperson can effectively demonstrate knowledge and appreciation of Chinese culture (and the Chinese people) is through knowledge of Chinese cuisine, its mysteries, and its mystique.

At the same time, the official business banquets for which China is famous have become one of the most controversial aspects of the country's Open Door policy, with officials accused of squandering hundreds of millions of yuan a year for an unnecessarily large number of elaborate banquets. In part because of their low salaries, officials throughout the country take advantage of their authority to spend public money on such banquets as one of the key fringe benefits of their positions. The government rule of ''four dishes, one soup'' is routinely ignored.

International conferences, which invariably include one or more banquets, have also proliferated to the point that they now cost the state more than five hundred million yuan a year. Party leaders in various cities attempt to control such expenditures through a number of imaginative means. The

202

city of Shenyang, for example, collects a "fat tax" on all official banquets. Despite the criticism and the tax, however, the banquets go on as more and more Chinese indulge themselves in a frenzy of eating high off the proverbial hog.

Good Chinese food (meaning that prepared of quality ingredients by an experienced chef) is, in fact, much more than nourishment for the body. Being the handiwork of an ancient culture that has been developed and refined over a period of 5,000 years, Chinese food is meant to please the palate, to feast the eyes, to ensure optimum health, and "to repose benignly on the stomach."

The Chinese are probably more food-conscious than any other people. Their vocabulary relating to foods is especially rich, and a polite, traditional greeting is not "How are you?" but "Have you eaten?" The Chinese "banquet meal" has even broader dimensions. It serves as a therapeutic roundtable at which one sloughs off the burdens of the day and reenergizes the spirit. (It is not only the growing numbers of affluent people who are conspicuous for their eating habits. The old saying, "The poorer one is, the more he likes to eat," is indicative of the traditional Chinese attitude toward food.)

To fully savor Chinese cuisine requires a certain degree of learning and aesthetic appreciation. It is not an automatic thing that comes with the food. Both host and guests must recognize and respond to choices well made, to dishes of exceptional quality, and to the ambience of the occasion (a lot of us are more apt to achieve this enviable state by getting a bit tipsy—something the Chinese approve of quite highly).

While the Chinese have traditionally eaten almost anything that grows, from snakes to birds' nests, they have over the centuries become masters at transforming the most questionable ingredients into gourmet delicacies.

The Yin/Yang Principle

Furthermore, the Chinese have traditionally been guided in their approach to eating by the ancient principle of *yin* and *yang,* which holds that everything in the universe is either positive or negative, wet or dry, cold or hot, light or dark, male or female, plus or minus, and so on, and that there must be a harmonious balance between these opposing forces if we are to stay right with the cosmos.

Within this thesis, every category of food—meat, fowl, vegetable, fruit, nut, liquid,—has its own specific yin or yang character and should be consumed in combinations and quantities that are balanced. (Yin foods are thin, bland, cooling and low in calories; yang foods are rich, spicy, warming and high in calories. Boiling foods makes them yin; deep-frying makes them yang.)

Further, the Chinese believe that each individual is constitutionally yin or yang or a combination of the two. These three types of people are described as "positive," "negative," and "nervous"—the latter being those who are mixtures of yin and yang. And this fundamental factor must also be taken into consideration in eating.

Be that as it may, there is a certain order one is expected to follow in eating Chinese food. Whether the reasoning is based on valid scientific principles or simply an age-old custom derived from other sources, the guidelines are part of the fabric of Chinese life and, generally speaking, are automatically followed by all.

In the Chinese lexicon, the five tastes of food—spicy, bitter, sweet, sour and salty—are intimately linked with the five primary elements of the Chinese cosmology—metal, wood, water, earth and fire—and with the five primary internal organs of the body.

The Chinese believe that peppery foods clean the lungs, that bitter foods relieve gastroenteritis, that sour foods refresh and strengthen the liver, that salty foods strengthen the kidneys and bones, and that sweet foods invigorate the spleen.

According to Chinese theory, the effects of various foods differ with the personality of the individual. They also believe that abalone calms the nerves and clears the eye; that almonds form a protective film on the stomach walls, thereby reducing the effects of alcohol; that bamboo shoots and burdock speed up metabolism and stimulate bowel activity; that carp speeds up blood circulation and the activity of the internal organs; that chestnuts are an excellent energizer; that dried orange peels stimulate digestion; that clams have a tranquilizing, restful effect.

Other foods with reputedly specific effects on the body that have long been famous among the Chinese include: ginseng, which helps regulate the functions of the glands; laver/seaweed, which reduces inflammation; and lotus root, which has a significant sedative effect that greatly benefits insomniacs and contributes to elasticity of the blood vessels, thereby benefiting people suffering from bleeding ailments.

Pickled plums have long been famous for relieving the effects of hangovers and refreshing the stomach and bowels. Red beans are noted for relieving fatigue and stimulating both the heart and urinary system. Garlic is noted for stimulating the internal organs as well as warming the body and aiding in the absorption of nutrients. Sesame seeds are reknowned as an energizer and in aiding digestion. Shrimp are also said to have a fast energizing effect and to be especially beneficial to people recovering from illnesses.

Regardless of whether any of these claims are true—and there is established scientific evidence to support many of them—Chinese food has long been prepared and consumed with more intelligence and more understanding of nutritional as well as psychological effects than existed in any other culture. Chinese doctors have been using diet to cure many diseases for more than two thousand years. As early as 200 A.D. they were writing learned treatises on the importance of a balanced diet.

The Chinese Ways of Cooking

The special character of Chinese food derives from the manner of preparation, the methods of cooking, the timing, the sauces used, and of course the ingredients.

Generally speaking, the first principle of a large share of Chinese cooking is to chop, mince, crush, shred, grind, score, dice, or slice all ingredients into bit-sized or paper-thin pieces. The second principle is that the food should be cooked quickly over a very hot fire so that the natural characteristics, including the minerals and vitamins, are left intact. The third principle is that a wide variety of spices and other taste enhancers such as coriander, aniseed, sesame, plum sauce, oyster juice, and soy are used.

The primary Chinese cooking methods are cold-mix, barbecuing, deep-frying, shallow-frying, roasting, sautéing, simmering, braising, steaming, and stir-frying. The cutting and the ingredients determine how long each dish is cooked. And being able to judge just the right amount of time to achieve the desired consistency, taste, and appearance is one of the key arts of Chinese cuisine.

Another distinctive characteristic of Chinese food is provided by the ingredients themselves—shark's fin, jelly fish, squid, sea cucumber, bamboo, birds' nests, tree fungi, roots, nuts, and numerous other exotic materials, along with the more common meats, fowl, seafoods, vegetables, and fruits.

Main Styles

Then there are regional differences in Chinese cooking that range from the subtle to the flamboyant and give it a variety and nuance unmatched by any other cuisine. The most comprehensive and popular of these regional "styles" of Chinese cuisine—which originated in the northern, southern, eastern and western regions of the huge landmass—are Guangdon (Cantonese), Sichuan, Jiangsu (Beijing), and Shangdong (Shanghai). Each of these regional schools has at least one hundred individual, distinctive dishes, and there are more than one hundred minor "schools" of Chinese cuisine.

The Mandarin or Beijing style of Chinese cookery is marked by refinements and subleties that originated in the kitchens of the emperors and members of the royal families during the long dynastic reigns of the past. Its variety of starchy dishes owe their origin to the cold, harsh winter climate of northern China.

Among the other characteristics of Mandarin cuisine are the liberal use of vegetable oils, sesame oil, garlic, vinegar, salt, scallions, and spicy sauces to enhance the flavor and warm up the body; the use of rice wine as a cooking "oil"; the popularity of wheat buns, rolls, and dumplings (baked, steamed, or fried); and an emphasis on deep-frying to ensure crispness.

Some of the specialities of Beijing cuisine are the famous Beijing (Peking) Duck (the original recipe for which is said to have been 15,000 words long), fried meatballs, mutton, noodles, meat buns and dumplings, cold sesame-spiced chicken with noodles, paper-thin wheat pancakes stuffed with fried shredded beef and green peppers, casserole of shark's fin with cabbage and soybean curd, ham and winter-melon soup, sweet-sour fish, chicken and black mushrooms, and bamboo shoots with mushrooms.

Cantonese is probably the best known of all Chinese cooking styles because so many people from this region spread around the world during the domestic turmoil of the 1800s and early 1900s. It is characterized by the use of dozens of contrasting sauces—sweet/sour or sharp/bland—with similar contrasts in colors and textures.

Oil is used sparingly by Cantonese chefs, and many dishes are parboiled before quick-frying. Half-cooking and steaming to preserve natural flavors is also typical of Cantonese cooking. Overall, Cantonese dishes are mild instead of spicy. Ginger is a popular ingredient, and rice is a mainstay of any Cantonese meal.

Some popular Cantonese choices are sweet/sour pork,* abalone in oyster sauce, meat buns, shrimp dumplings, "1,000 year-old" eggs, braised brisket of beef in sauce, chicken with bamboo shoots in sauce, shark's fin soup with shredded chicken, minced quail with lettuce, and baked prawns with spiced salt and chili.

Secrets of Chinese Chefs

The preparation of Chinese food is simple in concept and methodology, but successfully accomplishing each of the steps so that the result is both attractive

---

*It has been my experience that you can fairly accurately judge the merits of a Chinese restaurant by its sweet/sour pork. If the sauce is good and the meat is lean, tender and tasty, chances are all the rest of the food served by the restaurant will be good. But if the "pork" is gristle concealed under batter, no amount of the greatest sauce can transform it into something fit to eat—and chances are the remainder of the dishes on the menu will also be less than meets the eye.

and tasty requires a very high degree of skill—skill that generally comes only after years of dedicated apprenticeship to a master chef.

The ultimate secret of Chinese food, as in all great cuisines of the world, is first in its sauces and second in the way the ingredients are prepared and cooked. The various ways of cooking Chinese food—the *wok*, intense heat applied for short periods, the use of particular oils, spices and essences—are not mysterious at all. It is in the combinations and proportions of its sauces and ingredients that the exotic character and quality of Chinese food emerges. And here is where the master chef comes in.

Outstanding Chinese cooks and chefs have been coveted for centuries. The skill and creativity of the chef is, after all, what distinguishes a Chinese restaurant. Recognizing this, commercial entrepreneurs in major Chinese food centers such as Tokyo, Yokohama, Taipei, Hong Kong, Macao, and Singapore compete for the services of master chefs. And in these cities, where the food and beverage departments of world-class hotels are the primary revenue producers, master Chinese chefs are not only wooed and feted, they are publicized as celebrities.

Recognizing the value of trained Chinese chefs, the Beijing Friendship Service Corporation (BFSC) and the China Cuisine Skill Export Corporation (CCSEC) "exports" them to foreign countries. The BFSC was set up in 1980; the CCSEC dates from 1987. Together they have exported hundreds of chefs to over twenty countries. An estimated 10,000 Chinese chefs are now working abroad.

There are eight grades of chef in China. The top ones compete for gold, silver, and bronze medals in an annual National Cuisine Skill Contest in Beijing. In each contest, there are 80 gold medal winners, 120 silver medal winners, and 200 bronze medal winners.

Styles of Eating

Generally speaking, there are two styles of Chinese meals—family style and banquet style. The family style, in which everyone helps himself or herself from a number of communal dishes, is followed both in homes and in restaurants. Banquet-style dining most often occurs in restaurants, usually involves guests, is more formal, and typically takes place in a private room.

What is served at traditional banquet meals varies according to the nature of the event. There are customary dishes for wedding parties, birthday parties, memorial occasions, and other celebrations. In the case of business banquets, the hosts usually choose several of the more popular items as main dishes (which range from seven or eight to fourteen or fifteen), so there is ample food for every preference.

There is a great deal of special etiquette involved in dining Chinese style, not only in what is eaten but also in the order in which the various dishes are eaten, as well as the treatment of guests and where dining takes place.

Seating Etiquette

Eating arrangements are very important at meetings with Chinese, including meals—whether or not they are officially hosted. In the case of formal dinners, the host and chief guest sit on opposite sides of the table, facing each other. The chief guest is always seated at the "head" of the room, facing the door; the host with his or her back to the door. In most restaurant arrangements, this means the host is also closest to the door (and in a better position to give orders to the waiters as they come and go).

Other guests are seated to the left and right of the chief guest in descending order of their rank or importance. This means that the two lowest ranking members in the party may end up seated to the immediate right and left of the host—just the opposite of what a Westerner might expect. In Chinese etiquette, the left side is the seat of honor.

The thinking behind the Chinese-style seating arrangement is simple and logical. It assures that the host will have a direct view of the main guest, and only slightly oblique views of other guests of importance.

Foreign guests who are not familiar with the Chinese custom of seating should not rush to sit down. They should wait for the host to indicate where they are to be seated. At this point, the chief guest may get up and serve the host the first drink, who then reciprocates. Thereafter, others take turns offering drinks to both the host and guests. The official toast in China is *Ganbei* which literally means "dry glass," but is our equivalent of "Bottoms up." The toast drink officially favored by government dignitaries is *maotai*, a fiery liquid made from sorghum. Generally, guests are expected to *gan bei* only the first toast. Subsequent toasts—and there may be many of them—can be sipped.

At more formal gatherings, the host will generally make a brief speech, welcoming the guests and making other suitable comments, and then lead the group in a *Ganbei* toast. The chief guest normally responds with a few comments of his own and a toast, but not until after the second or third dish has been served.

When the host picks up his chopsticks, that is the signal for everyone to begin eating. It is a special honor for the host to serve an individual guest with his own chopsticks—something the foreign business host can easily do to indicate respect and appreciation for one or more of the guests. There are usually a pair of serving chopsticks on the table for use by the host. If there is none, the practice is to use the reverse end of the host's own chopsticks. The host will serve the chief guest and two or three associates (those easily reached). Then those associates will serve the other guests nearest them. In some very formal situations, the hosts serve the guests each time a new dish is brought out, thereafter letting them help themselves if they want seconds from the same dish.

It is the responsibility of the host and the host's side—not waiters or servants—to see that the guests' drinking glasses are refilled. It is also customary for the host to accompany each guest to the door when a meal or party ends. Ranking guests are normally accompanied all the way to their automobiles, and the host waits until they drive away before going back inside.

A typical Chinese dinner for special guests will consist of ten to fifteen courses (although Shanghai is trying to reduce the number of dishes by more than half!), beginning with a platter of cold cuts. This is followed by a variety of dishes that usually covers the gamut of the five basic tastes—sweet, sour, salty, spicy, and bitter. A sweet dish is served about midway in the meal (many foreigners think this is the end of the meal and fill up too soon). The meal usually ends with a fish dish (which signifies abundance), soup, and some kind of dessert, such as fresh fruit. The accepted way of indicating that you have had enough is to leave some food on your plate.

Chinese banquets usually start at 6:30 P.M. and end at 8:30 P.M. Just as in diplomatic protocol, the host group arrives first and forms a line in a reception area to greet each visitor. There is usually a period of casual chatting in the reception room when tea may be served before the guests are directed to the adjoining dining room.

The Quick-Gorge Syndrome

People not familiar with Chinese banquet-style meals typically eat too much too soon, partially if not completely spoiling the overall experience for themselves. At a meal for twelve, for example, four appetizer dishes will be served at the same time. Novice diners almost always partake as if these were the main-course dishes. Shortly thereafter, out comes another four dishes, several of which are likely to be more filling than the first round. Once again, novice diners take full portions. By the time they finish this round, they have often have enough to eat.

Then four *more* dishes—generally the best—are served. Finally, when the last round arrives, newcomers to the Chinese way are in pain. You can generally figure that in a party of six or more people—when there is nothing special to celebrate—there will be at least one appetizer, four mid-course dishes, and one or two ending dishes. On special occasions, there can be as many as twelve mid-course dishes.

Keep in mind that eating everything that is served to you can backfire in another way as well. The host will presume that you are still hungry and continue to add new helpings to your plate every time you clean it off. If you persist in eating all of a second or third helping, the host may feel you are saying the meal was inadequate.

Another thing to keep in mind is that plain white rice is generally served near the end of the meal—to clear the palate and give you that nice rounded feeling—unless you order it earlier.

It is also impolite to remove a dish from the Lazy Susan when serving yourself. Use the serving spoon or chopsticks on the plate if there is one. If there is not, use your own spoon or chopsticks. It is polite to use the reverse end of your chopsticks when serving yourself from the communal dishes or when serving others. Fried rice and chow mein are not considered main-course dishes. They are regarded as side dishes or snacks.

Rice Etiquette

It is invariably noted that the equivalent of "How are you?" in Chinese is "Have you eaten rice?" but in this reference "rice" has long since been more of a generic term for "meal" than just rice itself.

Most Westerners automatically think of rice as they do bread, as something to eat along with the other dishes—with the result that they are often mystified when rice is not served at the beginning of the typical Chinese meal, and are very surprised when it is served at the end—when they are often stuffed.

Chinese-style rice is not as glutinous or as sticky as the style preferred in Japan and is therefore more difficult to eat with chopsticks. This is especially true with Chinese-style chopsticks, which are larger and heavier than those favored by the Japanese. If you put some kind of topping on your bowl of rice, such as meat or vegetables, it is permissible to eat it with the curved porcelain spoon that accompanies most Chinese meals.

The use of chopsticks in China dates back to the Han Dynasty (206 B.C.–9 A.D.), if not before. Spoons were also in use by that period, well over a thousand years before such implements became commonplace in Europe. The Chinese word for chopsticks, *kuaitzu,* is said to have two meanings. In one it means "hurry"—possibly a reference to the fact that chopsticks allows one to pick up tidbits of food while they are still hot, thus hastening the eating. The second meaning is given as "little pieces picker upper." Although it is considered rude to lay your chopsticks across the top of a bowl or leave them sticking in a bowl, such etiquette is frequently ignored today, particularly in restaurants.

How to Order Chinese Food

One thing the foreign host should know for sure is how to order Chinese food in the proper sequence—which is based on beginning with nonoily foods, eating any oily foods midway in the meal, and ending with nonoily dishes. This arrangement makes it easier for the stomach to digest the food and enhances the pleasures of eating.

In ordinary family-style dining, the meal beings with soup. Next comes a cold-dish appetizer or "head dish." This is followed by the main entrées— various hot beef, pork, fowl, seafood, and vegetables. Plain white rice usually accompanies family-style meals. The last dish is most often fresh fruit

In a banquet meal, the cold head-dishes are always served first. These may be combination plates, with several different kinds of meat and vegetables on the same platter. The first two main-course dishes usually consist of one sautéed dish and one deep-fried dish. The next two mid-course dishes are always the spiciest, richest, heaviest dishes of the meal. The following two dishes should consist of one light dish, traditionally fish, and one sweet dish. The last main-course dish is a soup. The final dish is normally fresh fruit.

When there are eight or more main dishes, it is common to serve two sweet dishes midway in the meal. These dishes include such things as sweetened lotus seed soup with glutinous rice dumplings, fried apples, fried bananas, dumplings, and sesame seed covered sweet buns.

Testing Your Friendship

The egg is typical of how far the Chinese have gone in getting the most out of food sources. Virtually every egg known is eaten, either steamed, boiled, salted, marinated, or prepared in some other way. Eggs also play various roles in social customs. Probably the most famous—or notorious—of China's egg dishes is the so-called one-thousand-year-old duck egg, which, of course, it not one thousand years old, despite looking and smelling like it might be. The process of creating such eggs is to coat them in a layer of lime clay for six to ten weeks. The lime soaks through the eggshell, turning the egg white into a bluish brown and the yolk into a dark green. The taste that results is a cross between an overripe avocado and fish. Whether or not you eat 1,000-year-old eggs, and appear to enjoy them, may also be used as a test of your friendship for China. Normally they are eaten when nearly black, pungent, and slightly runny. Pieces of sweet-pickled ginger are usually eaten with them.

Shark's Fin Soup

Another popular Chinese dish that is often the subject of risque references is shark's fin soup, not only because it is nutritious, but also because it is widely believed to invigorate the body and to have considerable aphrodisiacal powers. Apparently because of this belief, it is a standard dish in wedding feasts and is traditionally served as the third course.

Actually, shark's fin soup may not always be made of sharks' fins. The fins of other fish are also used in the popular dish. After boiling, drying and, removing the skin and bones, what is left is a gelatinouslike substance that is yellowish white to reddish brown. This is used as the base for a soup that includes such things as crabmeat and roe.

Western businesspeople who order shark's fin soup for their Chinese guests, with suitable comments about its efficacy in sexual matters, demonstrate their knowledge of Chinese ways.

Drinking Your Way to Success

Drinking alcoholic beverages has a long and colorful history in China. Beer, wine, and spirits have been produced and used since ancient times, and were often the cause of great controversy. The manufacture, sale, and consumption of wine was prohibited and then repealed 41 times during the 2,400 years between the Chou and Mongol dynasties. In 1127 A.D., a publisher brought out a comprehensive distiller's manual covering all wines and liquors made in the country.

From earliest times, alcoholic drinks were invariably consumed in conjunction with food or at traditional ceremonies, such as marriages. Eventually they also came to be popular as recreational refreshments and for their supposedly stimulative qualities. One example of their latter role involved a school of poets who drank to stimulate their creative skills and became known as the "Drunken Dragons." One of the best of these poets, Po Li, was out boating on a lotus pond one night while totally soused. He leaned over to embrace the reflection of the moon in the pond, fell overboard, and drowned.

As in other Asian countries, drinking in China has also long been associated with establishing new personal, political, and business relationships, and in celebrating business and political events. Unlike Japan and Korea, however, where there is very strong pressure for everyone to drink to excess, the Chinese are much more tolerant of light drinking and abstinence.

Some of the common Chinese wines are *Shao-shing, Maotai, Ngkapei,* and *Meikweilu. Shao-shing* is a rice wine aged in earthenware jugs to a golden yellow color. Gourmets say it should be at least seven years old and is best when fifteen years old, that it should be served warm, and sipped from small cups. *Moitai*, the famous official drink of the Chinese government, is a potent wine made from sorghum. The alcoholic content is 140–150 proof, much higher than that of vodka, giving it a kick that is bionic. Not all Chinese businesspeople or officials are as immune to its effects as it often seems.

Many substitute water or some other colorless liquid for the powerful brew—
a ploy that foreign businesspeople should definitely keep in mind.

Meikweilu, literally "Rose Petal Dew," is a liquor named after the morning
dew found on rose petals in the district where it originated. *Ngkapei* is a
strong, blood-red liqueur that is stored in earthenware bottles and served in
small cups.

Probably the most notorious Chinese wine, and one that is occasionally
offered to foreign visitors, is *Sam Seh,* which means "Three Snakes," and
refers to the fact that at least one snake has been soaking in the wine for at
least one year. *Sam seh,* a clear "white" wine, reputedly does wonders for
one's general health and stamina.

China's biggest producer of "snake liquor" is Wuzhou Longshan Distillery in Wuzhou City, five hundred miles west of Hong Kong in the Guangxi
Zhuang Atonomous Region, and long known as "Small" or "Little Hong
Kong." The distillery produces some eight hundred "tons" of liquor-with-
snake each year, and exports to forty countries. (Snakes, particularly poison-
ous vipers, which abound in the semitropical region, are also a popular item
on restaurant menus in Wuzhou.)

There are some even more exotic drinks in China. One that older Chinese
men use to commonly drink for their health was known as "rat wine." A
just-born baby rat, with its eyes still closed, is put into the wine to soak.
While usually not available all over the country, connoisseurs say that some
herb shops will make it on order.

As also mentioned earlier, the best-known Chinese drinking toast is *Gan
Bei!* (ghan bay-ee), which literally means "Dry Cup!"—in other words,
"Bottoms Up!" The Cantonese equivalent of this toast is *Yam Sing.* The
Cantonese also have a special toast that refers to sipping instead of bolting
one's drink: *Dap T'sau.* Another common Cantonese toast is *Yahm Pai,* which
means something like "Here's to Your Health!" or "Cheers!"—often said
at the beginning of a meal with any drink that is on the table: water, tea,
or alcoholic. It is a casual, friendly sign of recognition to everyone present
and a signal for the meal to start.

At the beginning of a friendly meal or dinner party, a host or hostess will
often raise his or her glass and say, "*Yam to pai!* Or, "Drink and enjoy
yourself!"

Generally the only toasts that everyone participates in are following remarks by the host and the chief guest when he or she responds (often after
two or three dishes have been served). Other individuals on the host's side
normally take the lead in toasting guests who are seated closest to them.
These toasts may involve only two people or everyone at the table.

When there is more than one table, the host, after his opening remarks,
will often go to each additional table to clink the glasses of each individual
at that table and then drink a toast to them. At official banquets, chief guests

are expected to follow this same custom when they respond, leaving their own table to the last.

In Chinese etiquette, the host is permitted to merely sip his or her drink—or not drink at all—in order to stay sober and properly discharge the responsibilities of the host. But most hosts, it seems to me, choose to join their guests in drinking—and are still able to take care of their host's duties.

A guest may turn the tables on a host by calling for a *gan bei* toast, in which case the host is expected to go all the way—or come up with an acceptable excuse for not drinking or drinking only lightly. Women, particularly if they are not ranking members of the party, are generally excused from the demands of the *gan bei* ritual.

Another common unofficial toast is *Ngo chien ni-i,* which is the equivalent of "Here's to you," or "I drink to you." If you are in Taiwan and want to toast the host or some other individual in your party without making it mandatory that they drain their cup or glass, don't say *Gan bei,* say *Su'i,* which means "Sip" instead of "Bottoms up."

But even if the host or some other party member proposes a "sip" toast and *anyone* in the party does a "bottoms up," it is considered a special politeness (or mark of camaraderie) for everyone to follow suit.

It is also custom for toasts to be proposed in between courses, particularly before the mid-course soup dish. This practice generally has the effect of prolonging the meal and turning it into a noisy party—and is used not only to express special interest or pleasure in the event, but also sometimes to demonstrate drinking prowess.

Refusing to drink an alcoholic beverage when being entertained by a Chinese host is regarded as impolite if not unfriendly, unless you have a good reason, such as an ulcer, high blood pressure, or an upset stomach and make the reason know to the host and party. In this case, joining the toast with water, tea, or a soft drink is acceptable. Tables will frequently be set with three glasses—one for a soft drink, one for beer, and another for toast drinks.

Another way of limiting the amount you drink during toasts is not to fill your cup or glass to the top. Using this strategy will allow you to participate in half a dozen or more *ganbei.*

The cost of drinks served at banquet dinners is not included in the "head rate" that is set for the party. The host designates the drink or drinks to be served, but the total is not added up until after the party is over.

Reciprocating Chinese hospitality can be expensive. Generally the higher the rank of the banquet guest, the higher the *biao zhem* (head rate) charged by the restaurant. The cost is related to the pomp of the banquet—not to the quality of the food—and is a way of showing respect and appreciation to the guest. If, as host, you prefer to choose the dishes you want served, you must advise the chef well in advance.

Hotels are, of course, experienced at helping guests arrange banquets. Some hotels have forms for guests to fill out when they want to hold a banquet at outside restaurants.

Because of the substantial cost of larger banquets, and the fact that the privilege of staging banquets at government expense has been abused so much by officials, the Chinese are now encouraged by the government to hold afternoon receptions instead of sumptuous dinner banquets for their foreign guests—a move that many foreign businesspeople appreciate. Still, the dinner banquet is such a deeply entrenched tradition in China that it remains the most popular way of greeting guests and celebrating special events.

Visitors in China should keep in mind that entertaining businesspeople and official guests is part of the business process in China and should not be regarded as done for personal or social reasons. The Chinese take this part of the business process seriously and can be put off by someone refusing to attend a reception or banquet for any reason within their control. The Chinese generally do very little if any socializing after a dinner is over. As soon as everyone has finished eating, the group ordinarily breaks up and everyone goes home.

Special Notes

In a private setting, such as your home, Chinese etiquette calls for a host who serves tea or any other kind of drink to guests to repeatedly insist that they drink it. If this invitation or entreaty to drink is not repeated two or three times, most Chinese will not touch the drink no matter how long they visit with you.

And just as in Japan and Korea, it is alright to pick up a bowl of noodles in China, hold it under your chin or even right up to your mouth, and to slurp while eating them. When the noodles are hot, the slurping helps to cool them. Otherwise it is just a natural noise made when you suck the noodles in with gusto.

Chinese like their hot drinks hot. Tea served in private settings usually comes in teacups that have tops to keep the heat in. Sunflower seeds may be served with tea as a small snack.

The typical Chinese restaurant roundtable is sized to accommodate twelve people, which is judged to be the maximum number of people who should be seated at one table.

It is customary for hosts to pay for the meals of driver-chauffeurs who are kept waiting during luncheon or dinner parties. The rate for drivers is about one-fourth or one-fifth of that of regular guests.

Glossary

Interesting and Useful Terms

Airen   *(aye-wren)*—Loved one. The current term for *wife*.

Back door   China's "unofficial" economy is known as the "back door." It is similar to the black market that exists in most countries where the flow of goods and services is tightly controlled by the state. "Back door" channels represent a significant part of China's trade.

Bai-jiu   *(by-juu)*—A powerful alcoholic drink that has a strong, burning taste, which foreigners often compare to homemade moonshine or "white lightning."

Bailandi   *(by-lahn-dee)*—The Chinese pronunciation of brandy, a popular gift item.

Bang   *(bhang)*—Faction or gang. Given China's social philosophy, people are invariably divided into groups and are primarily identified by the group they belong to. In the case of politics, these groups or *bang* are referred to as factions or gangs.

Bao che   *(bah-oh-chay)*—This refers to the practice of hiring a taxi by the hour or day and paying a flat fee. It can be very helpful when you have several places to go on the same day when the weather is bad or when you have to go to locations where finding taxis for the return trip might be difficult or impossible.

Bao-xiao   *(bah-oh-she-ow)*—China's system of putting work-related expenditures on the office or company expense account is known as *bao-xiao*. The system also includes the use of any personal equipment or accessory, such as an umbrella, that one uses in conjunction with work. For example, an employee willingly uses his own umbrella to come to work when it is raining, but once at the office or factory he expects the *danwei* or company to provide whatever is needed.

Basi pingguo   *(bah-suh peng-gwah)*—Carmelized apple, a popular dessert following Chinese banquet meals.

Biao shun   *(be-ow shune)*—Literally "per person," this refers to the charge you pay per person at a Chinese banquet-style meal—a figure that is normally agreed upon in advance when the meal involves several people and is in the nature of a party. Some restaurants require that banquet reservations be made two or three days in advance.

Big Road; Little Road—*Big Road* refers to China's major news media, which tend to reflect the attitudes and line of the government and to be dry and hard to digest. *Little Road* refers to the smaller, unofficial publications that carry popular news, including gossip.

Bu fang-bian (*buu fahng-bee-inn*)—"It is not convenient," a stock expression used especially by bureaucrats when asked a question or asked to do something. It is an institutionalized way of saying "no" without coming right out and saying it. Another version is *Bu quing-chu*—"I don't quite understand" or "I'm not too clear about it, which is used in the same manner.

Bu gongkai (*buu gong-kie*)—"Not open," referring to all places and things "closed" to outsiders, including areas involved with national security and political thinking.

Cha dian ` (*chan dee-inn*)—Teahouse, more commonly called *cha guan* in the North. One of the great public institutions of China for centuries, teahouses fell victim to revolutionary madness in the 1960s, but have since reappeared in growing numbers.

Chi ku (*chee-kuu*)—An old phrase meaning to "eat bitterness," in reference to the extraordinary hardships forced onto the Chinese by their governments and by nature over the centuries. Literally the term means to eat vinegar, and nowadays refers to jealousy—especially the jealousy the Chinese feel toward people who are economically better off than they.

Chu Kuo Tequ (*chuu kwoh tay-chu*)—Special Export Zone (SEZ). Now often called *Jingi Te Ou* or Special Economic Zones, or just *Tequ*, Special Zone. Special zones designated by the Chinese government as approved locations for foreign factories, and engaging in the import and export trade.

Dai Ji Juan (*die jee juu-inn*)—Literally "The Great Fist," this is a slow-motion dancelike exercise engaged in every morning at dawn or shortly thereafter by millions of Chinese. The stretching-out, exercise aspects of *Dai Ji Juan* are the first steps in a system that goes on to teach one of the most effective martial arts to have originated in China. As was often the case of China's martial arts, it was "invented" by a priest, not a military man. Only the military and elite upper classes could carry weapons. Ordinary people had to depend on their hands and feet to defend themselves, and out of this need, martial arts were developed. *Dai Ji Juan* is said to keep one limber, healthy, and vital by helping to maintain the life forces of the body in proper balance.

Danwei (*dahn-way*)—A "workplace" or "unit." In China most people are intimately linked with their workplace, which may be a farm, office, factory, school, etc. The *danwei* is much more than just a workplace, however. Its importance is suggested somewhat by one's unit in a tightly structured military organization, but it goes well beyond that. Without a *danwei* one is virtually a nonperson. It is the basis by which each person is identified, and by which each individual is controlled. Approval must be obtained from the *danwei* for many of the things that are a part of one's individual freedoms in Western countries—marriage, changing jobs, moving, obtaining ration cards, etc. In one very real sense, the *danwei* are the building blocks of society in China, often taking precedence over the family. *Danwei-zhuyi*, or *danwei*-ism, refers to such situations as people telephoning some office and identifying themselves only by their *danwei*, not their own names.

Dengji   (*dunge-jee*)—Registration system. As part of China's internal security system, records are supposed to be kept of all visits by Chinese to the offices and homes of foreigners. In the early years, this system was rigorously enforced, with assigned "watchers" recording every move foreigners made and reporting every visitor they had. Enforcement slacked off rapidly in the late 1980s, and is now mostly ignored.

Doujiang   (*douh-jee-ahng*)—Milk made from bean curd. A popular breakfast food.

Dui   (*duu-we*)—This is the closest word to *yes* that exists in Chinese. It really means *correct*. *Shi*, also sometimes used to mean *yes*, actually means *to be*. The Chinese seldom use any form of *yes*. The usual practice is to repeat the verb form used in the question (as is the case in Japanese as well).

Duibuqi   (*duu-we-buu-chee*)—I'm sorry ("face you not").

Dui wai yinxiang   (*duu-we wye yeen-shee-ahng*)—The outside world; a term that is pregnant with meaning in distinguishing between China and other countries.

Gan bei   (*ghan bay*)—"Bottoms up." This popular toast generally means what it says: you drink the whole thing in one chug. If you prefer drinking in moderation, just smile and say, "Sui bian," which figuratively but politely means "You do it the way you want to and I'll do it my way and stay sober."

Ganbu   (*gahn-buu*)—This word is frequently translated as *cadre*, and sometimes as *official*. It may refer to any level of government employee, from a clerk to the top political leader of the country. There are twenty-four grades of cadre, with the lowest being grade twenty-four and the highest number one. Generally, the ranks of individuals are not mentioned in references to them.

Guanxi   (*gwahn-shee*)—Connections. Given the rigid division of Chinese society (into families, villages, professions, schoolmates, workplace), divisions that are difficult or impossible to cross because it is virtually taboo to make contact with someone with whom you do not have a recognized and sanctioned relationship, *guanxi*, or "connections," are the oil of life. The Chinese spend a great deal of their time, energy, and income on nurturing their connections and trying to develop new ones. The foreign businessperson wanting to succeed in China would do well to imitate the Chinese and build up his or her own network of *guanxi*, in and out of government.

Gu dong dian   (*guu dong dee-in*)—Antique shop, a favorite shopping place for visitors in China. In Beijing, Liu Li Chang is noted for its *gu dong* (which is also used in reference to an old-fashioned person).

Gwei Lo   (*gway low*)—Foreign devil, a term used in China for many centuries in reference to foreigners.

Hai shen   (*hie shuun*)—Sea slugs. Considered a great delicacy by the Chinese, sea slugs are often offered to foreign guests as something very special (also, it seems, sometimes in the nature of a test, to see how deeply committed an individual is to China!).

Hukou   (*huu-kow*)—Household Registration Certificate. This is the I.D. certificate that all Chinese must carry. It allows the Chinese authorities to keep track of everyone in the country, to control their movements and actions. To *cha hukou* is to check their I.D., often done by officials to harass people. Colloquially when people are overinquisitive, a Chinese may sarcastically ask: *"Cha hukou?"* (What are you doing?)

Iron Rice Bowl—This refers to guaranteed lifetime employment. In other words, the person with a job for life will never have to worry about having an empty rice bowl—i.e., going hungry. In actual practice, employment is no longer guaranteed for life throughout Chinese industry, but the government tries to make sure that everyone is gainfully employed.

Jishu jiaoliu   *(jee-shuu jee-ow-lee-uu)*—Technical exchange. This is the term the Chinese use to describe a presentation made by foreign interests wanting to introduce their technology into China. The Chinese may take the position that they should get *all* of the technology during the presentation, whether or not they intend to sign any kind of contract with the company making the presentation.

Joss—One of the most used words in Chinese, *joss* means "luck," something the people previously had to depend upon to an extraordinary degree, not only in respect to the vagaries of nature but also in their everyday affairs, since their rights were subject to arbitrary interpretation by anyone superior to them.

Kai-fang   *(kie-fahng)*—Open Door policy, introduced by then Vice-Premier Xiaoping Deng in 1978.

Kai-shui   *(kie-shuu-ee)*—Boiled water. Since public water purification systems are rare in China, it is important that visitors who do not have access to treated water drink only boiled water (or bottled drinks).

Kaolu   *(kow-luu)*—"I'll/we'll consider it." A very common expression used to put someone off, to delay something, or to avoid making any kind of commitment; sometimes because the individual approached does not have the authority to respond and must consult with other members of his or her unit; and sometimes because the individual simply doesn't want to be bothered.

Kao-shi   *(kow-shee)*—Examinations. Although exams in China are no longer as long, rigid, or impractical as the exams of Imperial China, they are still difficult and important, and responsible for much of the stress faced by China's young. Examination month is known as "Black July."

Kao ya   *(kow yah)*—Beijing duck or Peking duck, one of Beijing's most popular specialty dishes, also featured in many Beijing-style restaurants around the world.

Laisee   *(lie-suuh)*—These are red envelopes used to present "lucky money" to people as a gift.

Lao   *(lah-oh)*—Old. It is still a compliment to be called *lao* in China. Respect for the aged in China is not only steeped in the culture, it is also reflected in the law, the aged having many services and privileges denied to younger people.

Leng tsai   *(loong-t'sie)*—Cold hors d'oeuvres, usually the first dish in a Chinese banquet. The cold cuts usually include chicken and various kinds of seafood.

Lian-ai   *(lee-inn-aye)*—This is a new term, concocted in recent times, to mean romantic love between a man and a woman. In feudal China, the concept of romantic love was not unknown but it was not sanctioned by society and there was no word for it. This does not mean, however, that men and women in old China were not capable of romantic love and did not engage in it when the opportunity presented itself. However, there were few opportunities, at least for most people, because the two sexes were kept separated most of the time. On the other hand, sexual activity by itself was not regarded as a sin by the Chinese, and pornographic literature reached dazzling and no doubt dizzying heights during the long feudal age.

Lijie   (*lee-jee-eh*)—Etiquette or rules of behavior, also often translated as "rites." If all of the rules governing traditional Chinese behavior were put into a book and thoroughly explained, the book would be several thousand pages long. Long before Confucius, who was born in 551 B.C., the Chinese had developed a meticulous system of personal and private behavior that applied to virtually every action of their lives. As the generations passed, Confucianists and other scholars equated obedience to this highly systemized behavior with ethics and philosophy and the moral welfare of the nation. To follow all the dictates of *li* was to be upright and moral and guarantee peace and progress in the nation.

Strict obedience to traditional etiquette has, of course, changed with the times, but *li* is still of vital importance in everyday life in China. On an official level, however, much of what passes as sincere manners (and ethics) is no more than form, as in two diplomats saying nice things and toasting each other.

Liumang   (*lee-uu-mahng*)—A term that originally meant "vagabond" but is now used to refer to the street hoodlums often seen in China's major cities. Combined with *shua* (*shua liumang*), it is often used to describe the actions of a man deliberately feeling a woman on a crowded bus.

Luxinshe   (*luu-sheen-shay*)—China Travel Service (CTS).

Mandarin—In New China, Mandarin refers to the national language, which is the language that developed in the Beijing area. Mandarin is as different from the other "dialects" of China as French is from Italian. Education throughout China is conducted in the national language, but millions of Chinese continue to speak their own native language-dialect in their daily lives. In dynastic China, the word *Mandarin* referred to the class of scholar-officials who administered the laws of the country and were generally also the largest landowners.

Maotai   (*mah-oh-tie*)—This is the fiery alcoholic drink favored by the Chinese in toasts. It is made from sorghum.

Mei-yu fa-zi   (*may-yuu fah-jee*)—"There is nothing you can do about it" or "It can't be helped," an expression that one often hears in Taiwan in reference to situations that actually cannot be changed or that appear hopeless. It may also be used as an excuse to avoid making any effort.

Mian'ao   (*mee-in ow*)—The padded cotton coat that is so important to residents of northern China in winter.

Naixin   (*nye-sheen*)—Patience—something foreigners are constantly being told they must have to get anything done in China.

Nei-bu   (*nay-buu*)—"Internal" or "inside" in the sense of being restricted to those who are on the inside of an office or organization. The word is used in reference to printed materials or publications that go beyond what is available in the general news media, several of which flourish in China. The largest such publication, *Reference News*, has a circulation in excess of ten million. Any Chinese can subscribe to the paper, but foreigners in China are not supposed to buy or read it. The most exclusive of these "internal" publications are called *nei-can*, which are available only to higher-ranking government officials.

Nei-hang   (*nay-hahng*)—An expert, literally "inside the profession." By the same token, a novice is known as *wai-hang* or "outside the profession."

Nei wai yuobie   (*nay wye yuu-oh-bee-eh*)—"Never forget there is a difference between Chinese and foreigners!"—a common saying.

Pai-ma-pi   (*pie-mah-pee*)—"Pat the horse's rump," an interesting way to say "brown-nose" or curry favor with someone.

Pa ma-fan   (*pah mah-fahn*)—This literally means "to fear trouble," and is an expression the Chinese commonly use when they are afraid some action is likely to get them into trouble.

Pengyou   (*pung-yoh-uu*)—*Friend*, one of the most important words in Chinese dialogue with foreigners. Most Chinese have what often appears to be an obsessive desire to put their relationship with foreigners on a "friendship" basis as rapidly as possible. One of the reasons for this is that the Chinese have traditionally been conditioned to avoid any kind of interaction with strangers, making it imperative that they establish a personal relationship with someone before discussing business or anything else of substance.

Pin yin—"Phonetic transcription." This is the officially accepted system for writing Chinese in Roman letters. The system was first adopted in 1959 and put into universal use in China in 1979. This is the system that changed Peking to Beijing, which is closer to the actual pronunciation of the capital of China—but it also made the Chin Dynasty into the Qin Dynasty (win some, lose some!).

Renao   (*ray-nah-oh*)—This is more or less the opposite of *privacy*, for which the Chinese have no word and little or no concept. By itself *renao* means "hot and noisy," and refers to the kind of relationships the Chinese have with family and friends, especially, when they are eating and drinking in public places.

Renminbi   (*wren-men-bee*)—Literally "People's Money," *renminbi* is the national currency. It is broken down into ten jiao or mao. There are ten fen to each jiao. Bills come in denominations of a hundred, fifty, ten, five, two, and one yuan; coins in five, two, and one fen.

Shuan yang rou   (*shuu-inn yahng roh-uu*)—Mongolian mutton casserole, a popular specialty of some Beijing restaurants.

Tong ju   (*tong-juu*)—"Living in," a reference to a man and woman living together before they get married, a practice that became fairly common in China when men were not allowed to marry until they were twenty-eight and women could not marry until they were twenty-five. Now the age limits are twenty-two and twenty.

Tongzhi   (*tong-jee*)—Comrade. Use of this term is common now only at official parties and functions with political overtones. Young people, unless they are avid partyliners, do not like it.

Transaction—The Chinese tend to be exceptionally prudish in matters concerning sex. Generally, explicit sexual terms are taboo. The commonly accepted word for sexual intercourse is *transaction*.

Waiguoren   (why-gwah-wren)—An "external country person," in other words a foreigner, or what the Chinese call non-Chinese, with a neutral nuance. Also: *wai hang* (foreign businessman), *wai bin* (foreign guest), *waiguo pengyou* (foreign friend), *lao wai* (friendly for "foreigner"), *da bizi* (derogatory for "foreigner").

Xie xie   (*shay shay*)—Thank you.

Xiu-xi   (*show-she*)—Until the 1980s, it was customary for most urban Chinese to take a midday nap break for about two hours in the winter and up to three hours in the summer. This nap time was not part of the lunch period. Workers ate their lunch before noon and then took their *xiu-xi*. China's constitution guarantees the right of all Chinese workers to have their daily midday nap time (Article 49 says: "The working people have the right to *xiu-xi*"). The custom is said to have grown out of the age-old practice of Chinese farmers getting up at sunrise, then taking a long rest during the heat of midday. The custom has been gradually diminishing since the early 1980s, and in some city offices and factories is banned.

Wan-sui!   (*wahn-swee!*)—"10,000 years!" or "Eternal life!" This is the Chinese equivalent of Japan's *banzai*, and Britain's "Long live the king!" or whoever. It is shouted on auspicious occasions, as a grand gesture toward someone being honored.

Wei   (*way*)—This is China's telephone "hello" and is more or less the equivalent of "yes" when it is used in answering the phone. Because of the vital importance of establishing respective social rank, protecting "face," reluctance to get involved in new situations and identify themselves or their office directly and immediately over the phone, it often takes several *weis* before one succeeds in getting a conversation going, and the caller generally has to take the initiative. It is not uncommon to hear *wei* repeated ten or fifteen times during a telephone conversation.

Yang Guizi   (*whang gwee-jee*)—"Foreign devil," what many Chinese used to call foreigners, and an image that has not totally disappeared from the consciousness of some.

Yanjiu   (*yahn-jee-uu*)—"I'll/we'll study it." Another very common expression used to avoid making any kind of commitment. Often used with *kaolu*.

Yin/Yang—In Chinese philosophy and cosmology, *yin/yang* refers to the plus-minus, positive-negative, hot-cold, male-female, dark-light makeup of all matter and force in the universe. In traditional Chinese thought, all things have either a basically *yin* or *yang* nature, and for things to be right with the world these forces must be balanced. The food that one eats must have a proper *yin/yang* balance for the individual to maintain health; a building must conform to the *yin/yang* of the site in order to prevent bad luck and other negative forces from afflicting the occupants, etc.

Yonguan bumen   (*yoh-uu-gwan buu-mane*)—"The concerned parties," an old expression referring to mystical "other people." Now used to refer to people without saying exactly who, as in "Gen younguan bumen lianxi" (Let's contact the concerned parties).

Youyi (*yoh-uu-yee*)—Friendship. The Chinese believe that a foundation of friendship must be established before parties can engage in business with each other. Unlike in the U.S. and other countries in the West where business is often conducted on a product and price basis with little or no personal involvement, the Chinese do not put business in a separate impersonal category. The key to becoming friends with the Chinese is not at all complicated. All you have to do is be friendly, polite, honest, sincere, and not patronize them.

Yuan (*yuu-inn*)—One of the several words for the currency of China. The yuan comes in one hundred, fifty, ten, five and one yuan denominations, plus five and one jiao or mao denominations.

Zhao-daisuo (*jah-ow die-suh-oh*)—Guest houses. The government maintains a large number of *Zhao-daisuo* houses for use by higher officials when they travel.

Zhongguo tong (jong-gwah tong)—"China expert," a compliment paid by Chinese to foreigners who show some knowledge of China.

Zidian (*jee-dee-inn*)—Dictionary. An English-Chinese dictionary that gives the Chinese equivalents in pin yin (Roman letters) can be very helpful to the visitor in China.

Zili-gengsheng (*jee-lee-gung-shung*)—Self-reliance, something that both Chinese and foreigners must have to live and work within the Chinese system.

Zou-hou-men (*joe-uu-how-mun*)—"Taking the back door." This is a reference to going to or using an unofficial economy that exists in Chinese, where one can buy things and get things done that are not available or are impossible in the official economy. Old-timers say the "back door" market in China is much larger and more elaborate than a "black market," and that it forms a vital part of the overall economy.

Business Vocabulary

Accept—Jieshou (*jee-eh-show*)

Act on behalf of someone—Dai (*die*)

Additional charge—Fujiea fei (*fuu-jee-eh-ah faye*)

Advertise for (help wanted)—Zhaopin (*jah-oh-peen*)

Advertisement—Guanggao (*gwang-gah-oh*)

Agency—Daili (*die-lee*)

Agent (company)—Dailishang (*die-lee-shahng*); person—dailiren (*die-lee-wren*)

Agreement—Xieyi (*shay-yee*)

America—Meizhou (*may-ee-joe*)

Appointment, make one—Yue (*yuu-eh*)

Arbitrate—Zhongcai (*joong-tsai*)

Assign/entrust—Weituo (*way-tuu-oh*), weipai (*way-pie*)

Assistant/Vice Managing Director—Fu Zongjing Li (*fuu chong-jeeng lee*)

Australia—Aodaliya (*ah-oh-dah-lee-ah*), Aozhou (*ah-oh-joe*)

Australian dollar—Aodaliya yuan (*yuu-inn*)

Bank—Yinhang (*yeen-hahng*)

Bank of America—Meizhou Yinhang (*may-joe yeen-hahng*)

Banquet—Yanxi (*yahn-she*)

Beer—Pijiu (*pee-juu*)

Beijing (Peking) food—Beijing cai (*bay-jeeng t'sai*)

Be seated (at a banquet)—Ru xi (*rue she*)

Book/reserve—Yuding (*yuu-deng*)

Brand—Paihao (*pie-how*)

Brochure, pamphlet, leaflet—Shuomingshu (*shu-oh-ming-shuu*)

Bushel—Pushi'er

Business—Yewu (*yay-wuu*); trade/deal—shengyi (*shung-yee*); buy/sell—maimai (*my-my*); trade/deal—jiaoyi (*jow-yee*)

Business circles—Shang jie (*shahng jee-eh*)

Businessman—Shangren (*shahng-wren*)

Busy season—Wang ji (*wahng jee*)

Buy—Maijin (*my-jeen*)

Buyer—Maifang (*my-fahng*)

Canada—Jianada (*jee-ah-nah-dah*)

Cancel—Quxiao (*chuu-she-ow*)

Cantonese (Guangdong) food—Guangdong cai (*t'sai*)

Capital (money)—Zijin (*zuh-jeen*)

Cash (check)—Duifu (*duu-ee-fuu*)

Catalog—Mulu (*muu-luu*)

Chain store—Liansuo shangdian (*lee-ahn-suh-oh shahng-dee-inn*)

Charge—Shouxufei (*show-shuu-fay*)

Cheap—Pianyi (*pee-ahn-yee*)

Chemical fertilizer—Hau fei (*how fay*)

Chemicals—Guagong (*gwang-gong*)

Chicago—Zhijiage (*chi-jah-guh*)

Chinese food—Zhong can (*chong t'san*)

Claim—Suopei (*suu-ah-pay*)

Collect—Shouhui (*show-whee*)

Commission—Yongjin (*yong-jeen*)

Commodity—Shangpin (*shahng-peen*)

Company/Corporation—Gongsi (*gong-suh*)

Compensation—Buchang (*buu-chahng*)

Confirm—Queren (*chu-eh-wren*)

Contact/get in touch with—Lianxi (*lee-ahn-she*)

Content (ingredients)—Hanliang (*hahn-lee-ahng*)

Contract—Hetong (*huh-tong*)

Cooperate—Hezuo (*hay-zwoh*)

Cost—Chengben (*chung-bun*)

Cost, expense—Feiyong (*fay-yo*)

Cost, insurance, freight (CIF)—Dao an jia (*dah-oh ahn jee-ah*)

Counteroffer—Huan pan (*hwahn pahn*)

Countersign—Fu qian (*fuu chi-inn*)

Cubic meter—Li fangmi (*lee fahng-mee*)

Currency—Huobi (*hwoh-bee*)

Customer—Guke (*guu-kay*)

Customs—Haiguan (*hie-gwahn*)

Customs duty—Guan shui (*gwahn shuu-ee*)

Cut price—Jian jia (*jee-inn- jee-ah*)

Damage—Sunhuai (*soon-hway-ee*)

Date of delivery—Jiaohuo qi (*jow-hwoh chee*)

Deadline—Qixian (*chee-she-inn*)

Deferred payment—Yanqi fukuan (*yahn-chee fuu-kwahn*)

Deliver—Jiaohuo (*jow-hwoh*)

Demand, needs—Xuqiu (*shu-chee-uu*)

Deposit—Yajin (*yah-jeen*)

Design, pattern—Huase (*hwah-suh*); huayang (*hwah-yahng*)

Develop—Kaizhan (*kie-zhan*)

Dining room, restaurant—Canting (*cahn-teeng*)

Disagreement—Yiyi (*yee-yee*)

Discount—Zhekou (*chay-kow*)

Distributor—Jingxiaoshang (*jeeng-she-ow-shahng*)

District, region—Diqu (*dee-chuu*)

Documents—Danju (*dahn-juu*)

Dollar (U.S.)—Meiyuan (*may-yuu-inn*)

Dozen—Da (*dah*)

Draft—Huipiao (*whee-pee-ow*)

Economy—Jingji (*jeeng-jee*)

Electrical equipment—Dian qi (*dee-inn-chee*)

Employee—Renyuan (*wren-yuu-inn*)

England—Yinguo (*yen-gwah*)

Entertain—Yanqing (*yahn-cheeng*)

Equality and mutual benefit—Ping deng huli (*peng dung huu-lee*)

Equipment—Shebei (*shay-bay*)

Estimate—Guji (*guu-jee*)

Europe—Ouzhou (*oh-uu-joe*)

Examine, test, inspect—Jianyan (*jee-ahn-yahn*)

Exhibit—Zhanpin (*chahn-peen*)

Expire, fall due—Daoqi (*dah-oh-chee*)

Export—Chukou (*chuu-kow*)

Exporter—Chukou shang (*chuu-kow shahng*)

Feast—Jiuxi (*juu-she*)

Finance—Jinrong (*jeen-rohng*)

Fire, dismiss—Jiegu (*jee-uh-guu*)

Firm offer—Shipan (*she-pahn*)

First class—Diyi liu (*de-yee lee-uu*)

Flexible—Linghuo (*leeng-hwah*)

Foreign businessman—Wai shang (*wie shahng*)

Foreign capital—Wai zi (*wie zuh*)

Foreign trade—Wai mao (*wie mah-oh*)

Franc—Falang (*fah-lahng*)

Free on Board (F.O.B.)—Jiao Huo Tiaojian (*Jow hwah tee-ow-jee-inn*)

Freight—Yunfei (*yuun-fay*)

Fuel—Ranliao (*rahn-lee-ow*)

Gallon—Jialun (*jee-ah-loon*)

Give up, call off—Fang qi (*fahn chee*)

Government—Zhengfu (*chung-fuu*)

Gross weight—Mao zhong (*mah-oh chong*)

Guarantee—Danbao (*dahn-bow*); baozheng (*bow-chung*)

Guest house—Bin guan (*bean gwahn*)

Handle, deal in—Jingying (*jeeng-yeeng*)

Hardware—Xiao wujin (*she-ow wuu-jeen*)

Hire—Guyong (*guu-yong*)

Hong Kong—Xiang Gang (*she-ahng ghang*)

Hong Kong dollar—Gang yuan (*ghang yuu-inn*)

Hotel—Fandian (*fahn-dee-inn*)

Import—Yinjin (*yeen-jeen*)

Imports—Jinkouhou (*jeen-kow-how*)

In bulk—San zhuang (*sahn juu-ahng*)

In common use—Tong yong

Inflexible, rigid—Siban (*she-bahn*)

Inquire—Xunjia (*shune-jee-ah*)

Inquiry (letter)—Xunjia dan (*shune-jee-ah dahn*)

Insurance—Baoxianfei (*bow-she-inn-fay*)

Interest (money)—Lixi (*lee-she*)

International—Guoji (*gwah-jee*)

Invest capital—Chuzi (*chuu-zuh*)

Invitation card—Qing tie (*ching tee-eh*)

Invite—Yaoqing (*yah-oh-ching*)

Invite to dinner—Qingke (*ching-kuh*)

Invoice—Fapiao (*fah-pee-ow*)

Iran—Yilang (*yee-lahng*)

Italy—Yidali (*yee-dah-lee*)

Japan—Riben (*ree-ben*)

Japanese yen—Riyuan (*ree-yuu-inn*)

Joint venture—Hezijing ying (*hay-suh-jing ying*)

Kilogram—Gongjin (*gong-jeen*)

Kind/type—Pinzhong (*peen-chong*)

Label—Shangbiao (*shahng-bow*)

Law—Falu (*fuh-luu*)

Letter of credit—Xinyong Zheng (*sheen-yong chung*)

Letter of guarantee—Baozheng han (*bow-chung hahn*)

Loan—Daikuan (*die-kwan*)

London—Lundun

Los Angeles—Luo Shanji (*low shahn-jee*)

Machine—Jiqi (*jee-chee*)

Mail (post)—Youji (*yow-jee*)

Manager—Yewuyuan (*yay-wuu-yuu-inn*)

Manufacture/make—Zhizao (*chi-chow*)

Manufacturer—Changjia (*chahng-jee-ah*)

Market—Shichang (*she-chahng*)

Market price—Shi jia (*she jee-ah*)

Meet—Huijian (*hwee-jee-inn*)

Minimum quantity—Qiding liang (*chee-ding lee-ahng*)

Model—Xing (*sheeng*)

Name card—Ming pian (*ming pee-inn*)

Negotiate—Qiatan (*chi-ah-tahn*)

Negotiate payment—Jie hui (*jee-uh whee*)

Net weight—Jingzhong (*jeen-chong*)

New Year's Day—Yuan Dan (*yuu-inn dahn*)

New York—Niu Yue (*new yu-oh*)

Notice, notify—Tongzhi (*tong-jee*)

Order—Ding, dinggou (*ding, ding-gow*)

Origin, source—Laiyuan (*lie-yuu-inn*)

Output—Shuchu (*shuu-chuu*)

Packing—Baozhuang (*bow-juang*)

Parts—Lingbujian (*leng-buu-jee-inn*)

Pay—Changfu (*chahng-fuu*)

Pay back—Chang huan (*chahng hwahn*)

Payment by installment—Fenqi fu kuan (*fun-chee fuu kwahn*)

Payment for goods—Huo kuan (*huu-oh kwahn*)

Permit—Yunxu (*yuun-shu*)

Place an order—Ding hou (*ding ho-uu*)

Plan—Jihua (*jee-whah*)

Policy—Zhengce (*chung-tsuh*)

Pound—Bang (*bahng*)

Port—Kouan (*koo-uu-inn*)

Price—Jiage (*jee-ah-guh*)

Price list—Jiamu dan (*jee-ah-muu-dahn*)

Principle—Yuanze (*yuu-inn-zuh*)

Private (not government)—Siren (*suh-wren*)

Produce—Chuchan (*chuu-chahn*)

Product—Chanpin (*chahn-peen*)

Profit margin—Lirun'e (*lee-ruun'uh*)

Quality—Zhiliang (*jee-lee-ahng*); zhidi (*chee-dee*)

Quantity—Shuliang (*shuu-lee-ahng*)

Quota—Ding'e (*ding-uh*)

Quote, offer—Bao (*bow*)

Retailer—Lingshoushang (*leng-sho-uu-shahng*)

Revoke—Chexiao (*chuh-she-ah-oh*)

Russia—Ewenguo (*uh-wren-gwah*)

Sales confirmation—Xiaoshou querenshu (*she-ah-oh-sho-uu chuh-wren-shuu*)

Sample—Huoyang (*huu-oh-yahng*)

Sample book—Yang ben (*yahng bun*)

Seasonal—Jijiexing (*jee-jee-uh-shing*)

Sell—Xiaoshou (*she-ah-oh-sho-uu*)

Service charge—Shouxu fei (*sho-uu-shu jay*)

Service desk—Fuwu tai (*fuu-wuu tie*)

Settle accounts—Jie suan (*jee-uh swan*)

Shanghai (Shandong) food—Shandong cai (*shahng-dong t'sai*)

Ship (send)—Zhuangyun (*juu-inng-yuun*)

Shortage—Duanshao (*duu-inn-shah-oh*)

Sight—Jiqi (*jee-chee*); sight draft—jiqi piao (*jee-chee pee-ow*)

Sign—Qian (*chee-inn*); qianshu (*chee-inn-shuu*); qianzi (*chee-inn-zuh*)

Sign one's name—Qian ming (*chee-inn ming*)

Singapore—Xinjiapo (*sheen-juh-ah-poe*)

Size—Chicun (*chee-t'sune*)

Slack season—Danji (*dahn-jee*)

Spain—Xibanya (*she-bahn-yah*)

Spare parts—Beijian (*bay-jee-inn*)

Specifications—Guige (*gwee-guh*)

Specified packing—Zhiding baozhuang (*jee-ding bow-chung*)

Square meter—Ping fangmi (*ping fahng-mee*)

Square yard—Ping fangma (*ping fahng-mah*)

Staff member—Zhi yuan (*jee yuu-inn*)

Standard (quality)—Biaozhun (*bee-ow-june*)

Sum of money—Bi (*bee*)

Superior (quality)—Shangdeng (*shahng-dung*)

Supplier—Gongxiao-shang (*gong-she-ow-shahng*)

Sweden—Ruidian (*ruu-ee-dee-inn*)

System—Xitong (*she-tong*)

Television—Dianshiji (*dee-inn-she-jee*)

Terms—Tiaokuan (*tee-ow-kwan*)

Tokyo—Dongjing (*dong-jeeng*)

Ton—Dun (*dune*)

Trade—Maoyi (*mah-oh-yee*)

Trade show—Jiaoyi hui (*jee-ah-oh-yee whee*)

Unit price—Dan jia (*dahn jee-ah*)

Value—Jiazhi (*jee-ah-juh*)

Valid—Youxiao (*yoh-she-ow*)

Volume of business—Chengjiao liang (*chung-jee-ow lee-ahng*)

Western food—Xi can (*she t'san*)

West Germany—Xide (*she-duh*)

Wholesale—Pifa (*pee-fah*)

Abbreviations of Important Organizations

ATCM	Academy of Traditional Chinese Medicine
CAAC	General Administration of Civil Aviation of China
CAAFS	Chinese Academy of Agricultural and Forestry Sciences
CAAS	Chinese Academy of Agricultural Sciences
CAFS	Chinese Academy of Forestry Sciences
CAMS	Chinese Academy of Medical Sciences
CAS	Chinese Academy of Sciences
CASS	Chinese Academy of Social Sciences
CATCM	Chinese Academy of Traditional Chinese Medicine
CCPIT	Chinese Council for the Promotion of International Trade
CIBTC	China International Book Trading Corporation
CITIC	China International Trust and Investment Corporation
CMA	Chinese Medical Association
CNCCC	Chinese National Chemical Construction Corp.
COSA	China Ocean Shipping Agency
COSCO	China Ocean Shipping Company
CSCEC	China State Construction Engineering Corporation
CSHR-DC	China State Housing & Real Estate Development Corporation
CSSC	China State Shipbuilding Corporation
FTB	Foreign Trade Bureau
FTC	Foreign Trade Corporation
GFTC	Guangzhou Foreign Trade Center
GITIC	Guangdong International Trust and Investment Corporation
MOFTEC	Ministry of Foreign Trade and Economic Cooperation
SAIC	State Administration of Industry and Commerce
SINOCHEM	China National Chemical I/E Corporation
SINOPEC	China Petro-Chemical Corporation
SINOTRANS	China National Foreign Trade Transportation Corporation